The History of Britain in Africa

John Hatch

The History of Britain
in Africa

From the Fifteenth Century
to the Present

André Deutsch

FIRST PUBLISHED 1969 BY
ANDRE DEUTSCH LIMITED
105 GREAT RUSSELL STREET
LONDON WCI
COPYRIGHT © 1969 BY JOHN HATCH
ALL RIGHTS RESERVED
PRINTED IN GREAT BRITAIN BY
EBENEZER BAYLIS & SON LTD
THE TRINITY PRESS
WORCESTER AND LONDON
233 96008 2

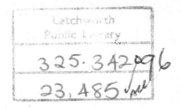

Preface

In this book I have attempted to trace the main factors in the story of relations between African and British people from the sixteenth century to the 1960s. Inevitably I have had to be selective and to rely on certain generalizations. The object of this work has been to show how British actions have affected African life and the ways in which contact with Africans have influenced society in Britain. I hope that the story told here and the analysis of the underlying factors affecting both peoples will contribute to greater understanding by Africans of the British and the British of Africans. For each have much to offer to the other in the effort to build a single human society in the last third of the twentieth century.

My debt to many previous authors is obvious. I am particularly grateful to the work done on African historical records by Basil Davidson and on the economic bases of the imperial era by Michael Barratt Brown, from both of whom I have drawn extensively. Discussions with René Dumont, Thomas Balogh and Roger Opie have greatly helped me to sort out the complicated economics of the modern scene. My son, Barrie Hatch, has assisted with some of the statistics, and I have had valuable editorial assistance from Michael George and Michael Alexander of André Deutsch. The staff of Faustus antiquarian bookshop, Hampstead, kindly searched their nineteenth-century journals for African references.

I am happy to express my gratitude to Gillian Hollings, who, as so often before, has both helped with the research and done most of the typing. My thanks are also due to Christine Hewitt and Courtney Collier who endured some dictation. I am always grateful to my wife who has to suffer my periodic literary 'pregnancies' but is still willing to type out long quotations from ancient volumes. Responsibility for everything in the text is, of course, mine alone.

Houston and London, 1966–68

Contents

List of Maps

Chapter 1

Prologue

In the year 1530 William Hawkins of Plymouth sailed in his 250 ton *Paule of Plimmouth* for the coast of Brazil. In the course of his voyage he put in to the coast of Guinea and traded there with the Africans. From them he bought 'elephants' teeth' or ivory. This is the first confirmed direct contact between a Briton and the African continent.

In the following two years Hawkins sailed again to Brazil. In 1540 he sent the same *Paule* to Guinea and Brazil with John Landye as her master. The bills of lading provide a character-picture of this original Anglo-African trade. The outward cargo included matchettes, combes and sarpes (hand bills), copper and lead mellios (bracelets), woollen cloth and nightcaps. The *Paule* returned to Plymouth carrying twelve elephants' tusks.

The English came late into European trade with West Africa. The Portuguese had made their first contacts on the Guinea coast nearly a hundred years before Hawkins' visit. Their trade in gold dust, ivory, pepper and slaves had grown steadily since then. As early as 1482 they had built the great fort of Elmina. This gave them a stronghold from which to try and maintain the monopoly of African trade granted to them by the Pope and confirmed in treaties with Spain. But the coast was long and could not be entirely patrolled by the Portuguese. Certainly Spanish and French traders broke the monopoly and probably merchants from other European countries followed their example. For, from the end of the fifteenth century onwards, Europeans knew something of Barbary's riches, and trade to Guinea was a natural extension from the Barbary coast.

It may even be that a few English merchants found their way to Barbary and Guinea before William Hawkins. If they did, however, their records remain silent. The only evidence we have of English participation in African trade at this time is negative. It is reported that in 1482 two Englishmen, John Tintam and William Fabian, were preparing a fleet for a voyage to Guinea when their plans were vetoed by Edward IV after protests from John II of Portugal. A similar abortive plan was reported in 1488. It seems almost certain that a few English merchants would have known of the African trade from their Portuguese acquaintances. Hakluyt reports that the Island of Madeira was discovered by an Englishman who was supposed to have sailed later to the African coast in a boat made from a tree without sail or oar. Certain Englishmen were also believed to have accompanied the Portuguese Prince, Henry the Navigator, at his siege of Ceuta in 1415. But the Portuguese were very jealous of their commercial monopoly, employing an army of spies to report from European ports on any preparations for voyages likely to break it.

In any case, neither Britain as a whole nor any one of her disunited national units, was strong enough to challenge the Portuguese monopoly. England was still a remote off-shore island of Europe, her economy dependent on the export of wool and much of her trade on European merchants travelling in European ships. Her sailors seldom ventured farther than the wool markets of Flanders or to carry timber from the Baltic and wine from Bordeaux. The Venetians and Germans controlled the larger part of England's export and import trade. Henry VII encouraged John Cabot to sail westward, but this brought little more than the discovery of the Newfoundland cod banks. Nor did the English share in the great fillip given to intellectual activity in Europe by the discovery of the new lands. It is significant that Caxton's first books were on such subjects as the history of Troy, the Morte d'Arthur and Chaucer's Tales, at a time when many continental presses were turning out books on geography. Caxton showed scant interest in the new geographic revolution, and without books on the subject Englishmen remained for the most part ignorant of the fresh vista which the world now took on for Europeans. Sir Thomas More in his *Utopia* of 1516 showed some recognition of the geographic revolution by locating his ideal society somewhere beyond Mexico. But it was not until 1549 that the Cambridge statutes established the study of classical geographers as a branch of mathematics. By this time, the work of Ptolemy had been a commonplace of continental knowledge for nearly a century, along with the many adaptations made necessary by the findings of the new explorations.

Yet this century was not wasted by the English. The new Tudor monarchy consolidated the centralized powers of the Crown and put it on a sound economic basis. Their political system was more adaptable and enduring than that of any continental state. Under Henry VII, and to a lesser extent his successors, English fleets began to emulate the example of the Venetians, Spaniards and Portuguese. Although their main colonizing interest remained in Ireland, their forced disengagement from Europe gave them a greater national cohesion, preparing the way for expansion across the oceans. Moreover, during this period the English experienced great religious, economic and social revolutions. The subsequent seizure of church lands seriously damaged the political power of the land-owning group. The change from agriculture to sheep farming, together with the appearance of gold and silver from across the Atlantic, destroyed the established price mechanism of medieval England.

The hundred years from the mid-fifteenth to the mid-sixteenth centuries saw Europe's relations with the rest of the world transformed. With the exception of the few Italian merchant cities, Europeans had stood in a semi-colonial status to Asia throughout the Middle Ages. Whereas Asian goods had had a ready sale amongst wealthy Europeans, most of the trade between the two continents was in the hands of Arabs. Indeed, Europe itself, with its skins, hides, wool and timber, had little to offer in exchange for the spices, silks, cottons, precious metals, porcelain, ivory and other luxury goods imported from Arabia, India and China. Even to buy the gold and ivory transported across the Sahara to the North African ports, the Europeans had to rely on Arab middlemen able to provide goods needed by the Africans in exchange. For there was little produced in Europe at this time that was of any use to Africa. Yet, during the same period, a string of commercial city states along the East African seaboard was flourishing from their exchange of African minerals for commodities imported from Arabia, India and China. It is no exaggeration to suggest that at this time international trade from certain areas of Africa was more advanced than that of any part of Europe, with the exception of the Italian city states.

One of the ways in which Europeans could break through this colonial status was by overcoming their ignorance of geography. They had but a hazy idea of where the goods they coveted originated or who had produced them. The valuable trade from Asia, on which so much of Europe's aristocratic life in the Middle Ages relied, was almost entirely dependent on the skill, knowledge and enterprise of the Arabs. It was the European sense of frustration stemming from this ignorance, allied to fears that Islam might seduce their faith as well as drain their specie, which provoked the Crusades; and the Crusades took the Europeans into the centre of the market lying between Asia and Europe. The revelation fired ambitions to quit the role of customer and rival the Moslem merchants. The Crusades brought Europeans new wealth and a fresh geographic perspective; they inspired ambitious monarchs to set traders, sailors, map-makers and ship-builders to provide the means for turning the flank of Islam, seeking the sources of Asian luxuries and Guinea gold for themselves.

Already the Venetians, Genoese and Pisans had proved that the Arabs need not be left with a monopoly of commercial profits. They had penetrated to Egypt and the Near East, competing with the Arabs, accepting the same commercial principles. Venetian commercialism supplied the model for the wider European expansion which began early in the fifteenth century. Its object, like that of the Venetians, was to expand and control trade, rather than to take territorial possession. Where it did occur, the purpose of territorial expansion was to protect commercial monopoly from invasion by rivals.

The first serious imitators of the Venetians were the Portuguese. From 1415 onward their sailors, often with the help of Venetians and Genoese, and armed with the knowledge acquired from Arabs, slowly penetrated the Atlantic Ocean southward along the coast of Africa. They sought the gold, ivory, ebony, pepper and slaves which they had been accustomed to buy in the Barbary ports. By the middle of the century African slaves were being used on Portuguese farms and gold dust was being imported from the Guinea coast. Before the end of the century, Bartholomew Diaz had been blown round the Cape into the Indian Ocean, and Vasco da Gama had sailed round the continent to the Indian market of Calicut on the Malabar coast. Meanwhile, another Portuguese, after visiting Egypt and India, had sailed in an Arab dhow down the East African coast as far as Sofala.

Within a few years the Spaniards were established on the other side of the Atlantic, Magellan had found his way westward around the world and the Pope had divided the newly-discovered lands between

Spain and Portugal. The Iberians, expelling the Arabs from their peninsula after learning what they could from them, had undermined the commercial strength of Islam and broken the trading monopoly of Venice. Western Europe had broken out of the Middle Ages, discovered the globe and laid open hitherto unimagined trading potentialities.

England was not yet ready to participate seriously in this growing enterprise. She was still green, rural England, slowly emerging from the Middle Ages. During the fifteenth century, whilst the Iberians were crossing the oceans, the English continued their vain pursuit of a European empire. Only the outcome of the Hundred Years' War with France finally convinced them that this dream was over. Yet no sooner were their European adventures concluded, than the English were plunged into civil war, the Wars of the Roses. Those who might have been following the pioneering example of the Portuguese and the Spaniards were caught up in the turmoil at home. Although this civil war was fought between rival gangs of nobles, it did have wide social significance. In economic outlook, the Yorkists were supported by slightly more progressive southerners and the Lancastrians by old-fashioned northerners. So Edward IV's victory led to greater co-operation between the crown and the city merchants who supported him. This, in its turn, had some little influence on Britain's commercial position. Edward used the wealth supplied by the merchant class to build new fleets capable of shipping wool, tin and cloth as far as the Mediterranean. On the other hand, his brother Richard restored the power of the old nobles who had little interest in commerce. Again, two years later, when in 1485 the Battle of Bosworth provided Henry Tudor with the English throne, an economic interest was at stake. The rising merchant class had once more secured victory over the landed nobility; the new monarch was supported and influenced by this new class; and England hesitatingly awoke from her rural medieval sleep.

Something of the spirit of European society at this time may be gleaned from the burning of Joan of Arc and the murder of Edward's two young sons in the Tower. The former instance is one not only of brutality, but of the power of witchcraft which had become widespread as the secret religion of the masses throughout the Middle Ages. It can be seen as a mixture of nature worship with revolt against authority of Church and State. It was this force from amongst the masses which

Joan mobilized against the English invaders, aided by the emotions of incipient nationalism; it was because the authorities feared this force that she was burnt. Belief in, and fear of, the supernatural had similarities with the supernatural beliefs of Africa.

Both the Hundred Years War abroad and the Wars of the Roses at home had only limited effects on the daily life of the English people. As we shall see later, they had important influences on the economic development of the country which eventually were to affect the relations of the English people with Africa.

During the second half of the fifteenth century England was comparatively prosperous. Feudalism was declining and industry growing, often leaving the old guild-dominated towns and moving out into the suburbs, villages and new towns. Production was becoming organized on a small capitalist or semi-capitalist basis, whilst the vast majority of the English people now lived as small peasant farmers. Increasing land prices, a growing population, the expanding wool market, steady prices, all gave evidence of this prosperity. Many labourers and peasant farmers supplemented their agricultural incomes by engaging in domestic industries, spinning and weaving in their homes. As the manorial system declined so peasant agriculture became the dominant form of life, although the accumulation of capital possible at this stage was not yet sufficient to sustain a fully capitalistic agriculture.

On the other hand, there were elements in English life less favourable to a peaceful rural existence, and others undermining the economic stability of this form of life. As feudalism retreated so the nobles lost their social functions, yet their habits of violence acquired from foreign and civil wars survived after their social usefulness had disappeared. They still kept bands of armed retainers, whom they protected from the course of justice. They began to develop new channels of wealth from sheep farming, displacing many peasants accustomed to the use of arable land.

Moreover, money began to displace land as the chief source of wealth, merchants gradually accumulating enough to challenge the power of the declining nobility. The medieval pretence that the church forbade usury disappeared in practice, if not in theory, many nobles themselves becoming heavy debtors to the new merchant class.

Thus the new shift in class relationships did not in any way narrow the gap between the few rich and the many poor. If it remained true throughout this period that England was still largely an agricultural country, with political and financial control vested in a small section, the activities of the wealthy still remained of major significance to the relations of England with the outside world. In the transition from feudalism to capitalism, internal struggles and conflicts by the time of the Tudors had undermined the power of the nobility; both the monarchy and the bourgeoisie emerged stronger from these struggles, ready for the alliance which was to mark the later Tudor period. Yet the rich, both the nobles and the increasingly powerful merchants, demanded goods which were to affect decisively the external relations of England. It was the demand of the wealthy for luxuries like spices, silks and ivory which first stimulated and then maintained imports from Asia via the Arabs, Venetians and Genoese, and later prompted English merchants to seek the sources of such lucrative commodities.

The advent of the new merchant class slowly altered traditional English foreign trade. Much of the trade with Asia had a one-way character. Few European goods were either suitable for export or were generally sought after by Asians. They had therefore to be paid for in bullion. This situation had a double effect on English merchants: in the first place, it led them to seek supplies of gold and silver; in the second, it stimulated their desire to go straight to the sources of the goods they wanted.

These impulses were further strengthened by economic changes. Throughout this period England was steadily turning from wool to cloth exports. As they became stronger, the English merchants organized themselves into a group known as the 'Merchant Adventurers' to gain control of their own trade. As Flanders' competition declined, especially after the invasion of the Netherlands by the Spaniards in the sixteenth century, the English cloth trade, further strengthened by Flemish refugee craftsmen, prospered independently. Moreover, the cloth industry was mainly organized on capitalist lines. The merchants bought wool, distributed it to spinners, sold the spun wool to weavers in their cottages, bought back the woven cloth, then handed it on to dyers and others who would complete the process to finished cloth. This whole business brought in large profits, allowing merchants to accumulate considerable amounts of capital for the first time, and so to seek fresh channels of investment. It was on this trade that Bristol, Hull and London developed into large ports.

The increase in commodity production and international trade during the later part of the fifteenth century, rapidly expanding during the sixteenth, brought ever-increasing demands for currency as a means of exchange. The crisis of currency shortage rose to a peak in the late fifteenth century, undoubtedly another factor in the feverish search for precious metals at that time. When this factor is coupled with the growing threat to the established trade routes to Asia, resulting from the invasion of Russia by the Mongols and the Turkish advance across Asia Minor driving the Arabs before them, the European need for geographic exploration at this time becomes clear. Interference with the trade routes and Arab markets brought steeply rising prices, whilst rapidly increasing foreign trade necessitated new sources of gold and silver. German, Italian and Flemish financiers invested in voyages led by intrepid seamen seeking the original source of Asian luxuries and Guinea gold. The knowledge and experience of the Arabs were eagerly sought by jealous merchants and monarchs, anxious not only to piece together the complex pictures of the African continent, and the routes around and within it, but equally determined to keep that knowledge to themselves. New experiments in ship-building were tested; the Iberians developed the caravel capable of sailing the turbulent Atlantic at increased speed, whilst the lateen sail was employed to make it possible to make way into the wind. The compass was adapted and improved, the astrolabe put to the calculation of latitudes and new maps were drawn, less romantic but more accurate than those of medieval times. It now became possible for the Europeans to break out and seek the sources of the wealth they were accustomed to having delivered to their doors.

Moreover, a rise in nationalist sentiment in Europe coincided with this fresh economic activity. Spain and Portugal had come to recognize the value of national sentiment in their long struggle against the Moors. The French and the English were likewise following the nationalist path in their battles against each other. The Hapsburg monarchy was establishing some kind of nationalist following in its struggles against the Turks. So, just at the moment when economic forces, allied to geographic and technical knowledge, were making desirable and possible the search for new trade routes, centralized national states were becoming discernable entities for the first time. These states took the form of a monarchy and court. Monarchies, in association with merchants or merchant groups with political power, threw their resources into new overseas ventures. And when, as a result of the early discoveries of precious metals and jewels across the Atlantic, bullion began to flood Europe, this stimulated rival states and their competing groups of merchants to seek their share.

Yet, although Europe was stirring in the ferment of new ideas, new knowledge and even greater rumours, interest was at first mainly confined to the continental countries. The Portuguese, the Spaniards, to some extent the Italians, the Germans and the Dutch, were all in one way or another involved. But the English had little or no part in it. England remained a small island outside Europe, inhabited by some five million people, producing good cloth, trade in which had usually been controlled by the Hansa towns or Antwerp. By the time that Henry VII came to the throne the Portuguese had already been exploring the west coast of Africa for over half a century. Two years after his accession, the Cape was rounded; five years later Columbus crossed the Atlantic; another five years and Vasco da Gama had sailed round the Cape to India and back to Lisbon. Even the first English oceanic voyage, that of John Cabot to Newfoundland and Labrador in 1497, was led by a Genoese sailor using the old-fashioned rounded English ships.

For much of the sixteenth century English trade was restricted to English ships. Corn and cloth were exported for bullion, whilst protection was given to home industries – what later became known as the 'mercantilist' policy. Meanwhile, the enclosure of arable land for sheep farming rapidly increased during Tudor times. The small peasant farmers who had flourished as the manorial system broke down now found themselves almost defenceless, although they did organize a number of protest demonstrations.

Increasingly during the sixteenth century the peasants were dispossessed, unemployment grew and a new proletariat of wage labourers came into existence. The enclosure movement inevitably caused land values to rise, thus stimulating still further enclosure, farming began to be organized on a capitalist basis and the new capitalist farmers took their position in the English economy along with small merchants. Prices rose rapidly, particularly as precious metals flooded into Europe, and by the end of the sixteenth century profits had been doubled and wages halved. Nevertheless, it was from this new growing accumulation of capital that English foreign trade and consequent contacts with the African continent were to develop.

Events in continental Europe also assisted this development in the English economy. In the second half of the sixteenth century European conflicts seriously disrupted the English cloth trade, particularly during the Dutch wars. Merchants were forced to seek other trading avenues and to diversify their exports from their heavy concentration on cloth. Meanwhile, the closing of the Antwerp money market forced the English government to look increasingly to English financial resources. The City of London became for the first time an important element in the English economy. Whether they wished to or not, the Tudors were driven inexorably into an alliance with English capital and commerce. By 1571 an Act was being passed fixing maximum rates of interest and thus, at least tacitly, recognizing money-lending as legitimate business. New trading companies were given monopolistic charters, whilst the development of joint-stock projects opened the way for direct links between finance and commerce. Whatever their public strictures, many members of the government, and even Queen Elizabeth herself, invested money in these ventures.

Unable yet to challenge the virtual monopoly of Spaniards and Portuguese in America, Africa and Asia, the English concentrated first on seeking alternative routes to the fabulous wealth of the East. The Cabots' voyages may seem of small importance compared with those of their contemporaries; but the cod fishing of Newfoundland and the fur trading with the Hudson Bay did provide the English with slow maturing stores of capital. They could be used to encourage other captains to rival the Iberians. By the middle of the century further expeditions to the north-east laid the basis for trade with Russia, Iceland and the Baltic. Thus, during the second half of the sixteenth century through a combination of the cloth trade, the enclosures and the new small, but important, trade routes to the north-west and the north-east, gold and silver were entering England in hitherto unknown quantities. Moreover, Englishmen were becoming masters of their own finance and economy instead of acquiescing in foreign control of the English economy as had been customary.

In view of the ways in which English traders and plantation owners were to treat Africans in later years, it is instructive to observe how the poorer people of England fared at this time. During the reign of

Henry VIII, as unemployment grew from the effects of the enclosure movement, laws were passed for dealing with the unemployed. In 1536 those categorized as 'sturdy vagabonds' were ordered to have their ears cut off and, if arrested for a third time to be executed. The parallel between the English treatment of their poor and their future attitude to Africans was drawn even more closely by an Act of 1547 which decreed that those refusing to work should become the slaves of the people who denounced them. They were then to be whipped to work, if necessary in chains, and if they escaped they were to be recaptured, brought back to their masters and branded. By Elizabeth's reign, any beggar over thirteen without a licence was to be flogged and branded unless an employer could be found for him, executed for a second offence, again unless somebody would employ him, and for a third offence executed without option.

What knowledge was there of Africa and Africans in the England of the fifteenth and sixteenth centuries, just preparing to establish her links with that continent? There was, of course, a fair amount of information available in Europe as a whole, and a great deal more in the Arab world. Not only were the observations of the classical writers, Herodotus, Ptolemy, and Pliny, there to be read; a number of more thorough geographical writers had offered their information. There were the works of al-Idrisi, the Arab Spaniard of the eleventh century; of Ibn Khaldun, the fourteenth century Berber. The Genoese merchant, Malfante, described his experiences in travelling to Tuat, a Saharan oasis, in 1443. His description seems to have been used by Florentines, who for a short period in the later fifteenth century established trade routes in North Africa. One of them, Benedetto Dei, claimed to have been in Timbuktu selling Lombardy cloth and serges in 1470. Above all there was Leo Africanus, the Moor. Leo was a contemporary visiting Timbuktu and the Sudanaic states in the early sixteenth century. He became a protégé of the Medici Pope Leo X, wrote his accounts of African society in Italian and taught Arabic in Bologna. He certainly gave Europe eye-witness accounts of the splendours of Timbuktu, the Songhai Empire and his 'fifteen kingdoms of the Negroes'. Then there was Cadomosto, the Venetian who sailed twice to Senegal in the middle of the previous century. His account of the country, people and customs he encountered was published as early as 1507. Later, in the mid-sixteenth century, de Barros, a

Portuguese civil servant, was to publish his account of his experiences as commander of Elmina Fort in the 1520s.

How much of this available knowledge actually came to the attention of Englishmen is difficult to judge. Merchants from the Italian cities had established themselves in North African towns during the fifteenth century, though their trading position dwindled as Portuguese, Turks and Spaniards invaded Morocco and Algiers. One must suppose that some English merchants learnt something of Africa in their trading contacts with the Italians. Certainly before the end of the sixteenth century English merchants were in Morocco, and a number of English craftsmen were employed there by the Emperor. It is known, too, that many Christian slaves were used in Africa before the end of the sixteenth century, some of them forming part of the Sultan of Morocco's army when he destroyed the Songhai Empire in 1590.

Moreover, Africans were by no means unknown, though certainly few in number, in European countries during the fifteenth century. The Portuguese soon followed their contacts with African societies down the west coast by bringing first a few slaves and then a number of African princes to their country. These princes were given an education in Portugal and received much attention. Probably a handful of African slaves were captured by English or Scottish pirates during this period, and there is a story, given credence by the Scottish poet Dunbar, of an African woman who became famous in Edinburgh society at this time.

The main African state during this period was the Empire of Songhai, successor to the two former Empires of Mali and Ghana, in the same north-western region. It was this area which had for many centuries been the meeting place for merchants bringing salt from the north and those from the south who would buy it with the gold of Guinea. The area had also both gained and lost from frequent invasion by the Islamic Arabs of the north.

Life in most African states of this time was mainly urban, although almost all the people were engaged in agriculture. Small villages were based on kinship units, the large towns consisting of many such units organized in wards around the royal palace. It was usual to build such settlements round the houses of kings and elders, with the majority of the people going out of town or village to the fields during the day.

In the east and north the towns were surrounded by a wall, leaving within an area large enough to shelter and even feed the urban population in times of emergency. Most towns and villages in this region of North-west Africa between the Sahara and the coast were linked by trade routes. The Hausa merchants in the east, the Yoruba in the south-west and the Mande in the west would travel these routes, although, as in Europe, their goods tended to be luxuries for the wealthy rather than necessities for the majority. Indeed, this was even more necessary in African trade, for the cost of transport was high, head loading being the only method in the forest, for lack of fodder and the ravages of the tsetse fly made animal transport impossible over large areas. Thus, most trading goods had to be of high value to justify the cost. The one necessity which had to be imported in this tropical, humid climate was salt. As in Europe, much of the trade had royal backing, the merchants being agents of the king rather than an independent class. Cattle, horses, beads, trinkets, metal ware, copper, cloth and cowrie shells (from the Indian Ocean; used as currency) were the known imported commodities; in return the Guinea area exported to as far away as the Mediterranean, and indirectly to Europe, gold dust, kola nuts, ivory, whilst domestic slaves had been traded to North Africa from the twelfth century onwards. Some local trading took place in the many market villages, usually an exchange of foodstuffs for manufactures. Textile manufacturing, in particular, was well advanced in certain towns. The life of the people was mainly occupied in agriculture, although some were also engaged in pottery, metal work and sculpture.

The West African kingdoms were divided, as in Europe, between the wealthy class, consisting of the kings and their courts, administrators, soldiers, artists, metal workers and the like, and the much poorer masses. Subjects were expected to pay tribute, usually in the form of gold dust or kola nuts, thus producing a surplus to maintain the elite.

These were the general conditions within the West African states, but by no means all Africans lived within state systems. Particularly in those areas where communication was difficult, no state system existed. Here people lived in various forms of kinship groupings in stateless societies based on traditional customs.

Africans in the fifteenth and sixteenth centuries, like societies outside the African continent, followed a variety of religious beliefs.

I Principal ethnic groups in early Africa

Various tribal religions, Islam and Christianity, all had followers in different parts of the continent. As in Europe, witchcraft also played a part in the life of many societies.

In East Africa political organization was somewhat different from the west. Here a string of port states, sometimes loosely grouped in what was known as the Zenj empire, had developed out of trade which was largely in Arab hands. The trade was extensive, providing evidence of considerably organized inland societies about which we still have much to know. Ivory, gold, slaves and iron were brought to the east coast and shipped to Arabia, India and China. The Arabs supplied most of the shipping, although the Chinese also took a prominent part until the end of the fifteenth century. But the production and carrying of the commodities internally was conducted by Africans bringing their goods to the coastal markets. Arabia, Persia, East Africa, India and China were linked around the Indian ocean in a vast commerce. There was also some influence from Malays, most of whom settled in Madagascar, though the cultivation of the root crops they brought with them from Indonesia spread down the east coast and later into the interior of the continent.

Contemporary descriptions offer us vivid pictures of life in Africa during the period when Europeans first began to make frequent visits to the continent. William Towerson noted in 1556 that the Africans he encountered in Guinea produced 'fine iron goods, spears, fish hooks, farming tools and swords that are exceedingly sharp on both edges'. Indeed, many of the African slaves taken across the Atlantic applied the techniques of tropical farming and mining which they had learnt at home in their new American environment to the profit of their masters. Much of the trade in Africa at this time was conducted by the barter system, although the beginnings of a money economy could be discerned in certain markets. They exported gold, ivory, cotton, hides, pepper and mutton to the oases of the Sahara and across the desert to Europe and Asia. The fact that they had learnt and practised sophisticated commercial techniques was borne out by John Lok in 1553, when he observed 'These people are very clever in their bargaining. They will not overlook a single bit of the gold they offer for sale. They use their own weights and measures and they are very careful how they use them. Anyone who wants to deal with them must do so decently for they will not trade if they are badly treated.' Some conception of the appearance of the best African cities at this time may be gained from a contemporary description of Benin, recorded at the beginning of the seventeenth century. 'When you go into it you enter a great broad street, which is not paved, and seems to be seven or eight times broader than the Warmoes street in Amsterdam. This street is straight, and does not bend at any point. It is thought to be four miles long.

'At the gate where I went in on horseback, I saw a very big wall, very thick and made of earth, with a very deep and broad ditch outside it. . . . And outside this gate there is also a big suburb. Inside the gate, and along the great street just mentioned, you see many other great streets on either side, and these also are straight and do not bend. . . .

'The houses in this town stand in good order, one close and evenly spaced with its neighbours, just as the houses in Holland stand. . . . They have square rooms, sheltered by a roof that is open in the middle, where the rain, wind, and light come in. The people sleep and eat in these rooms, but they have other rooms for cooking and different purposes. . . .

'The king's court is very great. It is built around many square shaped yards. These yards have surrounding galleries where sentries are always placed. I myself went into the court far enough to pass through four great yards like this, and yet wherever I looked I could still see gate after gate which opened into other yards. . . .'

Leo Africanus, whose descriptions of West Africa were translated into English in 1600, wrote of early sixteenth century Timbuktu: 'Here are many shops of artificers and merchants, and especially of such as weave linen and cotton cloth. And hither do the Barbary merchants bring cloth of Europe. All the women of this region, except the maid-servants, go with their faces covered, and sell all necessary victuals. The inhabitants, and especially strangers there residing, are exceeding rich, insomuch that the king that now is, married both his daughters to rich merchants. Here are many wells containing most sweet water; and so often as the river Niger overfloweth, they convey the water thereof by certain sluices into the town. Corn, cattle milk, and butter this region yieldeth in great abundance: but salt is very scarce here; for it is brought hither by land from Taghaza which is 500 miles distant. When I myself was here, I saw one camel's load of salt sold for 80 ducats. The rich king of Timbuktu hath many plates and sceptres of gold, some whereof weigh 1300 pounds: and he keeps a magnificent and well-furnished court. When he travelleth any whither he rideth upon a camel which is led by some of his noblemen; and so he doth likewise when he goeth forth to warfare, and all his soldiers rideth upon horses. Whoever will speak unto this king must first fall down before his feet, and then taking up earth must first sprinkle it upon his own head and shoulders: which custom is ordinarily observed by. . . . ambassadors from other princes. He hath always 3000 horsemen, and a number of footmen that shoot poisoned arrows, attending upon him. They have often skirmishes with those that refuse to pay tribute, and so many as they take, they sell unto the merchants of Timbuktu. Here are very few horses bred, and the merchants and courtiers keep certain little nags which they use to travel upon: but their best horses are brought out of Barbary. . . . Here are great store of doctors, judges, priests, and other learned men, that are bountifully maintained at the king's cost and charges, and hither are brought divers manuscripts or written books out of Barbary, which are sold for more money than any other merchandise. The coin of Timbuktu is of gold without any stamp or superscription: but in matters of small value they use certain shells brought hither out of the kingdom of Persia, 400 of them are worth a ducat: and $6\frac{2}{3}$ pieces of their gold coin weigh an ounce. The inhabitants are people of gentle and cheerful disposition, and spend a great part of the night singing and dancing through all the streets of the city. . . .'[1]

Timbuktu was, of course, an exceptional city. Its fame as a centre of scholarship reveals the importance attached to West Africa by Islamic academic circles. That the influence of Islam spread far beyond Timbuktu, however, is evidenced by numerous mosques and schools. Pilgrimages to Mecca by the emperors of Mali and Songhai were frequent; they revealed not only the extent of communications and ability to travel, but the degree of wealth accumulated in the empires. One Mali emperor took so much gold to Cairo on his journey that the value of the metal in Egypt became debased.

The activity which most clearly revealed the degree of stability in society was the conduct of trade. It was at the commercial cross-roads

[1] Leo Africanus, 'The History and Description of Africa done into English by John Pory', Hakluyt Society, 1896.

that political power was concentrated. Taxing of merchants here provided the means to sustain state and imperial organization. As the trade routes moved eastwards, so the empires extended their boundaries, Ghana being succeeded by Mali, in its turn giving way to Songhai. The extent of trade was also a measure of the security which had been established: several observers reported the peaceful, honest atmosphere which generally prevailed in these empires. Such stability was no doubt due in part to the comparatively easy customs of political transition. A king usually occupied the apex of the political pyramid, but his power was seldom absolute. A council of chiefs normally limited his authority in varying degrees. The chiefs, often elected from their own descent groups, supervised the officials who had responsibility for collecting annual tribute. Sometimes the council of chiefs would elect the king and unsatisfactory monarchs could usually be deposed. There were therefore few dynastic struggles, though kings had powers of patronage, often appointing relatives as rulers of provinces, and could use the wealth they accumulated from tribute to maintain their power by acting as arbiter between contending groups of chiefs.

This general description of African life applies only to the inhabitants of the capitals and the areas immediately surrounding them. In Africa, as in Europe at the same period, most people knew little of the way in which their government was conducted or of the individuals involved in it. The majority of people lived in rural villages labouring to grow food for their families. Agriculture was a virtually universal pursuit. Occasionally sufficient surplus could be produced to provide both the annual tribute to chiefs and to sustain a few craftsmen. More often the crafts, such as implement-making, had to be practised by farmers in their spare time. Almost all labour was manual, assisted only by such simple tools as hoes, axes and knives. The system of fallow rotation practised in Europe was also common in Africa. An area would be cultivated for a number of years and then left to return to bush whilst another district was cultivated. The use of manure as a fertilizer was rare. Various kinds of yams were grown in the forest, millets in the savanna.

Yet West African life did not exist only on a subsistence basis. As we have seen, there were always international markets, particularly for gold, salt and horses. There were also many domestic markets. For in addition to iron implements, pottery utensils and baskets produced throughout the region, a flourishing textile industry used locally grown cotton to weave into variously designed cloth gowns, whilst wood carving, brass work and terracotta modelling gave West Africa a reputation for great artistry. Again as in Europe, the demands of the wealthy, especially those at court, stimulated experiment in varieties of clothing, ornaments and the paraphernalia of official life. The barter or sale of such goods inspired the organization of lively markets throughout West Africa.

As we have already seen, many Africans did not live under state systems of government. The rain forests in particular held a large number of self-governing villages run by councils of elders drawn from descent groups or clans descended from a common ancestor. In such societies communal loyalty took precedence over the rights of the individual. The social order gained stability from the balance between different groups, land rights and authority deriving essentially from the community itself. Even within the empires many people lived in this fashion in villages remote from centralized government. There were smaller kingdoms too, like the Mossi and Hausa states, which tended to survive longer, with ruling dynasties marked by greater continuity than those of the great empires. Here, because government encompassed smaller areas, a greater degree of popular participation in its functions and involvement in its policies was a reality.

As in West Africa, so on the eastern side of the continent and in the central heartlands, trade was the crucial factor of society in pre-European times. Vasco da Gama described in his logbook the people he encountered in Mozambique during the course of his famous 1497–8 voyage to India: 'The people of this country are of a ruddy complexion and well made. They are Mohammedans, and their language is the same as that of the Moors. Their dresses are of fine linen or cotton stuffs, with variously coloured stripes, and of rich and elaborate workmanship. They all wear toucas with borders of silk embroidered in gold.'

How did the inhabitants of East Africa acquire such riches? Da Gama goes on to describe the occupation of the people of Mozambique and the goods they could command. 'They are merchants, and have trans-actions with white Moors (Indians), four of whose vessels were at the time in port, laden with gold, silver, cloves, pepper, ginger, and silver rings, as also with quantities of pearls, jewels, and rubies, all of which articles are used by the people of this country. We understood them to say that all these things, with the exception of the gold, were brought thither by these Moors; that further on, where we were going to, they abounded, and that precious stones, pearls and spices were so plentiful that there was no need to purchase them as they could be collected in baskets. . . . that there were many cities along the coast, and also an island, one half the population of which consisted of Moors and the other half of Christians, who were at war with each other. This island was said to be very wealthy.' Few European cities could have boasted such sights.

The logbook also gives us a description of the ships which plied this wealthy trade: 'The vessels of this country are of good size and decked. There are no nails, and the planks are held together by cords, as are also those of their boats. The sails are made of palm-matting. Their mariners have Genoese needles, by which they steer, quadrants, and navigating charts.' But where did the gold come from and why did Indians (and Arabs and Chinese) find it profitable to bring their luxury goods to this coast?

For answers to these questions – and fascinating answers they are – we are indebted to Duarte Barbosa, a Portuguese official who served in India during the first years of the sixteenth century and who described the trading centres around the Indian Ocean. He analysed the main trade of East Africa thus: 'And the manner of their traffic was this: they came in small vessels named zambucos from the kingdoms of Kilwa, Mombasa and Malindi, bringing many cotton cloths, some spotted and others white and blue, also some of silk, and many small beads, grey, red, and yellow, which things come to the said kingdoms from the great kingdom of Cambay (in India) in other greater ships. And these wares the said Moors who came from Malindi and Mombasa purchased from others who bring them hither and paid for in gold at such a price that those merchants departed well pleased; which gold they gave by weight.

'The Moors of Sofala kept these wares and sold them afterwards to the heathen of the Kingdom of Benametapa, who came thither laden with gold which they gave in exchange for the said cloths without weighing it. These Moors collect also great store of ivory which they find hard by Sofala, and this also they sell in the Kingdom of Cambay at five or six cruzados the quintal. They also sell some ambergris, which is brought to them from the Hucicas, and is exceeding good. These Moors are black, and some of them tawny; some of them speak Arabic, but the more part use the language of the country. They clothe themselves from the waist down with cotton and silk cloths, and other cloths they wear over their shoulders like capes, and turbans on their heads. Some of them wear small caps dyed in grain in chequers and other woollen clothes in many tints, also camlets and other silks.

'Their food is millet, rice, flesh and fish. . . . In this same Sofala now of late they make great store of cotton and weave it, and from it they make much white cloth, and as they know not how to dye it, or have not the needful dyes, they take the Cambay cloths, blue or otherwise coloured, and unravel them and make them up again, so that it becomes a new thing. With this thread and their own white they make much coloured cloth, and from it they gain much gold.'

Sofala, then, was obviously a rich centre for the purchase of Indian goods and for the collection of gold. But it was Kilwa which was the Queen of the coast. Barbosa describes it thus: 'there is an island hard by the mainland which is called Kilwa, in which is a Moorish town with many fair houses of stones and mortar, with many windows after our fashion, very well arranged in streets, with many flat roofs. The doors are of wood, well carved, with excellent joinery. Around it are streams and orchards and fruit-gardens with many channels of sweet water. It has a Moorish king over it. From this place they trade with Sofala, whence they bring back gold, and from here they spread all over Arabia Felix. . . . Before the King our Lord sent out his expedition to discover India the Moors of Sofala, Cuama, Angoya and Mozambique were all subject to the king of Kilwa, who was the most mighty king among them. And in this town was great plenty of gold, as no ships passed towards Sofala without first coming to this island. Of the Moors there are some fair and some black, they are finely clad in many rich garments of gold and silk and cotton, and the women as well; also with much gold and silver in chains and bracelets, which they wear on their legs and arms, and many jewelled earrings in their ears.'

To this picture Barbosa adds similar descriptions of other port cities, Malindi, Mombasa and others. Mombasa was 'a place of great traffic, and has a good harbour, in which are moored craft of many kinds and also great ships, both of those which come from Sofala and those which go thither, and others which come from the great kingdom of

Cambay and from Malindi; others which sail to the Isles of Zanzibar. . . .

'This Mombasa is a land very full of food. There are found many very fine sheep with round tails, cows and other cattle in great plenty, and many fowls, all of which are exceeding fat. There is much millet and rice, sweet and bitter oranges, lemons, pomegranates, Indian figs, vegetables of divers kinds, and much sweet water. The men thereof, are oft-times at war but seldom at peace with those of the mainland, and they carry on trade with them, bringing thence great store of honey, wax and ivory.'

In Malindi, 'they are great barterers, and deal in cloth, gold, ivory, and divers other wares with the Moors and heathen of the great kingdom of Cambay; and to their haven come every year many ships with cargoes of merchandise, from which they get great store of gold, ivory and wax. In this traffic the Cambay merchants make great profits, and thus, on one side and the other, they earn much money.'

We thus have a clear picture of the attractions of the East African coast for the merchants from across the Indian Ocean. But in each case the importance of gold is emphasized, and gold was certainly not mined in the coastal lands. Again Barbosa provides us with the key; 'Beyond this country (Sofala) towards the interior lies the great kingdom of Monomotapa (Benemetapa), pertaining to the heathen whom the Moors name Kaffirs. They are black men and go naked save that they cover their private parts with cotton cloth from the waist down. Some are clad in skins of wild beasts, and some, the most noble, wear capes of these skins with the tails which trail on the ground, as a token of state and dignity. They leap as they go, and sway their bodies, (and the tails which they wear) fly from one side to the other. They carry swords thrust into wooden scabbards bound with much gold and other metals, worn on the left side, as with us, in cloth girdles which they make for this purpose with four or five knots with hanging tassels to denote men of rank. They also carry assegais in their hands, and other bows and arrows of middle size. The arrows are not so long as those of the English, and not so short as those of the Turks. The iron arrow-heads are long and finely pointed. They are warlike men, and some too are great traders. Their women go naked, only covering their private parts with cotton cloths as long as they are unmarried. But when they are married and have borne sons they throw other cloths across their breasts.

'Fifteen or twenty days' journey inland there is a great town called Zimbabwe, in which there are many houses of wood and of straw. It pertains to the heathen, and the king of Monomotapa often stays there. It is six days' journey thence to Monomotapa. The road thereto goes inland from Sofala towards the Cape of Good Hope. In this town of Monomotapa is the king's most usual abode, in a very large building. And thence the traders carry the inland gold to Sofala and give it unweighed to the Moors for coloured cloths and beads, which are greatly esteemed among them; which beads come from Cambay. As regards Monomotapa these Moors say that the gold comes from a place yet further away towards the Cape of Good Hope, from another kingdom subject to the king of Monomotapa, who is a great lord, with many kings under him.' A later Portuguese observer, Dos Santos, who as a Dominican priest actually visted Central Africa, reported that gold 'is found in poulder like sand, in graines like beads; in pieces some smooth as they were melted, other branched with snags, others mixed so with Earth, that the Earth being well washed from them, they remayne like Honiecombes; those holes before full of red Earth, seeming as though they were also to be turned into Gold. As for that in stone, we have alreadie spoken. . . .'

The picture is now well-defined; gold was being mined in Central Africa, through the regions of modern Rhodesia, carried down to the coast, where Sofala was the nearest port, and there formed the basis of widespread trade across the Indian Ocean. At the time that Englishmen were first showing their earliest glimmers of interest in Africa, the East African coast was strung with city ports long engaged in sophisticated trade with Arabs, Indians and Chinese, based on gold mining in the heart of the continent, exchanging the metal for the cloths, spices and jewels of Asia.

The sixteenth century was a period of revolutionary change in Europe. The geographical discoveries led both to trade and to the plunder of the new lands of their minerals. The gold and silver and gems which crossed the Atlantic during the sixteenth century came to Europe to be used as currency and to build new political empires. The hazards of the early trade and the nature of the enterprises concentrated the newly-found wealth in a few hands. Great capitalists appeared for the first time in Europe, controlling a new kind of wealth which gave them the power to seek yet further channels by which to multiply their riches.

England played but a minor role in this great drama: the first act was but a preparation for the dominant role she was to take later. In the first part of the sixteenth century, her capitalists might have been only small-scale in comparison with their European fellows. They were, nevertheless, responsible for leading England out of the position of a backward agricultural country, in varying her economy, widening the gap between the few rich and the many poor, and promoting those pioneering ventures across the oceans which were to lead to the huge expansion of British seapower in the following century.

It was natural that these new wealthy Englishmen should have been content neither to see their fellows on the continent growing so many times wealthier nor to continue to rely on the continentals for their economic supplies. Yet at the beginning of the sixteenth century they did not have the power to challenge either the Portuguese monopoly in Africa and Asia nor that of the Spaniards in the New World. The voyages of William Hawkins in the 1530s were exceptional; they could not be followed by equal enterprise for another twenty years.

Nevertheless, before the mid-sixteenth century, pressures were building up in England for her merchants to compete with their continental rivals. From early in the century ships were fitted to make trading expeditions to the Levant. Hakluyt reports that in 1552 Thomas Windham made a second voyage to the Barbary Coast. There he traded 'linnen and woollen cloth, corall, amber, Jet, and divers other things well accepted by the Moores'. In exchange he collected 'Sugar, Dates, Almonds and Malassos or sugar Syrrope'. Windham's expedition was also apparently attacked by the Spaniards and aroused the wrath of the Portuguese who were offended by his trading with Barbary.

In the following year, 1553, the English once more called in the help of the Venetian, Cabot, this time to try and discover a way to Asia by sailing north-eastwards to the Arctic. Though it could not reach the Asian spices, this expedition brought Russia into the orbit of English trade, finding there both timber and valuable furs. The Russians were at this time almost entirely cut off both from European and Asian trade. Although they had a strongly centralized government,

their people seem to have been regarded by the English in very much
the same way as were Africans later. For this was the Russia of Ivan
the Terrible, whose people were described by English visitors as
'barbarous Russes' or 'the Barbarians'.

Within this early period of tentative English trading across the
oceans, William Hawkins's pioneering expedition to Africa was
followed by several voyages. But for many years they were infrequent.
One of Hawkins' captains, John Landye, visited West Africa in 1540,
also, like his predecessor, trading for ivory. In 1553 Thomas Windham,
having survived his hazardous journey to the Barbary Coast, took an
expedition to the Gold Coast and Benin. He was guided there by a
Portuguese pilot reneging on his duty to keep the Brazilian and Guinea
coasts reserved to the Portuguese and free from interlopers. His two
ships, the *Primrose* and the *Lion*, met in Madeira, sailed on to the Canaries
and the Island of St Nicholas, until at last they reached the Guinea
coast. Here they carefully avoided Elmina Castle, the centre of Portuguese power, and sold their goods for £150 worth of gold. But
Windham was not yet satisfied. He insisted on sailing further to Benin,
searching for pepper. From the Benin delta he sent pinnaces 50 or 60
leagues up the river where the crews were conducted to the court of a
king. This gentleman 'being a blacke Moore (although not so blacke
as the rest) sate in a great huge hall, long and wide, the wals made of
earth without windowes, the roofe of thin boords, opened in sundry
places, like unto lovers to let in the aire.' The king spoke Portuguese
and bartered pepper with them for their goods, even offering to give
them credit against their return. Windham and the Portuguese pilot,
however, quarrelled, Windham himself dying off the coast, and the
pilot dying on the return journey. It is some reflection on the dangers
and hardships of these early journeys that 'of seven-score men came
home to Plimmouth scarcely forty, and of them many died'. Some of
the merchants on the expedition were left behind in the king's territory.[1]

These English voyages to the West African coast, though hazardous,
continued as the trade was found to be lucrative. Lok followed
Windham in 1554 returning with £450 in gold, pepper and ivory,
estimated at ten times his risk capital. Further voyages were made
in the following three years. By the 1560s, Queen Elizabeth was

[1] See Richard Hakluyt, *Voyages and Documents*, Janet Hampden, OUP.

investing money in the Guinea expeditions, the profits of which were paid into the naval treasury.

The fact was that the initiative of the Portuguese and Spaniards had now provoked the envy of the other Atlantic European nations, the French, English and Dutch, just as the Iberians had emulated the Italians, the Italians the Arabs, and the Arabs the Indians and Chinese.

Yet this Elizabethan age was nothing like so glamorous as it has often been pictured. It was a time in which many of the most intelligent Englishmen were engaged in deep study of man, nature and geography. Their lives and those of the sailors and captains who made these pioneering voyages were often hard, needy and dangerous. It might sometimes bring great profit to those who had capital to risk, but many of the men who actually carried out the enterprises endured desperate hardships and, not infrequently, lost their lives.

It may be asked why it was the Europeans who sought out these new trade routes to Africa, Asia and the Americas. Why was it that neither the Africans nor the Asians found their way to the markets of Europe?

As we have already seen, this question does not take into account all the facts. The Arabs from Asia not only supplied European markets but actually occupied the Iberian peninsula. Nevertheless, it remains true that from the fifteenth century onwards, it was Europe which became the dominant power, conquering militarily and commercially the whole of the world.

If there had been mighty empires before, and, indeed, there were empires wealthier than those of sixteenth century Europe, in China, India, Africa and South America, they were never apparently strong enough to dominate Europe, whereas they themselves all fell in succession to European enterprise. As Michael Barratt Brown has pointed out, 'The three discoveries which Francis Bacon singled out in 1620 as those "which have changed the whole face and state of things throughout the world" were printing, gunpowder, and the magnet – all of them invented by the Chinese at least a thousand years earlier and brought to Europe by the Arabs. Our letters had their origin in Western Asia and our numerals in India, and were, also, brought to Europe by the Arabs.'[1]

---

[1] Michael Barratt Brown *After Imperialism*, pp. 26–7 (Heinemann).

Most of the ancient empires were either based on slavery or on peasant serfdom. They survived for many centuries, but never developed the productive power to dominate the world. The nearest parallels to the imperial enterprise of sixteenth century Europe were those of Greece, Venice and the Arabs. Yet here again were differences. These empires were based on merchants practising commerce and trade. Yet they never had the national unity or strength to sustain world-wide power, nor were they capable of using their accumulated capital to develop their own native industry on which to base sustained commercial imperialism. In both China and India, merchants were important in the growth of empires far more splendid than those of their contemporaries in Europe. But such was the centralized power of the emperors and the degree of monopoly in state manufacturing which they controlled, that the merchant class never gained that independence to be found in the Atlantic European countries. Indeed, that power could hardly be more clearly illustrated than in the case of China where, in the second half of the fifteenth century, a new political dynasty deliberately destroyed Chinese trade throughout the Indian Ocean, just at the moment when the Europeans, in the persons of the Portuguese, were entering that same maritime market. The lesson is still further pointed up by the early disintegration of the Spanish and Portuguese empires, where again centralized state power and the preservation of feudalism prevented the merchant class from obtaining that degree of initiative which it gained in France, the Netherlands and England.

The comparison between European and African conditions is more complicated. From the days of Egypt and Kush, there had been well-established states in Africa, which sometimes developed into empires. In the western Sudan, Ghana, Mali and Songhai succeeded each other in power and dominance. Kanem, Bornu and the Hausa states marched beside them. On the East African coast the loosely knit commercial cities in the Zenj empire traded across the Indian Ocean to Arabia, India and China. Even in Central Africa strongly organized societies developed, based on the mining of gold, whilst on the west coast kingdoms like that of the Kongo were established long before the European invasion. The Iron Age of Africa in the Middle Ages gave many of these states a social and economic equipment equal to that of many Europeans. Indeed, medieval Timbuktu surpassed most

European cities in learning, while the trade in an empire like that of Mali, as the market centre for the exchange of gold and copper for salt, silks, swords, and horses, exceeded that of many European markets. On the east coast, the export of gold and iron brought many Asian goods, including Chinese porcelain, to the trading cities.

The Europeans had certain advantages. External invasion of western Europe ended by the tenth century and allowed Europeans the security to fight each other, settle their own dynastic quarrels, and develop their own societies. In Africa, however, repeated invasions from Islam, the Almoravids, the Moroccans, the Turks, and eventually the Europeans, never allowed such a period of comparative quiet. Geographically, too, the proximity of western Europe to the oceans, following lessons learnt in the Mediterranean inland sea, was in sharp contrast to the difficulties of travel across the Sahara or through the rain forests of Africa. Whilst the problem of irrigation control in China and India had seemed to necessitate strong central government, so the African experiences in surmounting their natural hazards contrasted with those in the lightly watered, temperate climates of Europe.

Yet perhaps the greatest contrast was to be found in the different character of African and European societies. Generally speaking, African states were based on a fairly static communal structure. They balanced their economy between agriculture, mining and industry, and trade. Kano, for example, was one of the centres of the African textile industry. But it was an industry which never demanded the kind of semi-slave labour introduced into the European factories. Trade too, although centuries old, supplemented rather than dominated the economic life of African society. Those goods which were most in demand by Europeans, the ivory, gold, pepper, and later the slaves, were in plentiful supply in Africa. In exchange, the Africans could obtain all their basic needs. So the internal trade of the African continent plus its exchange of goods with other continents satisfied the needs of its people. Nor did Africa ever experience the inflation which Europe suffered from the sudden appearance of new metals and precious stones, nor the depression and unemployment, nor the religious influences extolling the virtue of labour. Even where there was hardship, the extended family in Africa provided its own natural social welfare scheme.

One can only speculate as to whether this comparatively stable, if uninspired, society would ever have stirred out of its calm passivity into something more akin to the aggressive, enterprising life of Renaissance Europe. For before it could approach the threshold of such change, its foundations were shattered. From the fifteenth century onwards the Europeans brought their new techniques and powers to the African coastline. Before the end of the sixteenth century, the Moroccan army, largely composed of Christians, slaves and mercenaries, exploited succession quarrels to destroy the Songhai Empire. The Turks seized the North African coastline as far west as Morocco for the Ottoman Empire. The Portuguese began to conquer East African cities, drastically undermining the trading entente established between African and Arab. A procession of European merchants besieged the West African coast, increasingly voracious for slave cargoes. Any chance that African society could build on its former achievements, that it might develop scientific, rational methods of economic or political progress, was destroyed at this time; the African continent became a focus for external forces essentially disruptive to indigenous evolution.

Chapter 2

The First Slave Phase:
1562-1713

The West African societies first encountered by the English in the sixteenth century revealed wide diversities. Their peoples spoke many different languages, practised a variety of religions and lived within varying social and political structures. Largely isolated between the two barriers of the Sahara in the north and the rain forests to the south, these African communities had been able to work out their own social development largely immune from external interference. From the conquests of the Almoravids in the eleventh century to those of the Moroccans at the end of the sixteenth century, West African societies had suffered no serious invasions. Yet, on the coast at least, they had been in peaceful communication with other peoples. The Portuguese had known them from the fifteenth century; when the English first arrived in Benin in the year 1553 they found that the Oba could speak, read and write Portuguese.

Many West African societies at this time were indeed sophisticated and well developed economically. Hand manufactures were common and widespread, whilst there was some mineral extraction from rocks, some oil production, smelting and the manufacture of various implements.

Along the main trade routes where wealth was increasing, society was organized politically through states and empires. Yet the kings and emperors who governed them were rarely complete despots. They were advised by councillors and had to listen to the wishes of their subjects. The growth of centralized government had brought a stratification into society within which people began to be identified in groups, clans or associations of craftsmen. Movement up and down the social ladder was frequent, sometimes provoking social conflicts.

Usually one of such groups would be responsible for government. A civil service bureaucracy of a rudimentary nature had developed and elders played an important part in government.

This was still, however, a mainly non-literate culture, depending on word of mouth to pass on its customs and traditions from generation to generation. Only where Islam had established itself, mainly in cities and towns, had literacy an important social base. In these towns, though, scholarship had developed to a high level with books being written and published, learning featuring prominently in society. Timbuktu was the finest example of this cultural pattern. Shortly after 1520 Leo Africanus wrote that 'In Timbuktu there are numerous judges, professors and holy men all being handsomely maintained by the king who holds scholars in much honour. Here, too, they sell many hand written books from North Africa; more profit is made from selling books in Timbuktu than from any other branch of trade'.

But in most of West Africa the economy was still based on subsistence. Families produced food for themselves, plus a little extra to pay their taxes and to exchange for simple implements. Blacksmiths produced weapons and tools to exchange for food, and a small surplus to contribute to their rulers. Trade was largely through a process of barter, although some little use was made of currency, usually in the form of cowrie shells. Employment depended almost entirely on the use of domestic slaves. These were usually drawn from the supply of prisoners of war or various types of malefactor. They provided the rulers and non-productive classes with their only supply of labour other than that contributed by all citizens through customary obligation. This was household, not chattel, slavery. The slaves had their place in family life, their rights as well as duties, and various methods of gaining freedom. Nevertheless, there was a certain amount of slave raiding in the area and also an organization of slave markets, whilst in a few regions, such as Mauretania, slaves were treated with a great deal more cruelty than was common elsewhere.

Education in these states was mainly restricted to vocational training in the practical skills required for a particular function in life. Thus, special instruction was given to children who would become metal-workers, weavers, boat-makers, drummers, soldiers, priests or medical men. There was also some teaching of the customs and traditional laws of society.

2 *

In this kind of society there was little stimulation towards scientific study. The established methods of the past were most important in cementing the structure of society. Neither scientific investigation nor the machines which such study would produce were demanded to supply the necessities for this kind of life. For this was largely a static society insulated from the troubles of the outside world, concerned with no more than its relations with immediate neighbours, and was almost self-sufficient.

If there was scant inducement to pursue scientific thoughts within these centralized states, there was even less in areas removed from the main trading routes. In the more remote areas little centralization had yet developed; society here rested on traditional methods of popular consent, with little organized government.

In the sixteenth century pressures from the outside began to influence these African societies. Invasions of Morocco by the Portuguese and Spaniards set off a series of chain reactions leading to political conflicts within that country. In their turn, these caused increasing interference with the caravan routes across the Sahara and with the markets situated at the Moroccan end of the trading paths. Eventually, as the Moroccans gained a sense of strength following their victories over the Portuguese and Turks, they attempted to take advantage of the dissensions developing within the Songhai empire. The central purpose of this policy was the old ambition of gaining control of the gold trade. For nearly thirty years, from 1590–1618, the Moroccans pursued this anti-Songhai strategy. In the end the central government of the Songhai empire was destroyed and its imperial unit fragmented into a number of tribal kingdoms. This was to have the effect of stemming the flow of gold itself and at the same time to contribute to the decline in the power of the region's cities. At the same time, the diversion of trade in the area from the traditional northward routes towards the Mediterranean to the new commercial attractions on the Atlantic coast aggravated the decline in the strength of the same cities.

Meanwhile Portuguese attacks on Egypt were countered by the Turks. The subsequent expansion of the Ottoman Empire and Turkish seizure of Egypt led to a disruption of trade along the north-east routes. The Turks then attacked westward along the North African coast, reaching Tunisia and Algeria. Unwilling to accept Moslem control of international trade with Asia and African states, Europeans now began to assert themselves. The growth of national consciousness based on the rise of merchant classes in Spain, Portugal, Holland, England and France strengthened this hostility towards the Moslem world. With a combination of increased financial and military power, always goaded by commercial interests, Western Europe opened a major campaign to capture the main trading channels of the known world. The Portuguese and Spaniards who led this campaign down the West African coast were soon followed by French, English, Dutch, Danes, Swedes and Germans. During the second half of the sixteenth century and throughout the seventeenth century these various European nationalities spent most of their time on the West African coast in quarrelling and fighting amongst themselves over their respective claims at sea and on the shores. Although a few attempts were made by European seamen to raid the interior and engage in looting, at this stage most of the West African states were far too strong for such activities to succeed. The basis of the relationship between the Western European traders and coastal Africans was mutual commercial interest. It was often confirmed by an alliance with an African ruler giving the traders of one European state exclusive rights.

During the early stages of this commercial partnership in the sixteenth century the only African goods of importance to Europeans were gold, ivory and pepper. Most of the luxury commodities such as silks, drugs, perfumes, spices and sugar were to be found in Asia rather than in Africa. Nor could Africa offer the opportunities for settlement to be found in America and the Caribbean, for the climate, diseases and difficult communications, together with the strength of African society, prevented European penetration of the hinterland or the establishment of plantations. It was, however, in the interest of both Africans and Europeans to exchange the gold, ivory and pepper for a variety of simple metal goods, cloth, hardware, and, later, spirits and fire-arms. Both sides were thereby cutting out the middlemen of North Africa.

The transition from the sale of these tropical products to the concentration on selling slaves to European merchants took place between the middle of the sixteenth century and the mid-seventeenth century. It was caused by the rapidly expanding demands for labour on the plantations of America and the Caribbean. It was not a difficult transition, for African rulers had been accustomed to bargain with each other for slave labour and even to export some slaves to the north. The European slave trade therefore appeared to them to be nothing more than an extension of their normal commercial practices. The African traders who had already established their connections for supplying gold easily changed from that commodity to slaves. To start with, the early slaves sold to Europeans were probably already enslaved (as prisoners or debtors) in their own land.

Yet, although the traders concerned may not have been conscious of the fact at the time, the change from normal commodity commerce to slave trading had a profound effect on African society. In conjuction with the conflicts developing in the north and north-east, it led to an increasing use of fire-arms, more intensive warfare, greater blood-shed and deepening insecurity. The profitable attractions of the trade shifted commercial activity from the camel caravans of the north southward to the slave coasts. Thus the centres of wealth and power moved from the savanna to the coast where European traders were wont to purchase their slave cargoes. Here the European traders leased land from local African communities to build forts in order to protect themselves, not so much from the Africans, as from their European rivals. These forts became islands of European strength, defended by small garrisons and protected from the gun-fire of off-shore vessels. The first trading fort of this nature was built at Sao Jorge de Mina on the Gold Coast, later known as Elmina. It was built of stone and to construct it in 1482 the Portuguese sent out ten caravels, two transports, a hundred engineers and five hundred soldiers.

The building of these forts in itself made little difference to African life. The forts simply provided centres for increased trade between Europeans and Africans. It was rather that the *nature* of this trade was to have a serious effect on the structure of African society.

In the first place, the rivalry between European traders led to frequent alliances between various European groups and different African communities. This in itself provoked hostility and conflict. Of even deeper significance, however, was the character of the trade. As the exchange of normal commodities changed to an obsession with the purchase of slaves, so provocation of conflict between Africans themselves rapidly increased. The alliances with the Europeans were now made for the purpose of slave-raiding against neighbouring communities. As a consequence, states and empires rose and fell and general violence greatly increased. Europeans and Africans in the coastal areas tried to prevent the growth of new rival states in the hinterland; yet they were unable to do so, because now, as the concentration of commerce moved southwards towards the coast, new centres of power were developing at strategic points where the new slave commodity could be supplied to the coastal region.

These disruptive effects of the slave trade in its infancy coincided with the Moroccan invasion of Songhai at the end of the sixteenth century. This also produced conditions of insecurity and violence. The great cities on which the empire had been based, Timbuktu and Gao, were ruined. Large areas of peaceful settlement surrounding the cities and towns rapidly decayed, and fell into disuse. The empire was fragmented, power devolving on smaller communities dominated by the strength of armies.

The effects of these twin disruptive elements were similar to those arising from parallel circumstances elsewhere. A tendency developed towards greater centralization of government. Already, in the sixteenth century, this was to be seen in such states as Benin and Oyo. Even in Songhai, before the invasion, the government had begun to take greater powers. In its turn, greater centralization led to the organization of professional armies and an increasing use of slaves within them. This whole tendency was strengthened as new arms were introduced into warfare, partly as a result of experience against foreign armies from the north, and partly because of the supplies provided by imports from Europe. Cavalry horses were now deployed, whilst the use of fire-arms rapidly spread from the coast into the interior. Such expensive methods inevitably demanded professional training. The call-up of amateur soldiers was not abandoned in time of emergency, but professional armies were maintained on a permanent basis. As in other continents, the existence of professional military organization increased the power of kings, adding to the trend towards greater governmental centralization and less popular participation. The new military skills and more sophisticated weapons meant, of course, that war became a much more destructive and a more frequent force in African life.

From Windham's first voyage to Morocco in 1551 until 1567 trade between England and West Africa was a regular, though only a minor part of England's maritime enterprise. During this period the names of Windham himself, Lok, Towerson and Fenner, all came to be associated with the West African trade. Their voyages were financed by a group of city merchants; generally the profits were as considerable as the hardships and deaths of the ships' crews. Through these activities and those of the French, with whom the English sometimes combined and at others fought, the Portuguese monopoly on the West African coast was broken.

Yet, towards the end of the period conditions for the Guinea trade became increasingly difficult. The voyage of George Fenner in 1556-7 illustrates the new hazards. Not only was Fenner attacked by Portuguese ships, but he also found the Africans hostile and unwilling to trade. By now the Portuguese, finding their diplomatic protests unheeded, had determined to use force. Through a combination of their coastal forts and their naval strength they were able to repair the breaches forced in their commercial monopoly. From this time English merchants seem to have abandoned reluctantly their promising Guinea trade.

One of the reasons for the new hostility of coastal Africans to Fenner and other English merchants of these years may have been their resentment of a new aspect of English trade. In 1562, John Hawkins, son of William, led the first English slaving expedition to West Africa. It may well have been that the introduction of trading in human beings brought an end to the promising trade in other commodities between English merchants and Africans. No doubt a further contributory factor to the suspension of this trade was the effect which English and French competition with the Portuguese in West Africa had already produced. Africans soon learnt to play off European rivals against each other, thus sharply raising the price demanded for their gold. Because the Portuguese had the only established position on the coast, it was they who were able, at least temporarily, to drive away their competitors by force of arms.

This first period of English slaving was much shorter than that of legitimate trade. In fact it only lasted six years, from 1562 to 1568. The fact that this overlapped some legitimate trade ventures – Fenner, for example, encountered difficulties on the west coast during the slaving expeditions – suggests that Africans had developed an antagonism towards English merchants from their fear of slavery.

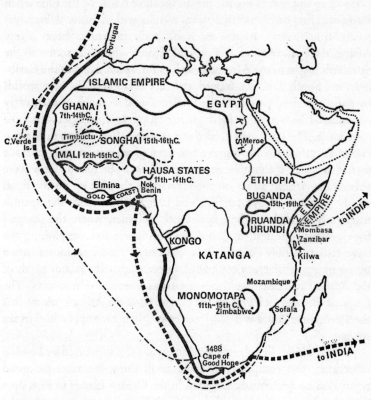

Empires and Kingdoms
approximate boundaries as far as known

Voyages of discovery & trade routes

➤ Bartholomew Diaz 1487-88
---➤ Vasco da Gama 1497-99
■■■■➤ English Voyages 16th C
··········· Trade routes to Arabia

2 Early empires and kingdoms; principal trade routes and
voyages of discovery

Hawkins did not, of course, invent the slave trade. At the time when Europeans first came into significant contact with Africans slavery was common in Europe, Africa and Asia. In the fifteenth century a few African slaves were taken to Portugal. From early in the sixteenth the Spaniards began to use African as well as European slaves in the Caribbean and South America. Indeed, the very division of the new worlds by papal sanction, on which the Iberians based so much of their early commercial power, was itself an invitation to interlopers into the slave trade. The Spaniards needed slaves in the West Indies, in Mexico and in Peru, but the Portuguese had been given a monopoly of trade to Africa where the only large slave pool was to be found. They were able to use African slaves on the plantations they set up on the small off-shore islands of West Africa and later in Brazil. But the Spanish monopoly of trade to their new world colonies, where the demand for slaves was greatest, excluded the Portuguese from exploiting the slave resources they controlled. It was only by devious means, often by no means satisfactory to Spanish interests, that the labour needs of the Spanish colonists could be met from Portuguese resources. The frequent shortage of slaves on the other side of the Atlantic meant that the Portuguese could not for long enjoy their monopoly in African slaving.

John Hawkins's first slaving expedition in 1562, supported by London merchants, was composed of three small ships. He used the good reputation he had already acquired in the Canary Islands to pick up a Spanish pilot who could guide him to the Guinea coast and to alert the Spanish buyers in Hispaniola of his intention to offer them slaves. On the Sierra Leone coast he secured 300 Africans, 'partly by the sword and partly by other meanes'. According to the Portuguese, Hawkins captured a Portuguese slaving ship and a number of other vessels. From here he sailed to Hispaniola, selling his slaves at such good prices that not only was he able to fill his own three ships with the proceeds, but also to load two locally hired vessels. The cargoes seem to have consisted mainly of hides, ginger, sugar and pearls. His voyage had not only broken the Portuguese monopoly of African slaving, but also the Spanish monopoly of trade to their own colonies.

The success of Hawkins's first voyage led to a second in 1564, in which Queen Elizabeth and a number of her Privy Councillors were secret shareholders. Yet the anger of Philip II and his Spanish govern-

ment at this English breach in their commercial monopoly was strong
enough to provoke the risk of war from Spain. The queen had no
intention of accepting the Spanish challenge at this time. She prohibited Hawkins from visiting the Spanish colonies a third time.
Nevertheless, a third voyage was made in 1566, though Hawkins
sent in his own place his captain, John Lovell. Despite the continued fury
of the Spaniards, the London merchants, having tasted the fruits of
slaving success, had no intention of abandoning them. The Spanish
ambassador in London wrote to his master, 'what they seek in Guinea
most are slaves to take to the West Indies. I will use all efforts to prevent
them going, but the greed of these people is great and they are not
only merchants who have shares in these adventures but secretly many
of the queen's Council. . . .'

So Hawkins sailed a third time in 1567 on a voyage which was to
end the English slave trade for over half a century. On this occasion
he had unusually substantial backing, for it immediately followed
Fenner's misfortunes and the end of gold trading. The merchants who
had been investing in legitimate trade now joined forces to support
the slaving expedition. On this expedition Hawkins took five hundred
Africans across the Atlantic, having captured them only after some
fighting. He also used violent means to reduce Spanish opposition
to his sales in South America.

It was after Hawkins had completed his trade and set sail for home
that there occurred the event which virtually brought an end to this
first period of English slaving. Caught by a hurricane in the Gulf of
Mexico, his small fleet took refuge in the Mexican harbour of San
Juan de Ulua. Here they were caught by the Spanish treasure fleet on
its way to load the annual supply of Mexican metals. Hawkins' expedition was almost totally destroyed, and only two ships, one commanded by himself and the other by Francis Drake, eventually limped
home in January 1569. The effect of this disaster, together with that
of Fenner at the hands of the Portuguese two years earlier, seems to have
convinced the English that, for the time being at least, they could not
challenge the might of Spain and Portugal. Trade with Africa, both
in slaves and goods, together with attempts to break the Spanish
monopoly across the Atlantic, came to an end. With the union of the
Spanish and Portuguese monarchies in 1580 the door to English trade
in Africa and the new world was not only closed but bolted. Hence-

forth, for the rest of the century, piracy against Iberian shipping replaced the merchant trading which for a short period had provided large profits and the prospect of expanding commerce. Now, as a consequence of Iberian might and monopoly, Englands' links with Africans were again severed.

It was not accidental that Englishmen made this first determined effort to trade with Africans during the second half of the sixteenth century. By this time traditional English trade in Europe was fast declining as the new trade routes developed and European religious influences turned against the English. It was a time of economic and social disturbance; metals from the new world entered the continent in hitherto unknown quantities; towns expanded, new towns were built and the urban population demanded manufactured goods. New industries developed to supply the growing demand for mercantile and naval ships. Although the development of world-wide trade from Europe brought new luxury goods and an extravagant life for the small wealthy class able to enjoy it, the decline of the old markets brought widespread unemployment and hunger to many Englishmen.

There was therefore every inducement to expand English trade routes. As we have seen, this attempt quickly encountered the high monopoly walls of Portugal and Spain. Yet conditions were developing in England in which a merchant and manufacturing class was gradually undermining the feudal structure. For a time it depended on royal monopolies. It tended to arise out of or to be absorbed into the land-owning class. But as money became more powerful than land, so the merchants developed a greater independence from both land-owners and monarchy. It was trade which would enable the new class to develop its profits and its power. As the importance of internal European trade and the cities it had raised to dominance declined, so opportunities for the new merchants of the European Atlantic seaboard expanded. In Spain and Portugal feudalism was still too strong to permit the merchant class that independence on which lasting power would be based. Feudal survivals even handicapped the French, but in Britain and Holland the new merchants gradually felt their strength and raised an open challenge to feudalism itself and the monarchies which were part of its system.

So the rebuff suffered by the young English merchant class from the Spaniards and Portuguese in its attempt to establish African trade did not destroy commercial ambition. Other trading channels were tried, to Russia, Scandinavia, the Levant, Hudson Bay, and, eventually, to the fabulous East Indies themselves. For the time being these attempts relied on the formation of chartered companies dependent on the grant of royal monopolies; but monopoly inevitably restricted the scale of trade and the profits derived from it. Not until the manufacturing sector of the new merchant class had acquired the strength to challenge the monopolist merchants could the class as a whole shake itself free from the trammels of feudalism and monarchical control. One of the principal factors which was to provide strength to the manufacturing merchants was the new demand invoked by the voyages of the merchant adventurers and the wars which they provoked. The stimulus given to manufacturing for all kinds of ship-building and provisioning, together with the production of military equipment, provided a sure foundation for the new manufacturing industries which were to take their place alongside traditional cloth production.

Meanwhile, however, relations between Englishmen and Africans languished. Drake and his fellows fell back on piracy against the Spaniards and eventually paved the way for the destruction of the Iberian monopoly by opening English sea lanes around the world. The incorporation of the East India Company in 1600 showed where the principal interests of English merchants were now focused. It was to be some years later before the more modest attractions of African trade were again to attract serious support.

But before the end of Elizabeth's reign a number of rather feeble attempts were made to revive English trade with the West African coast. A group of London merchants were granted a charter in 1585 to trade with Morocco and the Barbary Coast. Three years later a Portuguese renegade sold a patent to 'certain merchants of Exeter and others of the west parts and of London, for trade to the rivers of Senega and Gamba in Guinea'. But the crews of the three ships sent to trade with the Gambia encountered hostility from the Portuguese and Spaniards there. The wide estuary of the Gambia river invited commercial exploration for two hundred miles up its reaches. Yet at this time legitimate traders seem to have been discouraged by the pirates who used the river mouth as their base.

In 1592 Elizabeth granted a charter to another company to trade south of the Gambia as far as Sierra Leone. Yet these were but puny ventures compared with the trade of the Spaniards and Portuguese, or of the Dutch, who were now beginning to make serious inroads into Iberia's monopoly. It was not until 1618 that a more serious effort was made by Englishmen to rival the richly developing trade of other Atlantic states through the chartering of a Company of Adventurers of London trading to Guinea and Benin. It was this company which built the first English fort in Africa on James Island at the mouth of the Gambia, the site which was to become Bathurst. Rumours of rich trading opportunities and great quantities of gold up the river Gambia had been prevalent since the fifteenth century. Unfortunately for this company the Portuguese traders already established there killed all the crew of the first English ship, whilst fever decimated those of the second. Yet expeditions reached more than three hundred miles from the coast, one of them led by Captain Richard Jobson, who was to record his experiences in 'The Golden Trade or a Discovery of the River Gambia and the Golden Trade of the Aethiopians'. According to Jobson the Africans he encountered at Tenda in the interior, although never having seen white men before, received him with 'familiar conversation, fair acceptance and mutual amitie'. Apparently Jobson found favour with the Africans because he had no intention of slave trading, unlike other Europeans who had appeared on parts of the river.

Despite the promise of renewed trade between England and the Africans up the Gambia, the company lost money and soon ceased its ventures. Indeed, it was clear by this time that it was to be the Dutch, rather than the English or French, who would first successfully challenge the Spanish-Portuguese monopolies.

The Dutch, with their skill in ship building, their central trading position on the seas, the oceans and internal European trade, and, perhaps above all, with their freedom from the handicap of feudal institutions, quickly gained a paramount position in the commerce of the world. This was established not only across the Indian and Atlantic Oceans, in the Middle East and in the Baltic, but also on the African coast. It was they who first realized that in order to breach the Portuguese monopoly and take over control of the West African trade from the Portuguese, it was essential to command the coast itself. They therefore allied themselves with some of the coastal

Africans to drive out the Portuguese, built their own base, named Fort Nassau, and attacked the Portuguese strongholds. By 1632 the Dutch had succeeded in expelling the Portuguese from the Gold Coast, in the process capturing their two main fortifications, Elmina Castle and Axim.

In the meantime, although the English and French were also breaking through the Portuguese monopoly, they did so only as interlopers, avoiding where possible Portugal's fleets and forts. This kind of trade, whether for commodities or for slaves, could be conducted on a small scale by free-lance merchants. To compete with either the Dutch or the Portuguese, however, required much larger organization. In 1630, therefore, a new charter was granted to a Company of Merchants Trading to Guinea. After some years of failure, the company suddenly received a new lease of life when, in 1636, one of its ships arrived back in England with £30,000 worth of gold. This company, reconstituted in 1651, built forts and established factories on the west coast. In 1657, when in financial difficulties, it was taken over by the much more powerful East India Company, which had the influence derived from support by Oliver Cromwell.

During the first half of the seventeenth century all the major Atlantic European states began to develop at various paces the mercantilist concept of imperial policy. They based their imperial ideas on the value of expanding trade to the prosperity of their own countries. Believing that world trade had a certain static size, they naturally drew the conclusion that they could only expand their own share by diminishing that of their rivals. Thus trade was always accompanied by warfare, declared or undeclared. In particular, all these states, and especially England, resented having to pay from their own national resources for goods which they could only obtain from merchants of their rivals. Thus the English were impelled during this century to attempt, as a part of national policy, to seek control of those overseas markets dominated by the Dutch, the French, the Spaniards or the Portuguese. As they began to colonize the islands of the Caribbean and the mainland of America, they found it increasingly irksome to have to rely on supplies of slave labour controlled usually by the Dutch. This led them increasingly to seek positions on the slave coast between the Gold Coast and Benin. It also led them from time to time into open warfare with the Dutch.

This general policy was followed both under the Stuarts and by the Commonwealth, for in both cases it was the now powerful merchant class which guided commercial policy and dictated government attitudes to overseas trade. Indeed, many of Charles I's troubles arose from his lack of sympathy with the merchants; whilst the Navigation Act of Cromwell, confining imports to English ships, led directly to war with the Dutch. At the same time Cromwell seems, like Elizabeth, to have been more concerned with the threat of Spain than with either that of the Dutch, who had revolted against Madrid, or with the French. On one occasion he is believed to have considered forming an alliance with the United Provinces against the Spaniards and all who followed them.

Nevertheless, it was to be the Dutch first and then the French, who were to become the greatest rivals to Englishmen across the oceans. Neither the Spaniards nor the Portuguese ever developed an independent merchant class strong enough to capitalize on the new worlds which their sailors had discovered. Their national threats petered out as soon as the Dutch, French and English merchants had grown to maturity.

If it is possible to select one year in which the slave trade began its dominance in English commerical life, with all its consequences for Anglo-African relations, that year would be 1640. It was in 1640 that the colonists in Barbados began to plant sugar and it was sugar planting that led to the insatiable demand for slaves in the English Atlantic empire.

Barbados had been settled by English colonists from 1624. This was part of English expansion across the Atlantic following the example already set by the Spaniards, Portuguese and then the Dutch. Since the final failure by the end of the Hundred Years' War to colonize France, England had spent a century and a half in changing her social and economic structure, increasing her wealth and building her naval power. During the peaceful years of the reign of James I, this economic and military strength was used to lay the foundations of a new British Empire in America and the West Indies. The effort was reinforced when the strength of the navy was resuscitated by Charles I. English companies financed emigration, hoping thereby to create permanent markets for their manufactures across the Atlantic and to gain, in return, the products of the New World. Some people emigrated in order to practise their religious convictions in freedom; but most of the emigrants were attracted by the prospect of better living conditions. Free land was offered by such companies and, as this was a time of English land hunger, rising rents and unemployment, the attraction was multiplied. Craftsmen, who found work hard to come by at home, saw the chance of new opportunities, whilst the prospect of adventure and new riches tempted all classes. In addition, of course, the government was accustomed to deport convicts and also many of the prisoners taken in the Civil War. Nor was it unusual for youths to be kidnapped and sold into servitude in the New World.

These groups of immigrants were normally indentured to labour, a form of slavery, but one of a temporary nature which could, after a period, be followed by freedom. Lest it be imagined that the prospects of emigration suggested any vision of paradise, it should be remembered that at this time the voyage across the Atlantic was likely to take at least three months. The ships were very small and often in horrible condition. The danger of death from ship-wreck, dysentry or other diseases was correspondingly high. Thus voluntary emigration was always limited, and had to be supplemented by the press gang and the jailer.

The settlement of Barbados formed part of the English, French and Dutch challenge to the Spanish and Portuguese monopolies across the Atlantic. The English occupied the Bermudas in 1609, St Christopher in 1623, Barbados in 1624–5 and then the Leeward Islands. The French were in Guadeloupe in 1626 and Martinique in 1635. During the 1630s the Dutch moved into Curaçao, St Eustacius and Tobago.

From the Anglo-African viewpoint, however, it was Barbados which was first significant. For the first fifteen years the settlers in Barbados concentrated on producing cotton, tobacco and dyes. They had the financial backing of various syndicates formed by London merchants, the most important of which were those of Warner and his associates, who had previous experience in Guinea, and Courteen and his colleagues, who had Dutch connections. But in 1640 Dutch traders in Brazil encouraged the Barbadian settlers to begin planting sugar. They supplied them with the plants and with the equipment for crushing, boiling and pot crystallization. They also taught them how to wash the sugar to turn it from brown into white.

Within a few years the sugar trade to Europe became of major commercial importance. Whereas previously sugar was a rare commodity, it now quickly attained widespread popularity. Drinking sweetened tea and coffee became increasingly common in Europe. During the next ten years the value per acre of sugar plantations grew to treble that of the tobacco fields. Barbados came to be known as 'the brightest jewell in His Majesty's crown', for its exports to Britain were worth more than even those from Virginia or New England. Moreover, the cultivation of sugar in Barbados was approved by Englishmen, for it could not be grown in England and had previously been imported from foreign lands and through foreign traders. Colonial policy at this time approved the production of goods in the colonies only in so far as they did not compete with home production. Even tobacco was at times suspect, for tobacco could be and was grown in England.

The consequences of the establishing of sugar in Barbados and the immediately increased European market for its sale was a rapid growth of plantations, usually large, to justify the considerable capital involved. Planters, indentured servants and convicts multiplied. Yet this expanded population proved incapable of supplying the labour essential to the sugar fields. It was here that the connection between Barbados sugar-planting and Africa arose.

The only source of labour capable of filling the insatiable needs of the sugar plantations was Africa. For almost two hundred years now Europe had been engaged in the African slave trade aross the Atlantic and to Europe. The Indians of the Caribbean, South and Central America had quickly proved unsatisfactory for either plantation or mining labour, whose rigours had almost exterminated them. The Portuguese had supplied their own farmers with African slave labour from the fifteenth century. Their Atlantic colonies and those of the Spaniards had drawn on the same supply.

It was natural, therefore, for the Barbadian sugar planters to look to the same source. In any case, Negro slaves were cheaper than white indentured workers. Nearby Cuba was already the principal slave market of the region. European rivals to the Spanish and Portuguese monopoly had concentrated almost exclusively on contesting the slave trade from West Africa to the Spanish colonies and Brazil. The Dutch were combining their political with their commercial efforts to undermine the Spanish hold on the Low Countries. From 1621 the Dutch

West India Company had associated trade with Guinea to its West Indian settlements. By 1637 they had conquered much of Portuguese Brazil and proved their power to supply slaves from Africa to the planters. They had already begun to reduce or take over Portuguese posts on the West African coast. The Dutch, too, had aided their cause by destroying the sea power of Spain along the Atlantic lanes.

It was, therefore, to the Dutch traders that the English planters in Barbados turned first for their supply of slaves. Yet rapid increases in the value of the sugar trade, not only from Barbados, but from other English and French West Indian islands, quickly provided a tremendous incentive for English traders to turn increasingly to slaving. In any case, it was against all recognized mercantile policy to allow the needs of Englishmen to increase the profits of the Dutch. Under Cromwell's Commonwealth, Navigation Acts were passed making it illegal for Dutch ships to trade to the English colonies. Inevitably, though, ever pressing demand led to constant smuggling by aliens. At the time of the Restoration in 1660, therefore, Charles II granted a charter to an English group of merchants constituting the Company of the Royal Adventurers to Africa. Twelve years later it changed its name to the Royal African Company, the king himself being one of the shareholders. The object of the company was to supply English sugar colonies with 3,000 slaves a year at an average price of £17, or the value of one ton of sugar per slave.

The company quickly felt dissatisfied about being limited to supply only English planters. It sought to increase profits by selling some of its slaves at higher prices in the Spanish colonies, despite the objection of the English planters, who feared that such competition would raise the price of slaves. Like its competitors from Holland, France, Denmark, Sweden and Germany, the English company now sought to sell slaves wherever there were buyers. In 1663 the king granted dispensation from the Navigation Acts to allow Spanish ships to sell goods in English West Indian ports for the purpose of buying slaves for their colonies. Meanwhile, the English colonists themselves were protesting against the African Company's monopoly of slaving, demanded free trade in slaves and encouraged smuggling from interlopers. By now the profits of the slave trade had become so attractive that commercial circles began to argue as to whether its purpose was not more to sell slaves than to develop the sugar production for which they were supplied. It was a sign of the importance attached to the slave trade itself that slaving interests began to compete for the contract disposed of by the Spanish Crown for supplying slaves to Spanish America. This 'asiento', as it was called, was secured first by the French.

An alliance between an important section of the old landed classes and the new merchant class had supported the Tudors in their role of undermining feudalism, producing order out of chaos and creating stable government. It was the strength of this alliance that made it possible for Tudor monarchs to destroy the powers of the church and of the conservative section of the nobility. Defeat of these two elements was essential to produce the conditions in which England could enter the capitalist age. Yet the monarchy itself also became an obstacle to English economic revolution. The limited feudalism which still remained within it emerged again during Stuart reigns. The seventeenth century thus became a battleground between the new bourgeoisie and the monarchy for control of a state apparatus now crucial to ordering society in a manner allowing the new economic forces to mature. The victory of the new bourgeois classes and the settlement they arranged in 1688 gave England a decisive lead over her rivals in the race towards modern industrialism; in the seventeenth century it was this new bourgeoisie, largely activated by its merchant sector, which formed the progressive classes of England.

It was the newly-growing merchant class in Britain, as in Holland, which was responsible for forging the ever-strengthening links with Africa, the Caribbean and Southern America. At first the merchant adventurers had been but an off-shoot of a surviving feudal system. Their backers were mainly large, enterprising, aristocratic landowners who could count on their influence with the crown to secure royal monopolies. But this was a crude form of trade, based on the concept of buying cheap to sell dear and it usually concentrated on the purchase of luxury goods such as silks, spices and jewels. Although such activities incidentally brought encouragement to all aspects of shipbuilding and sailing, they did not promote the interests of the rising class of manufacturers. Indeed, the English cloth trade still had to compete with foreign textiles and the cloth manufacturers resented the imports which the early monopolist traders brought to their country. The Spanish empire demonstrated the negative outcome of such commerce. It remained subservient to the feudal system. Its merchant class remained small and politically unimportant, whilst much of the wealth gained found its way into the coffers of foreign protestant merchants through the practice of piracy. Indeed, the English merchant class itself found opportunities to profit from the social backwardness of Spanish imperialists; as the Spaniards could supply neither manufactures nor slaves to their own colonists, the English quickly developed smuggling techniques capable of providing both commodities to the Spanish colonies.

Elizabeth I had granted a charter to the African Company; during her reign the smaller merchants, anxious to combine manufactures and trade, had hardly begun to mount their challenge to royal trading monopolies. However, when Elizabeth's example was followed by James I and later by his son, English trade began to expand. The plunder which constituted the main objective of royal monopolies was considered a hindrance to the development of manufacturing and its expansion into overseas commerce. The object of this new class was to break the hold of the crown and the royal monopolists over the new colonies and to replace the inefficiency, extravagance and corruption common to monopoly companies by more virile, profitable and economically integrated commercial activities. As early as 1619 Sir Edwin Sandys, representing this new association between smaller merchants and the manufacturers, had not only won control of the Virginian company for its small stockholders, cleaned up corruption and attacked inefficiency; he had despatched his first ship of slaves to the colonies and was pioneering the growth of slave-owning plantations, supplying them with the labour of settlers, indentured workers and slaves. These were to provide the tobacco and cotton for British manufacturers and to create new markets for the goods produced in Britain.

Britain's general colonial policy in the seventeenth century was based on the concept, which was universal in Europe at the time, that the only purpose of colonization was to provide support to the home economy. So far as England was concerned this led, at first, to an obsession with seizing plunder and particularly bullion, usually from the Portuguese and Spanish ships crossing the Atlantic. It was believed that a country's wealth could be weighed in its specie. Moreover, most of the overseas purchases made at this stage of English commercial life were the luxury goods of Asia; as England produced virtually nothing which could be sold in that continent, imports could only be financed by offering precious metals in exchange.

At this stage English commerce was little more than a modern extension of medieval feudalism. A handful of large land-owners formed a sector of the court around the monarch and financed the early ventures into overseas trade. They were able to secure monopoly trading rights from the crown, the monarch himself often investing in such ventures. The real conflict was between the small group of royal favourites and the new type of merchant opposed to monopoly trading, working with the small but growing manufacturing interests. The activities of the monopolists in establishing their overseas markets and in using national resources to make war on their foreign rivals, did something in stimulating ship-building, promoting new commercial methods and encouraging the production of war implements to further the interests both of the new merchants and of manufacturers. In general, however, such activities raised barriers against the growth of manufacturing in the first half of the seventeenth century and against the development of unrestricted English commerce. The objectives of the monopolists in either seeking plunder or simply buying luxury goods cheaply in the east and across the Atlantic to sell dearly in Europe were inimical to those who wished to produce goods in England and sell them abroad. Indeed, some of the imports from Asia, particularly the textiles, were believed to compete with English manufactures, whilst the concentration of the monopolists on luxuries hindered the growth of a wider market for home-produced goods. As the concept of using tropical and semi-tropical colonies for the purpose of supplying scarce raw materials and later as markets for English manufactured goods began to strengthen, it led directly to a struggle between the manufacturing interests and the monopolists, concerned only with obtaining precious metals or adornments for the rich.

This struggle was reflected politically in the attempts of Parliament to restrict the powers of the crown in the Civil War and finally in the 1688 revolution. To both monarchy and Commonwealth the first consideration remained the accumulation of bullion in England. Yet whilst the monarchy and court thought of this in terms of wealth for a small group, the growing class of merchants and manufacturers used both parliament and Cromwell's Commonwealth to further their own wider and expanding economic interest. Moreover, their efforts were assisted by conditions in Europe. The English Civil War was only one of many conflicts besetting the continent during the seventeenth century. The efforts and resources invested in such conflicts caused an inevitable decline in the European market for normal trade during the last third of the century. In its turn this led to a reduction in overseas profits, evidenced, for example, in the collapse of the English African Company and in the need for the cloth manufacturers to seek new outlets for their trade. Economic causes were thus assisting political pressures to produce the final destruction of English feudalism and the royal monopolies which represented it in commercial life.

The causes of this conflict are also illustrated from the slave trade itself. This was still under the control of monopolist companies. It could be argued that the manufacturers who were producing goods to be exchanged on the West African coast for slaves received their profit from the trade. Yet the fact is that, because such enormous profits were made from slaving, they were usually reinvested in further slave expeditions instead of providing the capital needed for the expansion of manufacturing. It was not until the eighteenth century that sufficient capital accumulated from English commerce to provide the resources for a simultaneous development of slaving and manufactures.

The period between the Restoration of 1660 and the Revolution of 1688 was one of considerable commercial expansion. This was partially due to the alliance with Portugal and closer relations with the Spaniards and their colonies. The consequent progress might have suggested that the mercantile theory was not totally valid. The lesson that trade flourished whilst England was allied with at least some of her competitors does not seem to have been recognized. Yet the expansion of the American and Caribbean economies, added to the new markets opened in the Spanish and Portuguese colonies, provided the major factor in English commercial growth. And it was the capital accumulated from the exploitation of these colonial areas, together with the profits of the slave trade, which laid the economic foundations for the commercial and industrial triumphs of the eighteenth century.

The Restoration with its renewed monopolies was no more than an interregnum in the growing power of the merchant classes. The Parliamentary victory in the Civil War had marked the destruction of the power of the royal monopolies and thus had brought feudalism to an end. Though weariness with the Commonwealth allowed the monarch to restore the appearance of pre-Civil War conditions, the merchant class by now was far too strong to accept the restoration of real royal power. In 1688 it made this perfectly plain by supplanting the feudal-minded Stuarts with its own merchant prince, William of Orange. From now on, political power in Britain was independent of the monarchy and the feudal survivors who had surrounded it. Not only would political institutions be geared to serve the interests of the dominant merchant class at home; in future foreign and colonial policy would also be determined by economic rather than by political motives.

The settlement with Holland in 1688 committed England to war with France and the French were now succeeding the Dutch as England's chief competitors. They saw the decline of Spain as creating a vacuum which they must fill if they were to dominate the Continent. French success here would not only lead to restoration of the Stuarts and an overthrow of the 1688 settlement; but in so doing it could well substitute military despotism in England for control of government by the new English merchant classes. Moreover, victory for the French would certainly lead to their seizure of Spain's American colonies and the exclusion of the English traders from this lucrative market. Thus the war of the League of Augsburg, 1689–97, and the wars of the Spanish Succession, 1701–13, were fought not only in defence of English political power in Europe by blocking Louis XIV's pretensions in Spain, but to protect the interests of English commerce. Essentially, they were wars between rival merchant classes; it was the English merchants who emerged victorious. The peace which ended the latter war, the Treaty of Utrecht in 1713, provided Britain with vital keys to her future maritime and commercial power. Britain retained Gibraltar and Minorca in the Mediterranean; Nova Scotia and Hudson Bay in America were taken from the French; the merchants were especially satisfied by the allocation of the *asiento*, or monopoly for supplying slaves to the Spanish colonies. The Treaty was followed by a long period of peace, bringing rapidly increasing prosperity to British merchants. During the ensuing thirty years, exports from Britain increased by about fifty per cent. Holland had already declined as a competitor, whilst the French had to recover from the effects of the war and the peace treaty, still labouring under the handicap of a surviving feudal bureaucracy.

Chapter 3

The Slave Century

The century following the Treaty of Utrecht was one of prosperity and general stability in Britain. National life, balanced between agriculture, manufacture and commerce, provided a sound foundation for orderly and generally contented conditions. These three elements had expanded progressively, although never so rapidly as to cause serious social unrest. Having replaced the Spaniards and Portuguese as colonialists, beaten the Dutch at their own game in the commercial world, and then merged with them, Britain found herself in the eighteenth century faced only with the rivalry of France for international domination. The eighteenth century saw Britain emerge triumphant from conflicts with France, none of which seriously impinged on life at home. Perhaps the stoutest prop to this prosperity and contentment was the profitable slave trade from Africa across the Atlantic, together with the rewards of the plantation system which depended on it.

Within this scene of national prosperity, the city of London dominated economic life. Her population was fifteen times as great as that of any other English city. She was the centre of national and international trade, the home of industry and the greatest port in Europe. To a large extent London in the eighteenth century was self-governing, with her own magistrates, police and soldiers. During this time a vast majority of her people, the working class, lived in appalling slum conditions; yet during the eighteenth century some small proportion of the wealth which poured into the city began to be used for education, the beginnings of social reform – and to build many new churches. The city was prepared to accept the edicts of Westminster so long as they did not attempt to infringe on the ancient powers which she had been accustomed to employ to define her liberties. One should, perhaps, add the further reservation that London expected parliament and monarch to follow policies in conformity with what she saw as her economic interests. For, above all, London was the centre of banking, finance and commerce. Here the great merchant princes and banking magnates had their homes, usually on their business premises; their servants, apprentices, porters and messengers, were all allotted garrets or cellars. The river itself was an artery of wealth; London Bridge, until well into the century the only land passage across the river; the Pool a jungle of masts, with ships from the Orient, Africa, the Caribbean and America standing out in the road-way, loading and un-loading, for deep docks had yet to be sunk.

One of the consequences of this prosperous and stable age was the growth of a new humanitarian spirit. This may not have descended very far down the social scale, nor, of course, did it accept a scale of values which would appear humane today. Nevertheless, it was an age in which reform was accepted and, within limits, applied. In aspects of life like education, the treatment of servants, medicine, infant mortality and the building of hospitals, some slight start was made in humanizing relations between fortunates and unfortunates. At the same time, one should observe that the new wealth also brought an increase in the sense of sanctity of profit, appropriately accompanied by an ever-lengthening series of statutes against its invasion. Yet, with a reduction in the pressures to scrape a livelihood, with greater leisure and with increased comfort, some people were able to turn their minds and emotions towards securing a greater degree of benevolence towards peoples in a different station. It was this gradually expanding spirit of humanity which eventually enabled those who were, for various reasons, antagonistic to the slave trade to secure its abolition. Lord Mansfield's judgement in 1772 outlawed slavery in Britain; the campaign of Wilberforce and his friends culminated in the act of 1807 which prohibited the slave trade itself; and, finally, in 1833 all slaves throughout the British Empire were emancipated. There were, of course, many economic and political cross-currents within this campaign; nevertheless it only became possible to sustain as the spirit of humanitarianism gradually developed out of the prosperity of eighteenth century Britain.

The roots from which the prosperity of Britain flowered were commercial. The development of canals, the use of rivers and the building of Macadam's new roads all aided the transport and purchase

3

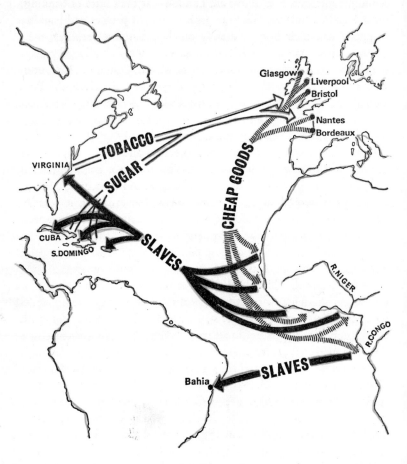

3 The slave trade

of goods in Britain. This inevitably stimulated overseas commercial activity designed to secure marketable commodities. In its turn, the export of British manufactured goods increased to pay for the growing imports. For the first time, overseas trade began to establish a link to popular, rather than only to privileged, tastes. Coffee, tea, sugar and tobacco consumption spread progressively during the century. Cotton was imported, manufactured in Lancashire and exported as cloth. Much of Lancashire's textile manufactures left Liverpool in ships bound for Africa, where they were exchanged for slaves, who were then transported across the Atlantic to the plantations. Ships returned from America or the West Indies with consignments of raw cotton, sugar and tobacco. Liverpool, particularly, thrived on this triangular trade, growing rapidly throughout the eighteenth century, until, by its turn, the city was inhabited by a population of 78,000, larger than that of any other provincial city, except Manchester-Salford, which had also prospered from a commercial base.

Having supplanted first the Portuguese and then the Dutch from their transatlantic monopolies, the British spent much of the eighteenth century in overcoming the rivalry of the French. They gained such commercial supremacy that half the slaves transported across the Atlantic came to be carried in British ships. In 1771, 23 slave ships sailed from Bristol, 58 from London and 107 from Liverpool; they carried a total of 50,000 slaves from the African coast.

The export of Lancashire textiles clothed the Negro slaves in the West Indies and America, and also bought those slaves in West Africa who were destined to labour in the cotton fields on the other side of the Atlantic. This commerce, however, had another effect. As manufacturing techniques improved, the cheap product of cotton cloth gradually undermined the indigenous cotton weaving in West Africa itself, as it did in India.

Some protests were roused against the slave trade, particularly by Quakers, from the seventeenth century onwards. They were lone and rather faint voices. The eighteenth century, however, saw stronger tones used. In 1750 Horace Walpole wrote, 'We have been sitting this fortnight on the African Company: we, the British Senate, that temple of liberty, and bulwark of Protestant Christianity, have this fortnight been pondering methods to make more effectual that horrid traffic of selling negroes. It has appeared to us that six-and-forty thousand of these wretches are sold every year to our plantations alone! It chills one's blood.' Nevertheless, throughout the century, it was the profits of the slave trade and the commercial activities which accompanied them which laid the foundations of British prosperity, initiated the beginnings of the industrial revolution and prepared the way for the tremendous expansion of wealth to follow in the succeeding century. The British plantation owners in the West Indies had powerful influence at Westminster so long as the mercantile system could be based on plantation labour. They could ignore humanitarian criticisms of slavery. Not until the British economy demanded a more efficient use of labour and commerce began to find the West Indian system a barrier to its further expansion, could the attack on the slave trade hope to gain practical success.

From the Revolution of 1688 to the mid-eighteenth century the British were engaged in a major accumulation of capital. The growth of a national debt and increases in taxation concentrated capital in the hands of the merchant classes on which the government increasingly depended to finance its wars. The huge expansion of trade arising out of monopolistic control of the colonies, added to the plunder from India, were vital factors in capital accumulation. And the acceleration of capital formation created its own chain reaction; new colonial possessions were acquired by warfare, whilst the existing colonies gained rapidly from increasing investment. Between 1734 and 1773 the white population in the British West Indies increased from 36 to 58 thousand, with a corresponding rise in the slave population. It has been calculated that by 1790 £70 million was invested in the West Indies compared with £18 million in Asia and that the British trade to the Caribbean was almost double that of the East India Company. Those who controlled the West Indies formed a political lobby in Britain, a part of the British bourgeois class with a vital influence on British political life.

England and France had destroyed Dutch commercial power by the early years of the eighteenth century. At the Treaty of Utrecht in 1713 it was the British who secured the *asiento* to supply 4,800 slaves a year to Spanish America. The contract lasted until 1750. The second commercial struggle was between Britain and France, continuing through most of the eighteenth century, with Britain decisively victorious. The French were never as successful in conducting the West African slave trade as the British. Up to about the middle of the eighteenth century it is estimated that the French never exported more than 8,000 slaves a year, whereas the British figure was at least 16,000 at the same time.

On the windward coast, from Gorée to Sherbro Island, the slave trade was mainly conducted by independent merchants. This coast, with its many inlets and islands, was ideal for the interlopers who were trading on their own in defiance of the monopolistic companies. Many of the traders along this shore were half-caste, usually speaking Portuguese, acting on their own, and quite happy to conduct the trade with individual merchants. The only exception was along the river Gambia, where trade to the interior was based on the English fort erected on James Island in 1618. The French, however, could use their influence from the northern bank of the river.

Along the grain and ivory coasts trade was small during the seventeenth and eighteenth centuries. The value of pepper had declined and ivory was almost exhausted by the eighteenth century. There was some slave trading but it was of minor importance.

On the Gold Coast, however, there were many European forts, trading posts and slave hulks. The Dutch were established in Elmina, which they had taken from the Portuguese in 1647, and the English at Cape Coast. The Danes concentrated east of Accra, the Brandenbergers in the extreme west. At the beginning of the eighteenth century the Dutch controlled about half the trade on the Gold Coast and the English about a third, yet by 1785, when the Gold Coast was exporting about 10,000 slaves a year, the British controlled over half this trade.

It is significant of the changing pattern of British commercial life that in 1750 the Royal African Company, based on London, was dissolved and replaced by a Company of Merchants Trading to West Africa. This latter was open to all British merchants prepared to pay the fees and offered an opportunity for those sailing from Liverpool and Bristol to engage openly in the trade without undermining the London monopolists. The new company, indeed, did not itself participate in trade, but looked after British commercial interests and especially the maintenance of the forts on the coast, for which it was given an annual parliamentary grant. This recognition in Britain of the value of independent traders as against the royal monopoly company was in sharp contrast to the practice in Holland and played a considerable part in the growth of British commercial life from the mid-eighteenth century onwards.

As the demand for slaves continued to surpass the supply, so the area of the coast east of the Gold Coast came into the trade. The Niger Delta and the coast down to Gabon river were brought into the operations. This area, known as the Slave Coast, was again exploited by individual European merchants and companies rather than by the large national concerns. The attraction of profits soon led to supplies of slaves being made available there. But here forts were not built. The Africans learnt from the Gold Coast example that if they wanted to keep control of their land and of the slave supply the Europeans should not be allowed to build forts. The absence of forts along the coast also reduced the expenses of the trade and therefore avoided the need to organize large companies.

During the wars between France and Britain in the eighteenth century, West Africa played only a small part. Nevertheless, during the Seven Years' War Britain seized all the French posts, and, by the Treaty of Paris of 1763, although Gorée returned to France, Britain retained her other conquests. In 1764 the British government took over the company posts on the Gambia and formed the crown colony of Senegambia. This was the first time a British government had tried to administer an African territory. The colony received a constitution similar to that of the British North American colonies, with a governor, a nominated council, and a judicial system. However, the commercial development of the colony was never given sufficient attention, more time and effort being spent in opposing the French, who were gaining considerable commercial profits from Gorée. In 1783, at the Peace of Versailles, the French took their former posts back and the Gambia was returned to the Company of Merchants. This first experiment in British colonialism in Africa thus turned out to be a complete failure.

Yet it was Britain which emerged from the conflict with France as by far the most powerful nation in West Africa. By about 1785, of the 64,000 slaves carried across the Atlantic each year the British share was about 38,000. France came next with about 20,000, the Dutch and the Danes carrying no more than around 4,000 and 2,000 respectively. The profits from this trade largely accounted for the rapid domination Britain was gaining over the commercial and mercantile life of the world.

It was largely African chiefs and merchants who secured the slaves of West Africa and sold them to the Europeans on the coast. This was to them quite a natural extension of their earlier trade in other commodities, and no more than the kind of exchange in slaves that they had been accustomed to make amongst themselves. The rapid expansion of their sale of slaves during the seventeenth and eighteenth centuries is largely to be attributed to their increasing demands for European goods. This inevitably led to an increase in the enslavement of Africans by their own rulers, either as criminals or debtors, leading to warfare deliberately undertaken for the purpose of capturing prisoners for sale as slaves. This process itself was stimulated by the sale of firearms by Europeans in exchange for yet more slaves. The enslaved men, women and children were brought to the sea in long caravans, shackled to each other, supervised by armed guards. African brokers on the coast acted as middlemen between the African and European slavers, or European factors themselves took possession of slaves, to lodge them in forts or hulks until they could be transported across the Atlantic. Rulers along certain coastal areas not only insisted on preferential terms for the sale of their own slaves, but also levied purchase tax on slave transactions, thus augmenting their treasuries and power.

It is impossible to estimate accurately the number of slaves taken from West Africa to the transatlantic plantations. It is believed that between fifteen and twenty million were actually landed in the plantation colonies, and, as it is also calculated that for every slave landed another African lost his or her life, either in the dreadful conditions of the slave ships or as a result of the slave wars, the total loss to West Africa during these three centuries must have been in the region of thirty to forty million. The impact of this loss was obviously more severe in certain areas at varying times. Yet there seems some evidence that the loss of population was partially compensated by the stimulation given to population growth as a result of trade with Europeans.

Still more important than the population loss, the slave trade retarded orderly progress and development in West Africa. Concentration on the profitable nature of the trade discouraged the development of agriculture and industry. Tools, clothing and manufactures were more easily obtainable by selling men and women to the Europeans than by producing them in Africa itself. The arts of iron-working, pottery, textiles, the production of brass and copper ware, all deteriorated in the face of this cheap competition. Slave raiding and slave warfare destroyed political progress and created such uncertain conditions as to make any constructive future planning impossible. Life was for the moment; society itself had no stability or continuity. The inducements of the slave trade played a large part in the rise of Benin, Dahomey and Ashanti and in the growth of Oyo. Yet the obsession with acquiring wealth and power from the slave trade and the wars which fostered it, played an equally large part in their decline. Interstate wars and civil wars, all for the promotion of slavery, inevitably undermined the structure of those states which had been built on these very activities. Provincial rulers revolted against the centre in order to secure a greater share in the trade. One state invaded another for the same purpose. Recruiting, training and paying armies took the place of developing the peaceful pursuits of social life. Economic organisation was subordinated to the voracious, obsessive demands of securing the slave commodity in order to purchase more and yet more goods from European merchants. The development of those arts and techniques known in pre-slave trading days was almost entirely neglected.

An instance in 1781 illustrates the brutalizing effect of this trade. When the British slave ship *Zong* exhausted its water supplies in the middle of the Atlantic, 132 slaves were thrown into the sea on the grounds that deaths effected in this manner would be covered by insurance, whilst, if they had died from thirst, the owners would have had to bear the financial loss themselves.

Some idea of the nature of these transactions can be gained from the report of an English ship's captain, who in 1676 bought a hundred men, women and children. They were branded with the insignia of the Royal African Company, DY, indicating the Duke of York. For this cargo he paid five muskets, twenty-one iron bars, seventy-two knives, half a barrel of gunpowder and various pieces of cotton material.

At the same time the introduction of firearms and the experience of warfare strengthened African societies against the power of the Europeans in their coastal forts. At the height of the eighteenth century trade to Guinea it has been estimated that the gunsmiths of Birmingham were providing more than 100,000 muskets a year. This, of course, was greatly welcomed by the Birmingham manufacturers, yet at the other end of the trade it was giving Africans a firepower they had never before experienced. The results were revealed by a Dutchman, writing from Elmina Castle in the year 1700, in these words: 'The main military weapons are muskets or carbines, in the use of which these Africans are wonderfully skillful. It is a real pleasure to watch them train their armies. They handle their weapons so cleverly, shooting them off in several ways, one man sitting, another creeping along the ground or lying down, that it is surprising that they do not hurt each other.

'Perhaps you will wonder how the Africans come to be furnished with these firearms. But you should know that we sell them very great quantities, and in doing this we offer them a knife with which to cut our own throats. But we are forced to do this. For if we did not do it, they would easily get enough muskets from the English, or from the Danes, or from the Prussians. And even if we governors could all agree to stop selling firearms, the private traders of the English or the Dutch would still go on selling them.'

During these slaving years travel between West Africa and Europe was by no means confined to Europeans. The Portuguese had very early invited members of the Bakongo royal family to visit Portugal and one of them took holy orders there and returned as a bishop. It is reported that before the end of the sixteenth century the French had begun to invite Africans from Senegal to participate in the splendours of French civilization. Certainly, during the eighteenth century, it became quite customary for African youths to visit Britain in order to be educated and trained as agents for merchants trading with West Africa. One remarkable case, which incidentally demonstrates the apparent lack of colour prejudice in Britain at the time, was that of Job ben Solomon, a royal Fulani, who, after being sent across the Atlantic as a slave and imprisoned for escaping, was brought back to Britain by English merchants. There he not only proved his skill by translating Arabic manuscripts, but met the President of the Royal Society, various members of the nobility and was received by the royal family, the queen presenting him with a gold watch. Eventually, he returned home bearing valuable gifts. His story was published in England in 1734.

The Europeans also needed trained men around their forts on the West African coast. In 1695 the English sent a carpenter and a bricklayer to one of their Gold Coast forts in order to train Africans in their homeland. From that time onward, African names began to appear on

3*

the lists of fort personnel. Indeed, according to John Barbot, half the soldiers listed were 'blacks' and, according to the records of the Royal African Company in 1731 there were, '100 blacks instructed in mechanik Arts, as Smiths, Armourers, Carpenters, Coopers, Bricklayers, Brick-makers, Masons, Stone-cutters, Sauyers, Gardaners, Linguisters and Massages'. In the mid-1750s some British officials on the West African coast suggested that a number of Africans should be sent to England to be trained as builders. The suggestion was rejected, but many of them were actually trained at the forts themselves. According to Board of Trade reports there was a long list of skilled workers employed in West African forts. The forts were also the centre of considerable missionary activity in the surrounding towns, where European languages, reading and writing were taught. According to Barbot again, Africans were applying 'themselves to some particular profession or handicraft as merchants, factors or brokers, gold and blacksmiths, fishermen, canoe and house carpenters, salt boilders, potters, mat-makers, husbandmen, porters, watermen or paddlers and soldiers.' By this time African traders were accustomed to writing to merchants in Liverpool and were clearly keeping records. Indeed, during the eighteenth century, a number of African traders were sending their sons to school in England. In 1788 thirteen students from the coast were studying in Liverpool and London. As early as 1766 a school had been established in Cape Coast.

Meanwhile, the slave trade was making a profound impact on West African life, strongly influencing national and international developments there. Benin had become a powerful state in West Africa during the fifteenth century. Its strength was augmented by contact with the Portuguese before the end of the century. Its rulers were amongst the first to purchase firearms in exchange for pepper, slaves, ivory and cloth. Benin, as we have seen, was also one of the earliest West African territories to be visited by the English, Thomas Windham putting ashore there in 1553.

The city of Benin became one of the richest and best organized in West Africa. The most interesting eighteenth century account of life in the Benin kingdom is that of Olaudah Equiano. Captured as a boy along with his sister and sold as a slave to the West Indies, he travelled widely with his masters before securing his release. As a free man he continued to travel, visiting the Mediterranean, the Arctic and Central

America and played a part in the anti-slavery campaign, especially in the preparations for the foundations of Sierra Leone. He was married to a local girl in Cambridgeshire in 1792 after having written his autobiography which contains fascinating accounts of the society in which he was brought up, of his experiences as a slave and of his travels. From his recollections of childhood we are given a first-hand picture of life in Benin during the eighteenth century.

'.... the most considerable is the kingdom of Benin, both as to extent and wealth, the richness and cultivation of the soil, the power of its king, and the number and warlike disposition of the inhabitants. . . . This kingdom is divided into many provinces and districts, in one of which, called Eboe, I was born in the year 1745, situated in a charming fruitful vale, named Essaka. The distance of this province from the capital of Benin and the sea coast must be very considerable, for I had never heard of white men or Europeans, nor of the sea, and our subjection to the king of Benin was little more than nominal; for every transaction of the government, as far as my slender observation extended, was conducted by the chiefs or elders of the place. . . . We are almost a nation of dancers, musicians, and poets. Thus every great event such as a triumphant return from battle or other cause of public rejoicing is celebrated in public dances, which are accompanied with songs and music suited to the occasion. . . . As our manners are simple our luxuries are few. The dress of both sexes is nearly the same. It generally consists of a long piece of calico or muslin, wrapped loosely round the body somewhat in the form of a highland plaid. This is usually dyed blue, which is our favourite colour. It is extracted from a berry and is brighter and richer than any I have seen in Europe. Beside, this our women of distinction wear golden ornaments, which they dispose with some profusion on their arms and legs. When our women are not employed with the men in tillage, their usual occupation is spinning and weaving cotton, which they afterwards dye and make into garments. They also manufacture earthen vessels, of which we have many kinds. Among the rest tobacco pipes, made after the same fashion and used in the same manner, as those in Turkey.

'Our manner of living is entirely plain, for as yet the natives are unacquainted with those refinements in cookery which debauch the taste: bullocks, goats, and poultry, supply the greatest part of their food. These constitute likewise the principal wealth of the country and the chief articles of its commerce. The flesh is usually stewed in a pan; to make it savoury we sometimes use also pepper and other spices, and we have salt made of wood ashes. Our vegetables are mostly plantains, eadas, yams, beans, and Indian corn. . . . Before we taste food we always wash our hands: indeed our cleanliness on all occasions is extreme. . . . Our principal luxury is in perfumes; one sort of these is an odoriferous wood of delicious fragrance, the other a kind of earth, a small portion of which thrown into the fire diffuses a more powerful odour. We beat this wood into powder and mix it with palm oil, with which both men and women perfume themselves.

'In our buildings we study convenience rather than ornament. Each master of a family has a large square piece of ground, surrounded with a moat or fence or enclosed with a wall of red earth tempered, which when dry is hard as brick. Within this are his houses to accommodate his family and slaves which if numerous frequently present the appearance of a village. . . . These houses never exceed one storey in height: they are always built of wood or stakes driven into the ground, crossed with wattles, and neatly plastered within and without. The roof is thatched with reeds. Our day-houses are left open at the sides, but those in which we sleep are always covered, and plastered on the inside with a composition mixed with cow-dung to keep off the different insects which annoy us during the night. The walls and floors also of these are generally covered with mats. Our beds consist of a platform raised three or four feet from the ground, on which are laid skins and different parts of a spungy tree call plantain. Our covering is calico or muslin, the same as our dress. The usual seats are a few logs of wood, but we have benches, which are generally perfumed to accommodate strangers; these compose the greater part of our household furniture. . . .

'As we live in a country where nature is prodigal of her favours, our wants are few and easily supplied; of course we have few manufactures. They consist for the most part of calicoes, earthenware ornaments, and instruments of war and husbandry. But these make no part of our commerce, the principal articles of which, as I have observed, are provisions. In such a state money is of little use; however we have some small pieces of coin, if I may call them such. They are made something like an anchor. . . . We have also markets, at which I have been frequently with my mother. They are sometimes visited by stout mahogany-coloured men from the south-west of us: we call them Oye-Eboe, which term signifies red men living at a distance. They generally bring us fire-arms, gunpowders, hats, beads, and dried fish. . . . Sometimes indeed we sold slaves to them, but they were only prisoners of war, or such among us as had been convicted of kidnapping, or adultery. . . .

'Our land is uncommonly rich and fruitful, and produces all kinds of vegetables in great abundance. We have plenty of Indian corn, and vast quantities of cotton and tobacco. Our pineapples grow without culture. . . . We have also spices of different kinds, particularly pepper, and a variety of delicious fruits which I have never seen in Europe, together with gums of various kinds and honey in abundance. All our industry is exerted to improve these blessings of nature. Agriculture is our chief employment, and everyone, even the children and women, are engaged in it. . . . Our tillage is exercised in a large plain or common, some hours walk from our dwellings, and all the neighbours resort thither in a body. They use no beasts of husbandry, and their only instruments are hoes, axes, shovels and beaks, or pointed iron to dig with. . . . This common is often the theatre of war, and therefore when our people go out to till their land they not only go in a body but generally take their arms with them for fear of a surprise, and when they apprehend an invasion they guard the avenues to their dwellings by driving sticks into the ground, which are so sharp at one end as to pierce the foot and are generally dipped in poison. From what I can recollect of these battles, they appear to have been irruptions of one little state or district on the other to obtain prisoners or booty. Perhaps they were incited to this by those traders who brought the European goods I mentioned amongst us. Such a mode of obtaining slaves in Africa is common. . . . When a trader wants slaves he applies to a chief for them and tempts him with his wares. . . . We have fire-arms, bows and arrows, broad two-edged swords and javelins: we have shields also which cover a man from head to foot. All are taught the use of these weapons; even our women are warriors and march boldly out to fight along with the men. Our whole district is a kind of militia: on a certain signal given, such as the firing of a gun at night, they all rise in arms and rush upon their enemy.'[1]

---

[1] *Equiano's Travels*, ed. Paul Edwards, Heinemann.

In this account we see how Benin's prosperity and power had come to depend very largely on the slave trade, and this emphasis on slavery is to be found in all contemporary records of West African life during this century. (Although it should be noted that Equiano, like other first-hand observers, made a sharp contrast between the domestic slavery traditionally practised by African society, and the sale of slaves for export.) A Swedish traveller, who was later to give evidence to the Privy Council Committee on the slave trade, described some of the effects of the traffic in this part of Africa during the same century. 'The Wars which the inhabitants of the interior parts of the country, beyond Senegal, Gambia, and Sierra Leone, carry on with each other, are chiefly of a predatory nature, and owe their origin to the yearly number of slaves, which the Mandingoes, or the inland traders suppose will be wanted by the vessels that will arrive on the coast. Indeed these predatory incursions depend so much on the demand for slaves, that if in any one year there be a greater concourse of European ships than usual, it is observed that a much greater number of captives from the interior parts of the country is brought to market the next.

The Moors, who inhabit the countries on the north of the River Senegal, are particularly infamous for their predatory Wars. They cross the river, and attacking the negroes, bring many of them off. . . . The French, to encourage them in it, make annual presents to the Moorish kings. . . . To enable them to fulfil this. . . . they never fail to supply them with ammunition, guns, and other instruments of War. . . . The publick Pillage is, of all others, the most plentiful source, from which the slave trade derives its continuance and support. The kings of Africa (I mean in that part of the country which I have visited) incited by the merchandise shewn them, which consists principally of strong liquors, give orders to their military to attack their own villages in the night. . . .'[1]

It was largely through such raids, counter-raids and the organization of military means to fight wars for the capture and sale of slaves that West African states rose to brief power and were then overcome by their rivals during the eighteenth century. Benin, at this time, was facing increasingly strong competition from rival slave traders,

[1] C. B. Wadstrom, Observations on the Slave Trade, quoted in Basil Davidson, *The African Past*, Penguin.

particularly in Yorubaland and the disturbed conditions which developed throughout the forest area as a result of slave wars made it increasingly difficult for her to maintain her supremacy.

As the consequences of continual warfare and the absence of constructive economic development took their toll, so Benin's fortunes began to decline. Now the kingdom of Oyo, organized in the heart of Yoruba territory, began to supplant the power of Benin. As happened elsewhere, when the internal strength of the Benin empire declined, an increasing number of its tributary states broke away from their allegiance. By the end of the eighteenth century the might of Benin had shrunk to tiny proportions; it had become the victim of its own former source of strength, its slave trade.

Benin was succeeded by Oyo as the most powerful of the West African states. Oyo built this position during the seventeenth century by impressing its military might, based on cavalry strength, on the peoples of Yoruba territory. Its power was noteworthy for the rule of its Alafins, who, though almost absolute in their rule, could nevertheless be removed if they became excessively unpopular. The second feature of the power of Oyo was the success of its slave traders in rivalry with those of Benin.

In the eighteenth century Oyo was able to widen its boundaries and build an extensive empire of tributary states. The Alafin stood supreme at the centre of this empire, though he was elected and, in spiritual matters, had still to look to the Oni of Ife. Much of his authority devolved through ministers and military officers, whilst in the provinces, the Obas, elected locally, ruled on his behalf. The towns had their own council which discussed local and national affairs. Oyo, indeed, bears witness to the traditional popular participation in African public affairs and policies. There were a number of occasions on which their Alafins were deposed, when they were supposed by tradition to commit suicide.

During the eighteenth century, the economic strength of Oyo grew as a result of its success in the slave trade. Although the sale of slaves provided its main resource, its inhabitants were still manufacturing pottery and spinning cloth. Yet, once more, the negative effects of the slave trade were to gnaw at the roots of the empire's prosperity. Rivalry for slaves provoked increasing conflicts. The southern areas nearest the slave markets of the coast prospered at the expense of the north. Yet again parts of the empire began to secede and, by the nineteenth century, disintegration, marked by internal conflict, drastically weakened the whole structure of the empire.

The third kingdom of importance during the slave period was Dahomey. In the eighteenth century the attractions of slave commerce on the coast tempted Fon rulers to attack the thriving slave centres of Savi, Whydah and Allada. The kingdom of Dahomey was based on these conquests and for the last two-thirds of the eighteenth century concerned itself almost exclusively with the slave trade. Fon policy was to defend their power along the coast and to extend their empire progressively further into the north in order to secure a regular supply of slaves. Some of the Dahomey rulers even established their own plantations, using slaves as labour.

Like other empires dependent on the slave trade, Dahomey was frequently involved in warfare, both to preserve its control of the trade and to obtain the slaves themselves. In particular, there was often war with neighbouring Oyo and, indeed, Dahomey's capital, Abomey, was invaded by the Oyo in 1738. Yet although the Fon were still constitutionally subject to the Alafin of Oyo and continued to pay tribute to him into the nineteenth century, they managed to preserve the autonomy of Dahomey, though constantly in conditions of conflict. The Dahomey state therefore became largely a military organization, its armies used to capture slaves from neighbouring territories.

As might be expected, the heavy concentration of slave traffic along the Gold Coast also provoked conflicts among African societies in the locality. In the seventeenth century the most powerful of these was the empire of Akwamu, a federation of a number of tribal communities ruled from a capital to the north of Winneba. During the first part of the century Akwamu was extending its frontiers and bringing new groups within its orbit; in the second half, the empire became even more closely associated with the operations of the slave trade. By controlling the roads from the interior to the coast and collecting tolls along them, the rulers of Akwamu were able to accumulate sufficient money to purchase arms from many of the European coastal forts. Accra itself, the capital of the Ga kingdom, was captured, along with small states on the coast, giving the empire control of the main part of the Gold Coast before the end of the seventeenth century.

It should be remembered, too, that the Europeans paid rent for their

forts, which augmented these traffic tolls. Levies on trade and the sale
of slaves to the Europeans provided the empire with a considerable
treasury. So strong had Akwamu become that, in 1693, its soldiers were
able to capture Christiansborg Castle from the Danes, hoist the empire's
flag, 'a black painted in the middle brandishing a scymiter' on a white
background, and compel the Danes to pay ransom for it the following
year when it was returned to them. Ten years later further evidence
of the power of Akwamu is seen in the agreement by the Dutch to pay
the imperial ruler five per cent on all gold trade, provided that he
would ensure that the trade routes were kept open and insist on his
subjects trading only with them.

Yet, once again, the effects of continual warfare to preserve the empire
and to secure the slaves upon which so much of its income depended
eventually brought about Akwamu's downfall. By 1733, internal
weakness arising from these conflicts left it at the mercy of the Akim
armies, who not only defeated its forces, but finally destroyed the
empire itself.

The successors to the power of Akwamu were the Ashanti in the
north-western forest area of the Gold Coast. From the last quarter of
the seventeenth century the Ashanti peoples began to organize into
some degree of unity, enabling them to develop an alliance based on
cultural and kinship ties, and then begin to expand their power. It was
at this time that Kumasi was founded as Ashanti's capital. It was also
from this period that the importance of the royal stool was recognized,
taking spiritual precedence over the stools of the other Ashanti states.
It was now that the golden stool was supposed to have fallen from the
heavens on to the knees of the first great leader of the Ashanti alliance,
Osei Tutu. The golden stool was believed to contain the spirit of the
Ashanti nation, with the major ruler, the Asantehene, as its custodian.

Ashanti continued to widen its boundaries during the early eighteenth century when it came into direct contact with the European
slavers. The kingdom could provide both slaves and gold to pay for
the firearms supplied by Europeans, and it also was able to collect
rents from Europeans who occupied coastal forts. Its wealth allowed it
to arm an impressive force, which, throughout the eighteenth century,
was continually fighting wars with neighbouring states. The principal
objective was to keep the channels of commerce to the coast free of
those who wished to cut them in order to profit from the important

traffic between the coast and the interior. It was largely the power of Ashanti to capture and collect slaves which supplied its strength and led to this continual warfare with rivals.

Ashanti groups were subject to their powerful neighbouring state Denkyira, to whom they had to pay tribute. Having become Asantehene and created some degree of unity amongst the Ashanti, Osei Tutu first turned against Denkyira. This powerful state was in control of most of the wealthy commerce with Elmina Castle, the main centre of European commercial activities. Its command of trade with the Dutch stronghold enabled it to establish a regular supply of firearms. In exchange, of course, Denkyira had to supply slaves and gold, part of which it secured from the Ashanti. To build their military power and commerce, therefore, the Ashanti had to break the stranglehold of Denkyira. Between 1699 and 1701 a war was fought between the newly-rising Ashanti and the established Denkyira, resulting in the destruction of Denkyira and increased cohesion among the Ashantis. From then on Ashanti had access to the coast, the trade which was conducted there and the European forts. Osei Tutu now turned against Akim, which had supported Denkyira, and brought this powerful state also under the suzerainty of the Ashanti. For the rest of the century successive Asantehenes were consolidating the cohesion of the Ashanti in wars against their rivals. By the end of the eighteenth century they had built the most powerful empire of the region, extending across modern Ghana, parts of the Ivory Coast and Togo. During the nineteenth century, the empire developed a strongly centralized system of government, with the Asantehene as the focus of a powerful bureacracy and army.

In the late eighteenth century, too, the newly-established partnership between the Ashanti and the Dutch faced the rivalry of the neighbouring Fante peoples associated with the British. Both alliances based their friendship on commercial operations, with the European forts as the foundation. Rivalry developed into conflict and in 1806 war broke out between the Ashanti and the Fante, resulting in the defeat of the Fante forces at Abora, near the coast. The Ashanti armies swept down to the beach, took Kormantin and Fort Amsterdam and besieged the British in Anomabu. The action was here inconclusive. The fort held out against attacks but the British had no forces to counter-attack and so peace was soon reached. But as a result of these operations, the Ashanti were recognized by British and Dutch alike as having major authority in this region of the Gold Coast.

It was not only these large and powerful empires which were affected by the European slave trade. Many smaller states, including a number of city states, found the demand from Europeans for slaves an opportunity to increase their revenues and to purchase goods from the outside world. Amongst these the city states of the Niger Delta were of particular importance. The low-lying coastal plain and the swamps extending across nearly three hundred miles of coastline and well over a hundred miles into the hinterland, forming the delta of the great river Niger, provided countless creeks and inlets ideal for conducting the slave trade. Markets grew in a large number of them and these market centres became virtually self-governing city states. From the sixteenth century onwards the growing demand for slaves enabled them to develop commerce and the governmental order essential for successful trade. Bonny, New and Old Calabar, Warri, Brass, Creek Town and Obutong were amongst the better known centres of this type.

As in Britain, so in Africa, it was the merchant class which dominated society for the purpose of conducting the slave trade. Amongst the delta towns the 'House system' was widespread. This allowed merchants engaged in the slave trade to co-operate for their common purposes, usually under the leadership of the head of a family, embracing all his relatives and assistants within his business. Members of the House would conduct the trade in slaves with European merchants and commercial affairs with other Africans. They might also organize their own plantation and their own systems of defence. Some of these Houses became large and powerful and were well known as commercial organizations amongst European merchants.

The delta city states had a particular vantage point in the slave trade, for their situation on river mouths and the coastline gave them control of the middleman trade. They conducted their business according to certain established customs, were good bargainers, insisted on their price and kept European factors very much in order. One description of a slave market at the end of the seventeenth century was given by the English captain, John Adams, who, writing about Bonny, referred to the city as 'the wholesale market for slaves, since not fewer than 20,000 are sold here every year. Of these, 16,000 come from one nation, called the Ibos, so that this single nation has exported, over the last twenty years, not fewer than 320,000 of its people; while members of the same nation sold at New and Old Calabar, in the same period, probably amounted to 50,000 more.' Adams further described the organization entailed in holding these markets. He wrote, 'the preparation for these markets generally occupy the Bonny people for some days. Large canoes, capable of carrying 120 persons, are launched and stored for the voyage. The traders add to their trade-goods by obtaining from their friends, the captains of the slave ships, a considerable quantity of goods on credit . . . Evening is the period chosen for the time of their departure, when they proceed in a body, accompanied by the noise of drums, horns and gongs. They generally come back at the end of the sixth day after their departure, bringing with them 1,500 to 2,000 slaves, who are sold to the Europeans the evening after their arrival, and taken on board the ships.'

Some idea of the character of trading relations between the merchants of these states and the English merchants may be gained from the records of an English ship, the Albion-Frigate, in New Calabar in the year 1699. On arrival the captain sent his emissaries ashore to ask the king to begin trading; 'He gave us to understand that he expected one bar of iron for each slave more than Edwards (the Captain of another English ship) had paid him. He also objected to our metal basins, mugs, beads and other goods and said they were of little value at the time.' The following day 'we had a conference with the king and principal natives of the country, about trade, and this lasted from three o'clock until night. But it had no result. They continued to insist on having thirteen bars of iron for a male, and ten for a female.' Apparently it took another four days of negotiation before the trading agreement was reached.

The merchant class in Africa was smaller and more simply organized than that in Britain, as well as certainly more heavily dependent on the kings, who both took a leading commercial role and demanded special privileges, but essentially it had been created by the same process. It was the slave trade which had supplied its initial raison d'être, which sustained it during its growth and which provided its most lucrative source of economic and political strength. The two merchant classes, British and African, understood each other and for at least a century and a half recognized their mutual interest and common purpose. The major difference, of course, was that whilst the British merchant class could turn its profits into constructive activities in its own country, the African merchants were selling the human resources of their own societies, reducing the able-bodied element of their own communities and, at the same time, undermining productive economic activity amongst their own people. They were also carrying on an essentially destructive activity through the warfare which was necessary for the capture of slaves.

It may seem remarkable that the very nation which had gained such colossal profits from the slave trade should be the same one to take the lead in abolishing it. The real picture was more complex than this. The ending of the slave trade was brought about by two complementary influences. From the middle of the eighteenth century onwards the character of British capitalism began to change. The easy profits of the slave trade no longer sufficed. Some of them were being invested in the growth of new British industries and the inventions which were to lead to mass production, much more attractive propositions. Manufactures and their sale abroad were gradually becoming more important than the sugar and tobacco plantation economy of the West Indies. At the same time, the British were losing their major stake in the European market to the French, whilst the long struggle to preserve the British monopoly in North America ended in the War of Independence.

With the decline in their economic importance and the shift of capitalist interest towards industry and manufacturing, the political influence of the West Indian planters' lobby was steadily reduced. They fought hard to retain their control over commercial legislation and their role in British economic life, but the trends of the day were moving against them. Nor did they help their own cause by bringing slaves back to England to serve their domestic needs in the ostentatious life to which they retired. When Lord Mansfield in 1772 pronounced his famous judgement that slavery was not recognized in English law, about 15,000 African slaves were living in Britain.

The decline of the West Indian planters' influence inevitably reduced the attractions of the slave trade. Moreover, as we have previously seen, investment in that trade itself to some extent handicapped the progress of the British industrial revolution. Towards the end of the eighteenth century, therefore, there was a double economic pressure against the British slave trade.

At the same time, the weakening economic attraction of slaving and the shrinking political influence of the planters progressively lent weight to the idealistic anti-slavery campaign. For, although the changing economic situation in Britain was a major element in making the abolition of the slave trade possible, it did not conceal the heroic efforts of the humanitarians. As we have seen, a handful of Quakers had begun to criticize the morality of slavery as early as the seventeenth century. The slave trade itself had been forbidden by the Catholic church, and, although this prohibition was honoured mostly in the breach, the Spaniards did not participate in the trade until as late as 1783.

It may be that the growing prosperity of the British middle classes as the eighteenth century advanced gave sufficient leisure and security to promote feelings of humanitarianism. Britain developed into a world power on the shoulders of a small professional army, an expanding navy and the success of her overseas trading ventures – not least in slaves. The burdens themselves in military and naval activity during the eighteenth century were carried by a very small minority. The expanding wealth of the country was enjoyed by many, though by no means all, Britishers. The rise in taste in literature, architecture and social habits was enjoyed by the nobility and the growing middle classes. There may also have been some rise in the standard of living of rural and urban workers, though one must always recall the horrible, insanitary hovels in which a large proportion of the British people still lived in the midst of the new plenty. Nevertheless, the new economic position of Britain and its accompanying refinements in attitudes did allow some reform in prison conditions, medical attention, education and nutrition. It was in this context that the agitation against the slave trade was able to make progress alongside the gradual encouragement of more humane conditions at home.

The campaign was conducted by methods of propaganda strikingly similar to those of the twentieth century. Evidence of the conditions in which slaves were captured, bought, sold, transported and treated on the plantations was gathered by a dedicated group of men. They wrote pamphlets, lobbied members of Parliament, put pressure on public men and conducted campaigns of public meetings throughout the country. Debates in Parliament were organized, commissions of enquiry set up and British public interest exploited to the full. The fact that in 1713 the announcement that Britain had obtained the *asiento* for supplying slaves to the Spanish colonies was celebrated by a torch-light procession in London, whereas less than a hundred years later Britain had taken the lead in abolishing the slave trade, bears witness to the impact made by this campaign on public opinion. As could be expected, it was bitterly opposed by the slave traders and plantation owners. Those who would abolish slave trading were denounced in Parliament and publicly accused of undermining the stability of society and the sanctity of the state, not least because they were held to be invading the rights of private property.

The first noteworthy name in the abolitionists' roll of honour was Granville Sharp. It is perhaps significant that Sharp was concerned, not only with slavery, but also with getting rid of the operations of press gangs, political corruption, flogging and abuses within the prison system, unemployment, alcohol and war. It was Granville Sharp who, almost single-handed, conducted the fight against slavery in England. Despite the general view that his cause was hopeless, he conducted the Somersett case in 1772 before Chief Justice Mansfield with such skill that Mansfield's judgement itself incorporated most of his arguments. These were based on the assertion that from the time of Magna Carta the only means of legally holding any English person was through serfdom. Serfdom had almost disappeared and Somersett could not be designated as a serf because his owner had never attempted to fulfil the contractual obligations demanded towards serfs. Sharp argued that he was being held in defiance of the historical traditions and precedents of English law.

Chief Justice Mansfield's verdict was that 'the exercise of the power of a master over his slave, must be supported by the laws of particular countries; but no foreigner in England can claim a right over a man; such a claim is not known to the laws of England.

'Immemorial usage preserves a positive law, after the occasion of accident which gave rise to it has been forgotten; and, tracing the subject to natural principles, the claim of slavery never can be supported. The power claimed was never in use here, or acknowledged by the law.' It is also significant of the mood of the time that when a decision had to be taken in Scotland, for Mansfield's judgement did not apply there, an even broader interpretation was accepted. In the case of Joseph Knight, in 1778, the slave system was held to be untenable, 'the dominion assumed over this Negro under the law of Jamaica, being *unjust*'.

The argument of the anti-slave lobby dwelt on the dehumanizing effects of slavery on the masters, whilst further suggesting that the slave system was an inefficient use of labour and therefore uneconomic for the slave owners. The propagandists also met the claim that the slave trade was essential as a maritime nursery in which to train seamen by showing that, on the contrary, it tended to lead sailors to their graves.

Granville Sharp was now joined by William Wilberforce, from inside parliament, and by Thomas Clarkson, who became responsible for much of the collection of facts and propaganda in the country. From 1789, for seventeen successive years, Wilberforce moved his anti-slave trade motion in parliament. His central thesis was that the British were a uniquely humane people, especially endowed with kindliness; and therefore, that the cruel trade was alien to their character.

It is a remarkable commentary on both the effectiveness of the anti-slavery campaign and the growing sense of humanity in Britain that Wilberforce was supported, not only by Pitt, who was his friend, but by Pitt's Whig opponents, Fox and Burke. It seems likely that this bi-partisan support would have brought abolition before the end of the eighteenth century if it had not been for the outbreak of the French Revolution. But all those humanitarians who were leading the campaign against slavery came from the middle class, and the middle class was terrified by the attacks on the established order across the Channel, particularly by the involvement of the masses in this assault. So the pro-slavery lobby, which had been passionately fighting for its preservation, secured an unexpected reprieve. The bitter hostility which it had already shown to champions of emancipation was redoubled in an atmosphere of insecurity conducive to vilifying the humanitarian. It was now easy for the planter lobby to return to the theme that the attack on slavery was an attempt to destroy the sanctity of private property comparable to the excesses witnessed in France. It seemed clearly relevant to the new situation to suggest that any interference with the slave trade would represent a grave blow to an important sector of commercial activity, vital to the national interest in war and in peace. The fact that the French were Britain's main trade rival only reinforced the argument.

Yet, despite war, the reprieve was only temporary. The impact of the French Revolution weakened as time passed. Though some of the prominent supporters of the anti-slave trade movement, like Burke, reneged on the cause, the dual impact of changing economic needs and humanitarian evangelism had bitten too deeply into the roots of slavery. Moreover, the anti-slave campaign was not confined to Britain. The Danes set an example by outlawing the trade to their citizens in 1804. All the American states had forbidden it by 1803, drawing on the Federal Constitution. By 1807 the British Parliament had so far recovered from the shock of events in France as to pass an act making it illegal for any British subject to participate in the African slave trade. In the same year, the American Congress adopted a similar measure, to be followed a few years later by the Swedes and Dutch. After the conclusion of the Napoleonic Wars in 1815 France also outlawed her slave trade, whilst Portugal and Spain limited their slavers to south of the equator.

These laws did not, of course, abolish the trade. In fact it is estimated that the number of slaves taken from West Africa actually increased following this legislation. Only Britain used her navy seriously to halt the slavers and it was some years before other states were prepared to allow British naval vessels the right to interfere with the suspected slaving ships sailing under their flag. So long as slavery itself was maintained in certain American states, constant demand ensured that the trade would continue. Even though the British navy sailed supreme during these years and a considerable section of it was stationed in West African waters to apprehend slave ships, the coastline was still too long and the waters too wide to allow complete success. What is more, the task placed a heavy burden on the men in the navy serving long periods in the tropical climate off the unhealthy African coast, the death rate being three times as high as in other foreign stations. Yet, between 1825 and 1865 it is estimated that 1,287 slave ships were taken and 130,000 slaves released. In spite of this action, during the same forty years it has been calculated that 1,800,000 Africans were shipped across the Atlantic to the slave plantations.

Despite the failure of this legislation, which represented the climax of the campaign to abolish the trade, the fact that the British were no longer able to engage in it was important from both African standpoint and for future relations between Africa and Britain. Not only had the main participants in slaving renounced the trade, but they were now active in securing its complete abolition. Final success in this task might still take many years' effort; nevertheless, the greatest naval power in the world had now become the declared enemy of the commercial exploitation of African men and women; it appeared certain that this fact would open a new chapter in the dialogue between British and African people.

Already, twenty years before the British proscription of the slave trade, a positive step had been taken towards the creation of this new relationship. The Mansfield judgement released about 15,000 slaves of African descent in England. It was not easy for them to integrate into English life and the members of the anti-slavery movement were concerned for their future. After some discussion it was decided to attempt to establish a new settlement for released slaves in Sierra Leone. The British government agreed to play a part by providing free passages and supplying provisions for the expedition. The first attempt was made in 1787, when four hundred and fifty Negro ex-slaves and sixty white prostitutes embarked for West Africa under the authority of Captain Thompson, of the navy. About eighty of the group died on the voyage, the rest being left on twenty square miles which Thompson purchased from a local chief. The summer rainy season made work almost impossible and the unhealthy conditions of the coastal area added to the misery of the community. There were more deaths and, although Granville Sharp sent out further provisions the following year, the settlement never took root. By 1790 the experiment had failed.

Sharp, however, did not despair. In 1791, against the opposition of monopolistic merchants, he established the Sierra Leone Company, hoping this time to underpin a new expedition by developing non-slaving trade to provide for a sounder administration. This time a governor, council, traders and craftsmen formed the hard core of the administration. Fresh slaves were provided from Nova Scotia, where unsuccessful attempts had been made to settle those who had fought for Britain in the American war. And on the new site of Freetown better hopes were entertained for the survival of the community. Although many difficulties were encountered and conflicts developed within the colony, it survived. In 1800 the Company was granted a Royal Charter and from that year received a grant from the British government to subsidize administrative expenses. Eight years later it became a crown colony.

The early years of the settlement were not very happy, for trade had not developed as it had been hoped and the company itself was not allowed to participate in the only profitable trade of the area, which was slaving. The French attacked the settlement in 1794 and burnt it down. There was continual discontent, the law courts set up by the Company were challenged, whilst the absence of any kind of forces to compel compliance with law invited unrest. It was Zachary Macaulay, governor from 1794 to 1799, who really ensured the survival of the settlement. He not only gained the confidence of the inhabitants, but invited them to share in framing their own laws. Yet the disappointment in commercial development soon led to the Company's dissolution. By 1808 the British government had been persuaded to take over the administration of the colony. It hoped in this way to establish a naval base on the West African coast which would enable it to protect British shipping there; later it was used as a base for anti-slave trade efforts. From this time onwards the colony expanded and became a haven for liberated slaves captured from the slave ships. The period which had seen the British merchants drawing a large proportion of their profits from human merchandise ended with some attempt to rehabilitate a few of their victims. The next era was to reveal what impact the new industrialism, partly the child of slave profits, would make on relations between Britons and Africans.

Chapter 4

Introduction to
the Nineteenth Century

At the end of the eighteenth century Europe knew little more of
Africa than a few areas of its coast. Parts of the North African coast
had had ancient contact with Southern Europe, but their hinterland
had been closed to Europeans throughout the Middle Ages, all the
North African countries being essentially part of Moslem society. A
few Christian slaves captured by Barbary pirates had returned home to
give vague impressions of society beyond the coast, but Europe knew
very little of North African life in the Sahara or of the caravan routes
which crossed it.

In West Africa, too, apart from voyages up the Senegal by the
French and the Gambia by the English, European knowledge was
confined to the slave coasts and a few incursions into the forest areas.
Traders on the coast may have heard rumours of the organized inland
states but they knew virtually nothing of the societies living there nor
of the towns and markets, the manufactures and trade across to North
Africa and Egypt.

In the south, the Dutch settlement at the Cape had survived and
expanded for a century and a half. Its frontier farmers were now pene-
trating well beyond the perimeter, but had only just begun, during
the second half of the eighteenth century, to come into serious contact
with African societies of the interior. The development of the Cape
settlement did, however, make one exception to the general rule that
European contact was confined to the African coast.

In the east, the Portuguese had captured and occupied most of the
small port states at one time or another in conflicts with the Arabs.
They had even made one or two expeditions into central Africa, but
these brought little information and did not survive as permanent

contacts. There had also been occasional journeys into the heart of Ethiopia, but again unproductive of lasting knowledge.

For three centuries Europe had traded with Africans, but the trade had been conducted almost entirely on the beaches or in the trading towns which grew up around Europe's merchant forts along the coast. Trade originally consisted of ivory, gold and pepper, but later was largely confined to slaves. Both the material and human commodities had been collected by Africans, transported to the coast by African traders and exchanged there for European goods. So, with few exceptions, Europeans had no occasion to travel into the interior where, in any case, communications were difficult and European traders often unwelcome. No European state had ever seriously tried to challenge the power of African societies or interfere with African control of territory.

The nineteenth century witnessed a major change. Nineteenth century Europe, and particularly Britain, experienced new impulses in its commercial, religious, scientific and, eventually, political, life. These factors all contributed their share to giving European life a new expansionist character. From a variety of motives they took Europeans for the first time into the heart of the African continent.

Pioneers in this fresh aspect of relations between Britons and Africans had begun to tread the new paths even before the end of the eighteenth century. In 1768 the Scotsman, James Bruce, seeking a new purpose to life after the loss of his wife, travelled into the interior of Ethiopia as far as the capital, Gondar, and then into the Blue Nile valley. In the last decade of the century Mungo Park completed his first expedition to the Upper Niger. In 1778 Sir Joseph Banks founded a dining club from amongst people interested in promoting African expeditions. From this club emerged the 'Association for the Discovery of the Interior Parts of Africa', which became principally responsible for the beginnings of serious expeditions into the heart of the continent. Its members were imbued both with a scientific interest, in uncovering the geographic facts of Africa, and with proselytizing fervour, bringing European knowledge and Christian religion to African peoples. In 1795 the Association financed Mungo Park's two-year expedition to the Niger. It was Sir Joseph Banks and his colleagues who persuaded the British government to finance Park's second expedition in 1805. Once the principle of government sponsorship for expeditions of exploration had taken root, government finance was made available to Lieutenant Clapperton, who crossed the Sahara and made his way to the walled city of Kano in 1825–6, and to Clapperton's personal servant, Richard Lander, who, with his brother, for the first time revealed the true course of the Niger in 1830. The British government even sponsored the German explorer Heinrich Barth in his Sudanese exploration of 1850–55.

Interest in the African continent and peoples was greatly stimulated by these explorations and the news of their discoveries. Indeed this, when combined with the excitement already induced by the passionate debate on the slave trade, caused British public consciousness of Africa and Africans to rise to new heights towards the late eighteenth and early nineteenth centuries. Intriguing parallels with arguments of the mid-twentieth century over Negro racial characteristics and culture appear in contemporary periodicals of the time. One of the most fascinating was a leading article written by Leigh Hunt in his *Examiner* in 1811. Not only does it demonstrate the concern of the time with cultural relations between British and African peoples, but also relates the fascinating story of a Negro ship plying between Sierra Leone and Liverpool.

'.... what conscientious trader to Guinea, with just philosophy enough to fancy that the negro was an inferior animal to the white, and just religion enough to assure himself that the Africans were undergoing the curse upon Ham's posterity, would have fancied, fifty years ago, that a negro would be declared a freeman and the traffic in slaves a felony?

'What led me away into these reflections was the following curious account in a paper of last Friday. It is not very ambitiously written, nor is the name of its hero quite so dignified as that of Oroonoko or Othello; but to those who can enter into the feelings just mentioned it will not want an air of romance, and to complete the effect, it is a romance happily realized:

' "The brig *TRAVELLER*, lately arrived at Liverpool from Sierra Leone, is perhaps the first vessel that ever reached Europe, entirely owned and navigated by negroes. This brig is owned and commanded by Paul Cuffee, the son of Cuffee, a negro-slave imported into America. Her mate and all her crew are negroes, or the immediate descendants of negroes. Captain Cuffee is about 56 years of age; has a wife (a negress) and six children, living at New Bedford, Massachussetts, of which state he is a citizen. – When Captain Cuffee's father (who had acquired his freedom) died, he left a family almost unprovided for; but he (the son) laboured hard to support them. He began trade in a small boat, and, after a while, almost by himself, built a larger vessel, in which he worked some years with assiduity. Having met a person wishing to impart some knowledge of navigation, his ideas were enlarged, and with his prospects he enlarged his efforts to succeed. Happily for him and his family, his mind received religious instruction from the Society of Friends, and he attached himself to that respectable body, adopted their dress and language, and is now a very respectable member of that community. When Mr Clarkson's History of the Abolition of the Slave Trade fell into his hands, it awakened all the powers of his mind to a consideration of his origin and the duties he owed to his people. With the view of benefitting the African, he made a voyage to Sierra Leone, and with the same object has come to England. Captain Cuffee is of an agreeable countenance, and his physiognomy truly interesting; he is both tall and stout, speaks English well, dresses in the Quaker style in a drab-coloured suit, and wears a large flapped white hat. His coming to London, to confer upon his favourite topic with the Directors of the African Institution.''

'A negro travelling on his own, unfettered account, is a curiosity at once; but a reading negro, – one who has thought well for himself and his race, – who comes over the Atlantic in his own vessel, – who instead of adopting sentiments of revenge against the whites, becomes a member of a society that worship peace, – and who, to crown all, is of a good countenance and a manly presence, – presents an excellent specimen of what freedom and instruction can do for the outcasts of his colour in the very infancy of their regeneration. He is not to be taken as an exception instead of an example, in this respect; for he is one of the few that have enjoyed the advantages of an early independence; he had laboured, read, thought, and felt for himself, and has become what he is; so that if numbers of his race have displayed marks of energy and free spirit under all the disadvantages of habitual slavery, is it but just to suppose that with his opportunities they would have acquired his information and expanded into his character.'

The editor then expatiated at length on the argument that Negroes in appearance and physique were inferior to Europeans. His comments provoked a long correspondence between those who were convinced of inherent Negro inferiority and others who took the sympathetic Hunt to task for suggesting that the Negro might be considered less aesthetically pleasing than the whites. The correspondence could well have been taken from the mid-twentieth century; but it revealed the interest stimulated in British circles of the early nineteenth century in relations between African and British peoples.

It is to the *Examiner* also that we are indebted for a glimpse into life in West Africa during the rumbustious years between the abolition of the slave trade and the regularization of the new commercial relations. The *Examiner* of January 28, 1816, summarizes a pamphlet it has received dealing with the complaints of a British merchant against a governor in West Africa:

'A pamphlet has recently appeared under the title of "British Justice in Africa; developed in Official and other Documents, concerning certain Proceedings at the British Forts on the Coast of Guinea: – to which is prefixed an Introduction by the English Editor. The whole submitted to the consideration of His Majesty's Ministers and both Houses of Parliament" . . . .

'This publication details the treatment of which Mr Hutton, a private merchant, received, in the first instance from the African Chiefs of Annamabooe – next, from the British Governor of that town, a Mr Dawson – and lastly, from the Governor and Council of Cape Coast Castle. – It appears that a custom prevailed among the Chiefs of Annamabooe, of paying the British merchants there at Christmas a complimentary visit, in order that they might be treated with liquor. On the 23rd of December the Chiefs called upon Mr Hutton for this laudable purpose. Mr Hutton was very busy, and sent word he would wait upon them as soon as he had quitted his storehouse, begging they would either wait or call again. – The Chiefs however were not to be so dismissed: they replied, that the Governor always waited upon them the instant they made their appearance at the fort, and that he must do the same. – Mr Hutton, deeming this a piece of insolence, remonstrated with the rum-seeking Chieftains, but all in vain; a sort of riot ensued; but no blows were struck: Mr Hutton finally not only refused to give them the liquor they had demanded with such violence, but told them he should either get them punished or break up his factory. – This had every effect but the desired one: they told Mr Hutton to quit the town immediately; they said they would themselves beat the gong-gong, and proclaim that they had stopped his trade; they intimated to the people to transact business with him at their perils. These threats were accompanied with divers African gesticulations and howlings, indicative of anything but "the meek-eyed peace".

'While Mr Hutton was meditating on proceeding for redress to the Governor of Annamabooe, that gentleman paid him a visit. Before they parted, Mr Hutton informed the Governor of what had passed, &c. when that Officer observed, that these Chiefs "were a bad set; that God knew, they had taken several Governors into the bush – (a Dutch term, bosh or basch, signifiying a wood or wilderness) – and frightened them fairly out of all the wits they ever had, playing the very devil themselves, or else finding them in the bush; but that, for his own part, having no taste for these adventures, and the bush having at all times a very salutary effect upon his mind, he never learned that the Pynims (Chiefs) had set foot in his fort, but immediately, all Governor as he was, whether he was writing or reading, packing his goods or serving his customers, he left what he was about, and waited upon them like a boy. – Having submitted to Mr Hutton's reflections these hints on the better part of valour, the Governor took his leave."[1]

'Not very well liking to be hooted or gong-gonged out of the place in this manner, Mr Hutton was proceeding to the Supreme Court at Cape Coast Castle for redress, when the Sable Chiefs stopped his canoe, and sent him word, that till he complied with their demands, he must remain a prisoner in Annamabooe. Upon this, Mr Hutton wrote to the Governor requesting his interference. – The Governor replied to Mr Hutton, that he would do his endeavour to make quietness, but he wished he had paid them their custom as usual; that he did not think it was much, but added, they were quite a bad set, and were much intoxicated. In another letter to Mr Hutton, he said, that the Chiefs had before complained of his using them ill; that some time ago he stopped their Sunday's allowance in liquor; that they required three ankers of rum as a settlement, – a demand which he disapproved; that Mr Hutton was at liberty to go to Cape Coast Castle, but the Chiefs expected to be better treated in future.

'Mr Hutton finding he could get no redress of the Governor of Annamabooe, availed himself of this very gracious permission of the

[1] Introduction pages 9–10.

4

African Chiefs, and laid his complaints before the Governor and Council at Cape Coast, – where, on the 27th of January, the Governor of Annamabooe, Mr Dawson, sitting as Vice-President, the case came to be heard. Here this Officer appears to have taken on himself the office of advocate for these dram-drinking Chiefs, and he accordingly made various allegations against Mr Hutton, though repeatedly checked by Mr White, the Chief Governor, who at length insisted on his ceasing. He still however persisted, when Mr Hutton declared that the allegations were false. "This [says Mr H] was the word, and this expression, – Sir, it's false. He called me next, a damned impertinent puppy. – I replied, he was the same, and what was worse, a damned scoundrel: for surely no man can restrain his feelings on such language; and being called a damned impertinent puppy, surely warranted me, at the moment, in returning the compliment as deserved." – p. 23.

'All this took place in the presence of these African Chiefs, and it certainly must have afforded them a fine specimen of British decorum and dignity. – However, the Governor and Council unanimously reprobated Mr Dawson's conduct, and recommended him to leave the Public Hall (the scene of contention) which he did, the Council also retiring nearly at the same time.

'Mr Hutton upon this retired to the room of a friend in the Castle, whither he was soon after followed by Mr Dawson. His unexpected appearance at first occasioned silence for some minutes, but on Mr Hutton's beginning a conversation with his friends, this Governor and Vice-President suddenly sprang upon him and seized both his hands. Mr Dawson, it seems, is a large and powerful person: Mr Hutton has no comparative strength nor stature, and, as he declares, is infinitely lighter than the wild animal by whom he was thus beset and pinioned. – "He knew" (says Mr Hutton) "his advantage in strength over me; and this, it is plain and is acknowledged by all, induced him to follow and treat me in the savage brutal manner he did. He seized my hands, and being a stout and powerful man, twelve or fourteen stone heavier than myself (who am not gifted with strength nor stature to face such an opponent in a pugilistic manner), he shamefully gave me several blows. I received one on each side of the face, one on mouth, and one under the left ribs, before the person present could separate us. The latter blow has occasioned me much pain: the two former being in my face, are visible to the world." – pp. 24–25.

'In explanation of this vulgar and violent conduct, the Governor of Annamabooe said, his object was to blacken Mr Hutton's eyes for his insolence. Mr Hutton observed, that after this unwarrantable and unmanly attack upon him, he hoped he would give him the satisfaction of a gentleman. To which the high-minded and dignified Governor answered, "Satisfaction, Sir. Do you want more satisfaction? Oh! wait a bit!" Mr Hutton, thus treated, again called upon the Governor and Council of Cape Coast Castle for protection and redress. In reply, they express much astonishment that he thought it necessary to complain to them, after seeking his own mode of satisfaction. The Governor had informed the Council that Mr Hutton (on being informed by him, that Mr Dawson should be talked to and made to keep the peace) had declared that he was satisfied; and therefore both the Governor and the Council refused doing anything more in the unfortunate business than transmitting the whole proceedings to the British Africa Company.

'To this Mr Hutton answers, that the Chief Governor, Mr White, had entirely misconstrued his meaning, for he had expressed himself as follows to him: – "That I was perfectly satisfied with myself in the manner I had acted, by sending Mr Dawson a challenge; and, for his refusal of it, exposing him to the country at large; and that it was gratifying to me, beyond expression, to find that everybody seemed to approve of my actions." Mr Hutton also adds, that he considers himself most scandalously used, again calls for redress, and announces his full determination to seek for justice in Africa and in England: – which, it should appear, he is now doing. – In the conclusion of his letter to the African Company, he states that several acts of outrage, even murder, had been suffered under the very eyes of office in Africa. – These things, of course, must be inquired into, for the character of the nation is implicated.'

The journals of the early nineteenth century not only provide us with a mine of information on British attitudes to Africa at the time, but also supply evidence of knowledge of that continent available in Britain, certainly read by many and related by more. Reports from the colonial registers abound, whilst editors then were certainly more willing than now to print long extracts from explorers and travellers. For instance, the *Quarterly Review* of January 1818 devoted forty-four pages to an account, published by permission of the Lords Commissioners of the Admiralty, of an expedition led by a Captain Tuckey to explore 'the River Zaire, usually called the Congo, in South Africa, in 1816'. The principal object of the exploration was to discover whether the Congo and the Niger were actually the same – as Mungo Park had suspected; the secondary aim was to gather 'information respecting an important part of "that ill-fated country, whose unhappy natives, without laws to restrain or governments to protect them, have too long been the prey of a senseless domestic superstition, and the victims of a foreign infamous and rapacious commerce".' Unfortunately for the guardians of the superior culture who made this journey to bring enlightenment to such unhappy people, many of them were unable to survive its rigours. The report attributes this to their own imprudence, for although 'spiritous liquors were not to be obtained; but excesses of another kind were freely indulged, to which they were prompted by the native blacks, who were always ready to give up their sisters, daughters, or even their wives, for the hope only of getting in return a small quantity of spirits.' When the same hospitality was offered by a local ruler the editor assumes that 'they were trained to this offensive custom by the European slave-dealers.' Nevertheless, whatever the officers of the expedition may have thought of their men's conduct, they themselves must have been agreeably impressed by their own reception. On the visit to the Chenoo of Embomma 'they sat down to an entertainment in a large apartment, where some chests covered with carpets served, at once, for seats and tables. The repast consisted of a soup of plantains and goats' flesh, a fowl cut in pieces and broiled, and roasted plantains in lieu of bread; some sweet palm wine, in a large silver tankard, was the only beverage. When dinner was ended, the king and his chiefs still appeared doubtful as to the real motives of the visit; at length an old man, starting up, plucked a leaf from a tree, and holding it to Captain Tuckey, said, "If you come to trade, swear by your God and break the leaf;" on his refusing to do so, he said, "Swear by your God you don't come to make war, and break the leaf:" this Captain Tuckey immediately did, on which the whole company performed a gran sakilla, a kind of measured dance, expressive of approbation; and the assembly then broke up apparently quite satisfied.'

Conditions in South Africa can also be traced from these old journals, whose accounts must have added considerable weight to the pleas of missionaries for government action to diminish the warfare between colonists and Africans. The *Asiatic Journal* of May–August 1835, for example, offered its readers an extract from the *Cape of Good Hope Literary Gazette* in which a John Centilvres Chase describes the trading relations between settlers and 'Caffres'. Writing in support of this trade, which some would have forbidden, this gentleman observed 'the traders penetrated along the coast in every direction, and settled themselves down with the consent of the chiefs on Caffre soil, building houses and opening stores; and such was the supply kept up in these nuclei of civilization, that travellers in the Caffre country declare that they found every want supplied with almost equal ease as if they had been within the colonial boundary. . . . It is supposed that more than one hundred of these trading stations were established, where European manufactures were taken in barter for hides, horns, and ivory. . . . the trade has gradually increased; so much so, that its returns are stated, for the year 1832, as equal in value to £34,000, whilst those for the following year are estimated as about £40,000 sterling.' And the writer concludes with a pregnant query: 'What shall we do now with, and what shall we do for, the Caffres? which I leave for consideration.'

But the frequent conflicts between white settlers and African communities, which had originated in the eighteenth century along the frontier between these rival societies, continued under nineteenth century British rule. The hopes expressed by the writer that British settlement might extend trading relations between European and African in South Africa were soon dashed by events such as that recounted in the *Quarterly Review* of February 1837. The question seems to have been not what to do *for* so much as *to* the Caffres. In an article on conditions in South Africa a report from the governor of the Cape on a punitive military expedition against the 'Caffres' is quoted: 'In the course of the Commissioners' progress in the census of the tribes of Gaika and T'Llambie, it was ascertained that their loss during our operations against them, has amounted to 4,000 of their warriors or fighting men, and among them many captains. Ours, fortunately, has not in the whole amounted to 100, and of these only two officers. There have been taken from them also, besides the conquest and alienation of their country, about 60,000 head of cattle, and almost all their goats; their habitations have everywhere been destroyed and their gardens and corn-fields laid waste. They have, therefore, been chastised, not extremely, but sufficiently.' It is salutary to note that the strictures of the Colonial Secretary to the governor are also quoted, including the pertinent passage; '. . . . to consign an entire country to desolation, and a whole people to famine, is an aggravation of the necessary horrors of war, so repugnant to every just feeling, and so totally at variance with the habits of civilized nations, that I should not be justified in receiving such a statement without calling upon you for further explanations.'

The abolition of the British slave trade in 1807 and the use of the Royal Navy to interfere with, and, where possible, to halt the continuation of the slave trade by other nationals, caused severe economic dislocation in West Africa. The early trade in commodities between Europe and West Africa had long been overshadowed by the traffic in slaves. This meant that the development of the African merchant class, usually dependent on its local rulers, had been almost entirely bound up with the sale of slaves and their exchange for imported European goods. The abolition of this trade, or at least its attempted abolition, accompanied by anti-slavery measures, deprived West African merchants of their only important commodity. There was some attempt to replace it by the export of palm oil, particularly from the Oil Rivers area, but the slave trade itself, through which communications had been developed throughout West Africa, on which all West African states in the eighteenth century had depended, and from which any immediate chance of future economic development rested, was suddenly removed. For long years, from the time when the Royal Navy first began seriously to interfere with slaving in the 1820s until Europe began to discover new needs which Africa could supply some thirty or forty years later, African trade with the outside world was drastically reduced.

Moreover, the effects of the obsession with the slave trade and with the European imports exchanged for slaves, had inevitably undermined local African manufacture and craftsmanship. Instead of this developing from the sound basis of textiles and metal ware, which had already been laid before the arrival of European traders, much of this production had been destroyed by the competition of European imported goods, the wars which accompanied the slave trade, and the uncertainty which was an inevitable consequence of the slavery period. It is reported that the Portuguese bought cloth from the Guinea coast and took it to Europe as early as the beginning of the sixteenth century. Benin textiles were particularly famous, but the textile manufacture along the coast, in places like Benin and Dahomey, was retarded as a result of European imports. Yet far enough away from the coast to be comparatively uninfluenced by the slave trade, Kano, in Northern Nigeria, continued to maintain a flourishing textile industry.

Similarly, African agriculture had remained largely stagnant in its methods and outlook during the same period. It is true that certain foods had been introduced as a result of commerce with the Americas, but the growth of a well-organized agricultural system capable of feeding the populations of stable societies was impossible during the turmoil of the slave years.

Then again, one must remember that a high proportion of the most able-bodied and most intelligent young men and women from certain areas of West Africa had been lost to their society through the mass transportations across the Atlantic. Though it is true that this impact tended to be regional and bore much more heavily on some areas than others, nevertheless it was an important factor retarding economic progress and a direct result of the slave trade.

Finally, one may also mention that the profits of slaving were so much greater than anything Africa had known before that they inevitably led to a concentration of trade on the coast, at the expense of the traditional trading paths to the north and east. As we have seen, new states and empires grew up around the slaving routes near the coast. This resulted in neglect of those inland areas which had traditionally been on trading routes to the Mediterranean and to Egypt. The consequence of this shift in commercial power and weakening of traditional routes was that the legitimate trading activities of western and northern Africans never expanded as might otherwise have been expected.

In short, the effects of the three centuries of slave trading was to create an obsession with an arid form of trade which not only reduced the virility of indigenous populations, but also gravely weakened the natural growth of commercial activities, the emergence of a strong independent merchant class and of progressive farmers who might have laid the basis for an agrarian-industrial revolution in Africa parallel to that in Europe. Of course, the bulk of profits from the slave trade went overseas to the European merchants, but those which remained in Africa actually hindered industrial growth there by being devoted to imported goods which undermined indigenous African manufactures.

The significance of the nineteenth century for Africa lay in the transformation of her economic relations with Britain. Strictly speaking this change began in the late eighteenth century and was virtually complete well before the end of the nineteenth. It was determined by changes in Britain, rather than by any notable development in African life.

In the middle of the eighteenth century Britain was the most prosperous nation in Europe, with a capital city inhabited by three-quarters of a million people. Her prosperity was founded on trade and enterprise, on the activities of her merchants, shippers and overseas agents, supported by her all-powerful navy. Provincial port cities like Liverpool, Bristol and Glasgow were rapidly expanding on the basis of the same trading interests as those which gave London its dominance – slaves, and the commodities produced by slave labour, sugar, tea, tobacco, cotton. A century later Britain was, however, the industrial heart of the world, her greatly magnified power and her much larger population sustained by industrialists rather than by merchants. The course of this revolution was influenced by Britain's relations with Africa and itself affected those relations.

The phenomenon which gave the leading role in the world's industrial revolution to the small islands of Britain was due to a large extent to Britain's eighteenth century export trade. The domestic market expanded steadily during this century, but exports multiplied astronomically. Africa played only one part in this tremendous expansion, but it was an important part. The slave trade not only rapidly increased during the eighteenth century, but, as we have seen, British slavers captured a large proportion of the commerce. Moreover, the slaves who were transported across the Atlantic provided the labour for the production of those tropical imports which in turn provided the foundations for British industrialism, as well as being a profitable commodity in themselves. Tea, sugar, and tobacco supplied the demands of the new working classes of Britain, but cotton, the raw material of the crucial textile industry, was of even greater significance. Meanwhile, the production of the manufactured goods, already stimulated by the traders who needed them to buy slaves, was induced to tremendous expansion by the growth of trade. Ship-building for slavers and navy demanded industrial innovation and development; the capture of rivals' markets through colonization and war brought new stimulation to industry; and the destruction of indigenous manufactures provided the opportunity for the production of substitutes.

The role played by the colonies in general and Africa in particular in this great British economic transformation has been described by Eric Hobsbawm in these terms: 'Behind our Industrial Revolution there lies this concentration on the colonial and "underdeveloped" markets overseas, the successful battle to deny them to anyone else. We defeated them in the East: in 1766 we already outsold even the Dutch in the China trade. We defeated them in the West: by the early 1780s more than half of all slaves exported from Africa (and almost twice as many as those carried by the French) made profits for British slavers. And we did so for the benefit of *British* goods. For some three decades after the war of the Spanish Succession British ships bound for Africa still carried mainly foreign (including Indian) goods; from shortly after the War of the Austrian Succession they carried overwhelmingly British ones. Our industrial economy grew out of our commerce, and especially our commerce with the underdeveloped world. And throughout the nineteenth century it was to retain this peculiar historical pattern; commerce and shipping maintained our balance of payments, and the exchange of overseas primary products for British manufactures was to be the foundation of our international economy.'[1]

The progressive dominance of industry over commerce within Britain was reflected in British African relations. Already, during the eighteenth century, despite the pre-eminent position of the merchants, British governments had begun to listen to the claims of industrialists. After all, landed interests still controlled government and in Britain the landowners had started to visualize the profits which could be made from industrial enterprises on their estates. So industry was able to persuade the government to adopt a policy of protection, entirely contrary to the wishes of merchants. This attitude of favouring industry

[1] E. J. Hobsbawm, *Industry and Empire*, Weidenfeld and Nicolson, pp. 37–8.
4*

against commerce was to influence the arguments over the slave trade, seeing its abolition as an incentive to the growth of industry; and it succeeded despite the fact that it was a highly profitable enterprise for one section of the commercial community.

In the longer term, though, it was the change in the character of trade between Britain and Africa which was to become most significant. In the first phase of the Industrial Revolution textiles played the vital role. The mechanization of the cotton industry paved the path for further technological innovation; it also enabled the Lancashire mills to manufacture mass-produced materials which swelled British exports – often at the expense of Indian products. And a large proportion of these textile exports were sent to Africa. At first the raw cotton was grown in the West Indies and the southern states of America; later, in the second half of the nineteenth century Egypt and Uganda also became important producing areas. In short, the industrialization of Britain changed the basic economic relationship between Britain and Africa; in place of slaves Britain now sought the continent's raw materials, palm oil, cotton, later cocoa, gold, groundnuts, copper; instead of firearms, liquor and metalware, she sent to Africa the products of her mills and factories. The relations of modern 'developed' and 'underdeveloped' economies were fixed.

This process occurred during the first phase of British industrialization. The second, beginning towards the middle of the nineteenth century, was marked by a renunciation of protectionism and the replacement of textiles as the powerhouse of industrialism by coal, iron and steel. For by now the overwhelming dominance of British industry had obliterated all fear of competition; British manufacturers desired simply the opportunity to offer their wares wherever they pleased, unhampered by tariffs, quotas or other restrictions. Free trade therefore became the Ark of the economists' Covenant. British industrialists, backed by the British Navy, now insisted that the world was their market place.

Other nations had now begun to follow the British lead by moving towards an industrial society. They were no longer content to buy for their needs from Britain and sought to build their own large-scale factories and workshops. But in order to do so they had to look first to Britain to supply the equipment. Capital goods therefore grew rapidly in demand from British exporters. In the Americas, in Europe and in the white-settled colonies, Australasia, Canada, and South Africa, the demand for British iron, coal and steel rose dramatically. Meanwhile textile exports still increased, though more slowly. They remained vital to British industry, especially as the huge Indian market was opened to Lancashire, but heavy industry now took the leading role. Textiles and cottons, which in 1830 had constituted over seventy per cent of British exports, fell to under fifty-five per cent by 1870. Heavy industrial exports rose during the same period from just over eleven per cent to nearly twenty per cent,[1] and when the middle of the century saw the opening of the era of overseas railway construction, the stimulus to the capital goods sector and to investment in it gained a powerful new thrust.

Once the slave period was ended Africa became no more than a marginal participant in these affairs. Nevertheless, she found, though to a much lesser extent than India, that her indigenous manufactures could not compete with the mass produced articles of Britain; and as there was insufficient political power to decree protection for her meagre infant industries, she came to be regarded as no more than a provider of food and raw materials to the maws of the great British industrial complex. Towards the end of the century, when minerals had been found in Southern Africa, she also shared in a minor way in the railway boom, though only to the extent that it served to facilitate the freightage of her materials to the coasts for shipment to Britain.

The production of such raw materials, as in the case of the mining extraction which developed later in the nineteenth century, was conducted usually by Europeans, individuals or companies. Thus again, the capital accumulated by such activities did not find its way into improved techniques or further investment in African industry and agriculture; it was expatriated and hastened the momentum of industrialism, commerce, agricultural growth and the national treasury in Britain. At the same time, agricultural development in Africa was never organized to provide food for the local population, nor were there the food surpluses which in Britain supplied one of the foundations of industrialization; the object in Africa was usually to produce export crops like cotton, cocoa, sisal or bananas. This again diverted

[1] Hobsbawm, *op. cit.* p. 89.

efforts essential for industrialization, as the profits from these export crops went to Britain and the British owners or managers of the estates on which they were produced then imported British manufactures which effectively killed local industries. Moreover, the expansion of production for export often reduced the amount of land devoted to food-growing for local consumption, leading to increases in malnutrition and decreases in human energy.

These processes were seen in their most tragic forms in India; but Africa also suffered from similar, if less dramatic, effects, particularly in Egypt. Productive land was there increased by twenty per cent, but almost entirely in order to produce more cotton for export to Lancashire's textile mills. The rapid growth of population was scarcely matched by increased local food supplies. Meanwhile, investors were paid their dividends out of these export revenues – foreign profits totalled half the total export value and over half the Egyptian budget. The result was that the vast majority of Egyptian people were kept in agricultural employment whilst landlord privileges and powers were sustained. The peasant masses, bowed under exorbitant rents and consequent debts, were thus rendered incapable of escaping from their traditional methods of production.

By the last quarter of the century, however, the position of Britain herself on the international economic scene radically changed. The hegemony which she had established over world trade was being challenged, particularly by America and Germany. Those who had previously been anxious to import British capital goods had put them to work in their own local industries. Countries which had formerly relied on British technology were now advancing faster in the field of technological innovation than the British themselves – and, of course, often had the advantage of starting their processes where Britain had left off. Moreover, as other countries became less dependent on Britain, so they followed the early British practice of protecting their industries against external competition – mainly from Britain. As the British economy became so firmly geared to overseas trade, the consequent reduction in the rate of expansion of international trade hit her particularly severely. And as wider industrial systems accompanied by greater productivity reduced manufacturing costs, whilst more efficient transport by sea and rail lowered the costs of primary products, so competition in the international markets sharpened and a period of general deflation ensued.

Most of Britain's competitors met this challenge by raising protective barriers and by seeking new techniques. Britain, with her heavy investment in overseas enterprise, concentrated increasingly on finance, shipping, insurance, brokerage and investment. Her industrial competitors were allowed to outstrip her without serious response. But she could not fail to respond to the direct challenge to her imperial position. She had been largely content during most of the nineteenth century to establish an informal empire based on industrial strength rather than political rule. Indeed, it seemed to most of her economic pundits that formal empire involved expenses inhibiting to her economic interests. In the white-settled dominions Britain had been promoting a devolution of political responsibility, leaving her directly governing only those imperial possessions from the past which seemed of economic or military strategic significance. When her rivals turned to acquire colonies in order either to imitate the British Empire, or to find outlets for their increasingly hampered foreign trade, or to gain control of potential raw materials, or any combination of these reasons, Britain could not afford to stand apart. For she saw that many of these acquisitions threatened her international power, on which the preservation of her trade routes depended. They might jeopardize her vital links with India, and could pre-empt new raw materials in colonial lands. Thus, to her existing empire she added, albeit with some reluctance, vast new imperial territories, particularly in Africa, and actively participated with other developed nations in the forms of financial imperialism which brought supposedly independent states under the financial control of the great powers. As Britain's foreign investments rose steeply in the later years of the nineteenth and early years of the twentieth centuries, even if partly through reinvestment of profits, a third form of imperial control was added.

In consequence of this urgent re-direction of British policies in order to meet the economic challenge to her international position beginning in the 1870s, the whole character of Afro-British relations was transformed. From trading partners they became ruler and ruled. Nor was there even the compensation of sharing the increased British investment which some other colonies enjoyed. Apart from the capital which flowed into diamonds and gold mining in South Africa towards the end of the century, there was little attraction for large-scale external investment anywhere in the continent. So, apart from the south, Africa suffered the imposition of colonial rule without any even long-term prospect of industrialization.

Chapter 5

From the Abolition of the Slave Trade to the 'Scramble' : 1

Two main influences had inspired the movement to abolish the slave trade: religion and commerce. Usually, the two complemented each other to produce a common outcome. Once the slave trade had been abolished by Britain it was in her commercial interest to prevent others from continuing it. Consequently, a British naval squadron was posted off the West African coast to intercept slavers, return them, usually to Sierra Leone, and there release the slaves. But if Christian influence was to replace British slavery, Britain could not remain content with her slight influence on the West African beaches. For, as we have seen, the trade itself was initiated far inland. To cut off the head of the trade on the coast would not destroy the roots in the hinterland. Nor, indeed, was it sufficient for the navy to conduct its anti-slavery operations off the coast. For the coastline is long and the ships committed to this unhealthy and unpopular station were necessarily few. Consequently, there were always interlopers and ships of other nations prepared to buy slaves and run the gauntlet of the British blockade for so long as they could be sold across the Atlantic. And this trade remained profitable until well into the second half of the nineteenth century.

Moreover, if Christian missions were to be enabled to perform their proselytizing work, they would need some protection when they had penetrated the fastnesses of the inland states. And missionary activity would hardly have appeared serious if confined simply to the coastal tribes. In any case, if missionaries were to abolish slaving, it was into the hinterland that they would have to turn in order to make converts of those who were actually engaged in the capture of the slaves themselves. Thus everything pointed to the necessity for increased British penetration of the West African inland areas.

Before this was possible, however, whether for commercial or for missionary purposes, more needed to be known of West African geography than the scanty impressions, largely based on rumour, that were available to the British people at the beginning of the nineteenth century.

Through a combination of scientific, geographical, commercial, humanitarian and governmental interests, throughout most of the nineteenth century exploratory expeditions were sent out to discover the facts of African geography. Britain took by far the largest share in this activity, although the French and Germans also participated. In the second half of the century the American journalist Stanley, later to be financed by the Belgian king, also played a part. But it was men like Mungo Park, exploring the Niger at the end of the eighteenth century and the beginning of the nineteenth, Denham and Clapperton, exploring the lands south of the Sahara during the 1820s, the Landers discovering the course of the Niger and linking it with the delta in the 1830s, who really brought serious knowledge of West Africa to Britain. Then David Livingstone, in his historic journeys from East into Central Africa, and Burton, Speke and Grant in his wake, increased British conceptions of life in the eastern highlands and central plateau. To this was added the knowledge gained by the French and Germans, and Stanley; indeed, on occasion, as with Heinrich Barth, these journeys were undertaken with British support.

For most of the century, Africa remained a continent of mystery, adventure and heroism to most British people. The travels of the explorers were followed with avid interest and excitement, but this was also laced with moral philosophy. The late eighteenth century and the nineteenth saw within many Christian sects in Britain a wave of evangelical enthusiasm for the conversion of non-Christian peoples to the Christian church. Thus, the central philosophy of those concerned with the exploration of Africa was to bring Christian enlightenment to peoples believed to be pagan or at least non-Christian.

But there was another, inter-locking element in this philosophy. It was assumed that Christianity was virtually synonymous with trade in its corrosive impact on slavery. Thus the triple and indistinguishable objectives of the British in their penetration of the African continent during the nineteenth century were to bring Africans within the British, Christian, commercial society.

So organizations like the London Missionary Society, inspired mainly by the Congregationalists, the Anglican Society for the Propagation of the Gospel and their Church Missionary Society, the Methodist Missionary Society, the Universities Mission, also Anglican, and the missions of the Scottish Presbyterian Churches, together with various Roman Catholic societies, all brought the gospels of nineteenth century Britain to the peoples of Africa.

As a commercial proposition, at least until the end of the century, the African continent was largely peripheral to the main British trading interests. It could never compare as a commercial or investment proposition at any time in the century with the United States of America or India. For most of the century, too, Canada, Australia and South America were much more important to the British economy. It was not until the discovery of diamonds and gold in South Africa during the last third of the century that investment in any part of the continent reached serious proportions, although it was moderate in Egypt throughout the second half of the century.

Nevertheless, there was some serious commercial interest in the development of trade to and from West Africa throughout the nineteenth century. On a national scale, the rate of this commerce might be small but it was still important to those who engaged in it and they in their turn made it appear significant to politicians. Much of British policy towards West Africa throughout this century was concerned with the affairs and the protection of those who had replaced the slave trade with other commercial activities. As commerce and proselytizing were often considered to be almost synonymous in Britain, it was held to be the responsibility of the British government to protect simultaneously the interests of British traders and of missionaries.

There was an earnest argument between Cobden and his followers, on the one hand, who feared that government activity might handicap commercial interests, and Palmerston, on the other, who believed that it was the government's responsibility to defend the British engaged in trade. Nevertheless, it was the Palmerston attitude which influenced policy in every government. Palmerston himself, in 1842, expressed most forthrightly the general outlook of the British of the mid-nineteenth century when he explained his conception of the purpose of divisions within the human race: 'It is that the exchange of commodities, may be accompanied by the. . . . diffusion of knowledge – by the interchange of mutual benefits engendering mutual kind feelings. . . . It is, that commerce may go freely forth, leading civilization with one hand and peace with the other, to render mankind happier, wiser, better.' It was this complex amalgam of deep humanitarian feeling, a bowdlerized form of Darwinism which held that Britain was proving herself to be the master and the educator of the world because she was the fittest survivor, together with a strong element of commercial expansionism, which characterized Britain's impact on Africa during most of the nineteenth century. There were often variations in the direction of government policies designed to safeguard commercial interests most efficiently. At times merchants were left to conduct their own affairs, though usually behind the protective screen of the navy; at others, direct governmental authority was imposed on the areas where trade was being conducted; or sometimes a consul would be appointed to ensure that trade was conducted in safety. Yet, although the methods might vary, the ultimate objectives remained unchanging; British commerce must be free to conduct its affairs as it thought best under constant protection from the British government. In this way the ultimate natural law would be fulfilled to the mutual benefit of British citizens and the lesser breeds of other lands. As Disraeli explained in 1863, 'There may be grave questions as to the best mode of obtaining wealth. . . . but there can be no question. . . . that the best mode of preserving wealth is power.'

The story of British relations with Africa during the first three-quarters of the nineteenth century provides constant evidence of this attitude. It was not a period in which the colonizing spirit prevailed. Indeed, it was generally believed that colonizing itself handicapped commerce by entailing unnecessary administrative expense and assuming responsiblities which would detract from the interests of trade. The central objective was to pursue the paths of commerce wherever they were found to be profitable, and, in so doing, undermine the evils of slavery and the slave trade. In order to ensure that this beneficent commercial interest was unfettered, trade to all quarters of the globe must be unhindered. It was therefore the duty of British governments to cut the bonds of monopoly and to destroy any barriers raised against the free exercise of commercial practices. For this, of course, was a period in which the long lead gained by Britain in the industrial race gave British manufacturers tremendous advantages over their competitors whenever free competition prevailed. At the same time, the paramount power of the British navy guaranteed that, when it was desired, all trade troutes could be kept open and any attempted restrictions removed.

At the end of the wars with Napoleon, the settlements along the Senegal, which had been seized by Britain, were returned to the French, but Britain retained the important islands of Mauritius and the Seychelles as strategic bases for the Indian Ocean. British merchants also retained their posts along the Gambia, which were linked to the British authorities in Sierra Leone. The British merchants who had concentrated on Senegal during the wars now returned to the Gambia and founded the township of Bathurst on an island at the mouth of the river. In 1821 the Gambia was annexed to Sierra Leone. Although it became an independent colony in 1843, by 1866 it was once more brought under the aegis of Sierra Leone and remained so until 1888, when it was again separated.

The Gambia was one of the earliest scenes of British commercial activity in Africa. A patent was granted to Exeter and London merchants in 1588 to trade with the river. Fort James, founded in 1618, was the oldest British dependency. But rivalry with the French prevented any lasting development of the area known as Senegambia. Many companies were formed to trade with the coast and up the river into the interior. The slave trade flourished, most of its victims being prisoners taken in war, brought to the coast tied 'by the neck with leather thongs, at about a yard distant from each other'.

But the opportunities for legitimate trade up the river – which was chosen by Mungo Park as the base for his Niger expeditions – were largely neglected by Britain. Most of the trade carried by the Gambia from the peoples living along its banks was directed by the French rather than the British. Nor was much attention paid to Sierra Leone. which for the first half of the century served mainly as a depository for those slaves freed from the slaving ships captured by the Royal Navy. The boundaries of the colony itself were gradually extended from time to time as the ex-slave population grew and the need to protect it from indigenous tribal communities became more urgent. Perhaps the most important event in Sierra Leone during this period was the foundation of Fourah Bay College in 1827. The College owed its inception to the evangelical spirit of the Church Missionary Society, which founded it originally as a Christian institution to train Africans for the priesthood, thence to carry the gospels from the settlement on the coast to the tribal areas of the interior. The foundation stone of the College building was laid in 1845 on the site of an old slave factory. The Governor who laid the foundation stone was himself of African descent, a doctor as well as Her Majesty's representative. The chaplain of the colony has left this description of the building erected on the site: 'The white walls of a large and noble building, rising in aristocratic loftiness, three good storeys high, as if by enchantment, from the palm trees which embosom it, and displaying its parapets in the quiet moonlight, like a structure of the fancy, which Spenser's pen might not have despised'. The college extended its hospitality beyond trainee priests, to prepare the descendants of the slaves for a variety of professional careers. This gave it a specially significant place in supplying the West African settlements with their cadres of doctors, engineers, priests and clerks. In 1876 the College was affiliated to the University of Durham. It owed its vital place in the West African scene to the continued support of the Church Missionary Society and then of Durham University. At the same time, the College recruited its students almost entirely from the Creole population, composed of the descendants of the ex-slaves. Within this small community English was the main language, trade the chief occupation and culture developed as an unsatisfactory amalgam, neither European nor African, separating the community sharply from the tribes of the interior.

It was, however, on the Gold Coast and around the Niger Delta that British policies had their greatest impact during the nineteenth century and off these coasts the major offensive was taken against the persistent slave trade. Here, the missionaries established most of their stations, offering practical training as well as spiritual enlightenment, and the most serious and prolonged attempts were made to find commercial substitutes for the human slave commodity that was now forbidden. It might be found possible to grow and export groundnuts from the Gambia or some palm kernels from Sierra Leone, but in the Gold Coast timber, indigo and gold and in the Delta more timber, pepper, rice, gum and ivory, all proved much more profitable. Above all, palm oil proved to be the best commercial alternative to the slave trade.

Two main issues were now involved in the continuing interest of Britain in West Africa during the post slave-trade period: the opening of trading opportunities to British merchants and the abolition of the slave trade conducted by others. In the Gold Coast the Ashanti kingdom had established itself as the most powerful military and commercial unit. The Fante on the coast, supported by their British allies, were considered by the Ashanti to obstruct the way to free trade with the outside world. As middlemen they were regarded as parasites. It was therefore the constant object of the Ashanti to conquer the coastal peoples who, once vanquished, were regarded as subjects of the Asantehene and their states as provinces of the Ashanti empire. Moreover, as the British Company continued to support the Fante, it was held responsible by Kumasi for the actions and provocations of its allies. In these circumstances, British policy, varying according to the personalities of its controllers and what seemed to be in the national interest of the moment, always played an important role in the commercial and political relations of the rival Gold Coast communities.

The abolition of the slave trade inevitably led to a decline in the fortunes of the Company of Merchants, which had been formed almost solely to organize this commerce. By 1821 the Company had sunk so low that it was abolished by Act of Parliament and its possessions on the coast transferred to the Crown. They were incorporated with the rest of the West African settlements under the authority of the government in Sierra Leone. But before the Company was abolished it sent the first British mission to Kumasi in order to negotiate agreements with the Ashanti. It was hoped in this way to halt the constant warfare between the Ashanti and the coast and to keep open trade routes into the interior. The following year, in 1818, the British government entered the scene by appointing a consul to the Ashanti court. His first action was to negotiate a treaty within which the Ashanti were recognized as suzerain over the coastal tribes. Already, however, merchants on the coast were showing an unruly independence of action which was to be repeated many times before the end of the century. They were very happy to accept the protection of the British government in any form in which it was offered; they were not prepared to recognize treaties signed by it if they appeared to interfere with their own commercial interest. In this case, the agents of the Company refused to recognize the Ashanti treaty and their subsequent activities were naturally held by the Asantehene to be a breach of British faith.

It is interesting to note contemporary observations of conditions in Ashanti at this time. On this first British mission to Kumasi in 1817, one of the travellers described his impressions of the Ashanti court in these words: 'an area of nearly a mile in circumference was crowded with magnificence and novelty. The king, his tributaries, and captains, were resplendent in the distance, surrounded by attendants of every description, fronted by a mass of warriors which seemed to make our approach impervious. The sun was reflected, with a glare scarcely more supportable than the heat, from the massive gold ornaments, which glistened in every direction. More than a hundred bands burst out at once on our arrival. . . . the horns flourished their defiances, with the beating of innumerable drums and metal instruments, and then yielded for awhile to the soft breathings of their long flutes, which were truly harmonious. . . .

'The caboceers, as did their superior captains and attendants, wore Ashantee clothes, of extravagant price . . . they were of an incredible size and weight, and thrown over the shoulder exactly like the Roman toga. . . . Some wore necklaces reaching to the naval entirely of aggrey beads; a band of gold and beads encircled the knee, from which several strings of the same depended; small circles of gold like guineas. . . . were strung round their ankles; their sandals were of green, red and delicate white leather. . . . rude lumps of rock gold, hung from their left wrists. . . .' The same writer, Thomas Edward Bowdich, also appears to have been deeply impressed by the Asantehene, Osei Tutu, whom he described thus: 'We cannot do justice to the King's sentiments either in detail or in expression; they were incredibly liberal, and would have ennobled the most civilized monarch; they seemed to break the spell which has shut the Interior.'

The failure of the 1818 treaty to preserve peace between the interior and the coast was reflected in renewed war between the Ashanti and the Fante in 1824. Once again, the coastal Fante were supported by the British. Despite this fact, they were soundly defeated and in the course of battle the British Governor himself was slain. Two years later, at Dodowa, the result was reversed, the Ashanti this time being put to flight by coastal armies reinforced by British officers.

Yet the expense of these engagements convinced the British government that its position on the Gold Coast was leading it into unreward-ing costs. It therefore tried to adopt a policy of withdrawal from the coastal forts. This, however, was strongly resisted by the merchants engaged in trade there, who were less concerned with the theory of governmental non-interference than with ensuring that their commer-cial activities were protected by the Home Government. In 1828, therefore, a compromise was reached in which a Committee of London Merchants trading to the Gold Coast took over control of the forts, set up its local administration, and received an annual subsidy of £4,000 from the government.

It was under the direction of George Maclean, who was put in charge of the Council's affairs in 1830, that the highest degree of positive policy from Britain was achieved. Maclean had only a semi-official role, but he clearly recognized the main needs of the British merchants. He saw that trade required peace and stable conditions and that these would not be secured until conflict between the Ashanti and the Fante was brought to an end. So, in 1831, he arranged a treaty by which the Asantehene surrendered his claim to sovereignty over the Fante, made a deposit to ensure the future good behaviour of his people, and agreed that, in future, Maclean should be the arbiter of disputes. Most impor-tant was the Asantehene's pledge to keep paths to the interior open and to prevent obstacles to trade being raised along them.

This treaty and the consequences which flowed from it brought a period of comparative peace, lasting fifteen years. It gave the Ashanti merchants direct access to the coast and it provided for the gradual development of a rough system of justice, removing to some degree the fears which had led to conflict. Although he had no constitutional right to do so, Maclean established his judicial authority throughout the coastal communities. In doing so he was wise enough to find a mean between traditional African law and the British sense of equity. He was bitterly attacked at times in Britain for refusing to outlaw all forms of slavery. What he did, however, was to use all his authority against the persisting slave trade and the practice of human sacrifice, whilst recognizing that the domestic form of slavery practised in African society was, for the time being, essential to its economic and social life. The dividends of Maclean's policy can be judged from the fact that between 1831 and 1840 Gold Coast imports increased from £131,000 to £423,000 and exports from £70,000 to £325,000. Of course, it is also clear from these figures that the central motivation in Maclean's policy was to provide conditions in which both British and African merchants could conduct their trade relations with maximum mutual profit and that this would be best secured if African and European kept their own functions. He therefore opposed suggestions that European merchants should pursue their trading activities into the interior.

Once again, however, in 1843, the dichotomy between those who favoured an administration run by the merchants themselves and those who believed that where British economic interests were concerned the writ of the British government should run, was exposed in the report of a parliamentary committee. As a consequence of this, the forts were once more taken under the control of the British government by the application of the Foreign Jurisdiction Act, which also legalized the application of British jurisdiction when accepted by custom or treaty. Maclean remained in the Gold Coast as Judicial Assessor, continuing his work with the consent of the coastal tribes. The following year, 1844, the Fante signed an agreement, known as the Bond, under which the chiefs of 'countries and places adjacent to Her Majesty's forts and settlements on the Gold Coast' gave certain guarantees against 'barbarous behaviour', and accepted the jurisdiction of the Queen's officers, thus adding their recognition to the situation which Maclean had created. It should be noted, however, that the signing of this agreement tacitly recognized the sovereignty of the Fante and their right to determine whether or not to accept the jurisdiction of British officers.

Yet, although this recognition was implicit in all the agreements made by Maclean, the fact was that Maclean's stewardship over nearly twenty years on the Gold Coast had inevitably established British influence in that area as a far greater factor than ever before. The British government and merchants now had the upper hand in relations both with the Ashanti and the coastal peoples. British commercial policy determined economic relations in the area, and, to a great extent, British conceptions of law were now guiding the development of the judicial system. From these foundations British influence was to grow into British control.

Even after Maclean's success, argument continued as to the correct extent of British influence on the coast. At this time there were still two other European powers concerned with the affairs of the Gold Coast, the Danes and the Dutch. The Danes, however, were bought out for £10,000 in 1850, their forts, including Christiansborg Castle, coming under British control. The Dutch remained until 1872, when they were also bought out for only £3,790, leaving Britain in sole control.

Nevertheless, the idea of Britain paying the expenses of its administration was still highly unpopular at home. An attempt was made to offset this when, in 1852, a 'Legislative Assembly of Native Chiefs upon the Gold Coast' was called together and persuaded to agree to an annual poll tax of a shilling per head. The tax, in fact, was never successfully administered, brought in much less revenue than had been hoped, and was abolished in 1861.

Voices continued to be raised against the whole concept of the British Treasury spending money on governing peoples overseas, especially peoples who appeared to be contributing little to British commercial prosperity. The clearest example of this opposition was evinced in 1865 when a Select Committee of Parliament reported, 'That all further extension of territory or assumption of government, or new treaties offering any protection to native tribes, would be inexpedient, and that the object of our policy should be to encourage in the natives the exercise of those qualities which may render it possible for us more and more to transfer to them the administration of all the governments, with a view to our ultimate withdrawal from all, except, probably, Sierra Leone.' The sentiments expressed in this report ran parallel to those in the Durham Report on the future of Canada, published in 1839, which made such a profound impact on British colonial policy. They bear witness to the strong current of opposition flowing through British political life during this part of the century against British expenditure on, or responsibility for, the government of colonial territories.

However, the 1865 report was probably more influenced by the renewal of Ashanti attacks in 1863 and 1864 than by any concept of political philosophy. This renewed warfare with the Ashanti closed almost all the trade routes into the interior and brought commerce virtually to a standstill. It again appeared to many with influential positions in Britain that British money was being spent on administration in an area producing too few profits to warrant it.

In fact, the renewal of the Ashanti wars showed something further. The merchants and their representatives on the spot concerned with Gold Coast trade had no intention of promoting self-government among the Africans nor of acquiescing in the removal of the protection afforded them by the British government. They were only concerned to ensure that the trade routes were kept open and that some authority was present to guarantee that bargains were kept. They had little objection when the British government tried to placate critics of its expenditure by transferring the seat of West African government once more to Sierra Leone in 1866, in order to economize on expenses. When the Fante established another alliance, first to make war against the Dutch and then against the Ashanti, the local British were prepared to support their coastal allies by military means in order to preserve their commercial interests; but they had no intention of allowing them to follow the precepts of the Committee's report and set up their own government. The Dutch were friendly with the Ashanti and had supplied them with arms. The Ashanti were prepared to come to the help of Dutch Elmina when it was attacked by the Fante and their allies. However, by now the Dutch were tired of their commitment in the Gold Coast and, as already seen, sold out their interests to Britain in 1872. The people of Elmina, however, now expected the Ashanti to come to their aid, rather than to leave them under the control of Britain and their Fante allies.

The ground was thus prepared for another trial of strength between the Fante and the British, on the one side, and the Ashanti on the other, who saw the takeover from the Dutch as yet another attempt by Britain to strengthen the middlemen of the Fante coast.

These attitudes were clearly revealed when, in 1871, the Fante tried to create a confederation to govern their own administration. Its object was not only to unite the coast against the Ashanti but also to build roads and schools and to develop the economic resources of their societies. A constitution based on an electoral system provided for a king president, a central assembly, a permanent executive and a system of magistrates. The British on the spot rejected the whole idea. Despite the fact that the educated Africans, who drew up this plan, asked for both advice and support from the British government, it was considered as an attack on British authority. Many of its officers were arrested; this first serious attempt to merge African with British precepts in a self-governing system ended by provoking hostility between its promoters and the British.

If the British in the Gold Coast were not prepared to allow the Africans to govern themselves, they were prepared to support them when it came to keeping the trade routes to the interior open. Once again, at the beginning of 1873, the Ashanti army invaded the coast, fearing no doubt that recent events indicated renewed support by Britain for the Fante middlemen. This time the British government decided to deal with the Gold Coast question decisively. Major-General Sir Garnet Wolseley was sent out as Administrator and Commander-in-Chief, with 2,500 British soldiers to stiffen the forces of the coastal people. Early in 1874 Wolseley and his armies decisively defeated the Ashanti, sacked and burned Kumasi and dictated peace to the Asantehene. The Ashanti had to pay an indemnity in gold, renounce all claim to authority over the coastal peoples, abolish the practice of human sacrifice, and ensure that the roads from the coast to the Ashanti kingdom were kept open for trade. This action marked the acceptance by the British government of full responsibility for the affairs of the coastal lands in the Gold Coast and for relations with the interior. A few months after the military victory, Disraeli's new Conservative government annexed the coastal areas and designated them, along with Lagos, as a new crown colony. The implications of the 1844 Bond were thrust aside and, without conquest, Britain imposed her rule on those same peoples whom she had prevented from setting up their own confederation. Meanwhile, the total defeat of the Ashanti and the burning of their capital so undermined the strength of the Asantehene and his colleagues that before long the Ashanti empire itself began to distintegrate. Conflicts, rivalries and confusion characterized the history of Ashanti for the rest of the century, ultimately destroying the power of this strong inland state.

During this same period British policy towards Nigeria revealed similar vacillations to those towards the Gold Coast. The main centre of interest was the Niger Delta, where trade in palm oil, replacing for British merchants their lost slave trade, was most profitable. Slavers still were prominent in the Delta area, mainly from Portugal and Brazil. Their operations, together with those of the new palm oil merchants, kept the area in a constant state of conflict, with frequent warfare between kinglets, slavers and traders. Off the coast a British naval squadron, composed during the 1830s and 1840s, of twenty warships and over 1,000 men, constituted a gauntlet challenging the operations of the slave traders.

Again it was the Africans who produced and sold the palm oil to British merchants. Indeed, local chiefs imposed port dues on visiting ships, whose crews then had to spend months in complicated bartering to complete their commercial negotiations. It was partly as a result of these difficulties that the practice began of mooring permanent hulks in the rivers to serve as trading posts, and, later, of setting up trading factories on the shores themselves.

Once again, too, the British traders on the coast expected their government to give them protection in their operations. It was for this reason that in 1827 the island of Fernando Po was occupied by the British navy to be used as a base for the protection of legitimate traders and to afford extra strength against the slavers.

But in Nigeria the British government participated more directly in commercial operations. Once the Lander brothers had verified the course of the river Niger, the river's well-populated banks offered an open invitation to imaginative traders for bargaining directly with local communities. Macgregor Laird, founder of the famous Birkenhead shipbuilding firm, took the initiative. He hoped to establish a permanent settlement at the junction of the Benue and Niger rivers to collect the products of the surrounding country. But as yet no protection had been discovered against malaria and only eight of the Europeans on his first expedition in 1832 survived. Richard Lander himself was killed by local Africans.

Another expedition was fitted out in 1841, but this time the government itself sponsored the venture, sending three ships up the river. It was inspired to do so by pressure from the anti-slave trade lobby in Britain, under the presidency of the Prince Consort. Not only was it hoped to abolish slave trading on the Niger, but an attempt was made to set up a model farm as an example to local inhabitants. Again, however, disease took such a heavy toll of the European adventurers that the expedition ended in a second failure.

Nevertheless, these efforts served to show local inhabitants that the British were concerned about this area. As in the Gold Coast, the jurisdiction of British consular agents had begun to spread. The naval base on Fernando Po had to be abandoned by 1834, again because of mortality amongst Europeans, but when Palmerston decided that it was time to appoint a British consul for the area, the island was again chosen as his base of operations. Palmerston's idea was that his consular agent should protect the interests of British merchants throughout the Delta area as well as use his good offices to suppress the slave trade. The man appointed, John Beecroft, like Maclean in the Gold Coast, had long experience of local conditions and peoples, and was in fact, at the time of his appointment, acting on behalf of the Spaniards in Fernando Po. He was able, through his local reputation, both to nego-tiate a considerable number of treaties outlawing the slave trade and to extend British influence along his part of the coast. By now, with-out any formal annexations or claims to territory, Britain had certainly become the most powerful European state along that part of the coast which stretched from Sierra Leone through Liberia, the Ivory Coast, the Gold Coast and Dahomey to the Niger Delta.

One of Beecroft's qualifications for his post was his experience in imposing what were considered to be the interests of British merchants on local African politics. He had been accustomed to impress the African trading community of the Delta with the paramount importance of British interests. On occasion he had been responsible for removing recalcitrant rulers from their kinglets or from positions of commercial authority when they showed signs of interfering with British trade. He had the reputation for tolerating no chief 'who took an independent line or showed signs of an anti-British attitude in trade or politics'.

It had become common for Britain to interfere with local political and commercial authorities along the Niger. There was a dual interest here, for the British objectives were both to undermine the slave trade and to promote their own commercial interests. These two objectives coincided, for where the slave trade was prevalent, local producers were reluctant to supply palm oil in place of the more lucrative trade in human commodities. In 1847, for instance, the leading priest of Bonny was removed for organizing African opposition against British merchants in his area.

But the most apparent example of the imposition of direct British interference came in 1851 with an attack on the island of Lagos, which had become a central haunt of slave traders. The king was deposed and his successor forced to sign a treaty outlawing the slave trade and human sacrifice whilst ensuring free trade and protection for the missions. In particular, the settlement at Abeokuta, fifty miles inland, was to be protected by this British move against the threats of the kingdom of Dahomey. Once again Palmerston had shown that the Colonial Office's opposition to the acquisition of further British colonies could be over-ridden when it appeared to be in the interest of the nation and particularly of her merchant class. The island was actually ceded in 1861, on the threat of further use of British force, and became a Crown Colony. Not only would it now be in a position to defend Abeokuta, but, at least as important, it would control the main trading channel for the palm oil trade. To the Jeremiahs, who alleged that this new possession would simply increase the list of colonial suppliants on the steps of the British Treasury, the Foreign Office could now point out that its commercial importance would soon ensure that it became self-supporting.

In the meantime, a further development had opened opportunities for much wider trading relations with the interior along the course of the Niger. In 1854 the enterprising Macgregor Laird, supported by a government subsidy, organized yet another expedition and sent his iron steamship, the *Pleiad*, up the Niger under the command of a naval surgeon, Dr Baikie. This time Baikie sailed his ship not only up the Niger, but also some 350 miles along the Benue before returning to the coast. The extraordinary feature of this expedition was that, in complete contrast to its predecessors, not a single life was lost. Dr Baikie had insisted on everyone under his charge taking a daily dose of quinine. The prophylactic was proved; in future it would be possible for Europeans to ascend the Niger, trade with its inhabitants and perhaps even reach the Moslem emirates of the north. Three years later, the government arranged a subsidy to support Laird in sending five annual expeditions up the Niger.

This open intervention, and the use of taxpayers' money by the British government to intervene in the trading relations of British merchants abroad, was, theoretically at least, directly opposed to conventional economic philosophy. Nevertheless, as we have seen, it was consonant with the practice of British governments. Here the government was taking the initiative in developing new trade routes in conjunction with attacking the abuses of the slave trade. It was encouraging British merchants to trade directly with the people of the interior and thus to undermine the African middlemen amongst the coastal tribes. Its action aroused anger amongst the European traders established on the coast, who found their relations with their African suppliers on the Delta seriously undermined. But trade was now pursued as far as Kano, and, as a result of the pioneering work of Baikie, a consulate was established in Lokoja for a number of years.

With growing prosperity in Britain, the demand for vegetable oils increased steadily. Although the price of palm oil was falling, the quantities exported from West Africa continued to increase until the 1880s. The opening of the interior along the Niger and the Benue played an important part in this trade. But the consequences in the area itself resembled those in the Gold Coast. Fierce competition had developed around the Delta with continual lawlessness and bloodshed. This was now to spread into the interior, as the whole basis of economic life was shaken. The merchants and sailing steamships up the Niger could undercut those at the mouth, and similar ships were able to carry freight more quickly and cheaply than the old sailing ships between Britain and the African coast. But this direct trading inevitably damaged the interest of both European and African on the coastal areas. Warfare became common. Some of the middlemen, notably Ja Ja of the Bonny trading House, showed sufficient commercial and political shrewdness both to resist the trend and to take advantage of it by monopolizing the trade in palm oil, cutting out British merchants and creating a centre of power for themselves. But the warfare continued, gravely upsetting political stability in the hinterland and on the coast. Nor were many Africans able to resist British pressure in the manner of Ja Ja. The British consulate was moved from Fernando Po to Calabar. Henceforth consuls were able to call in the navy to destroy any chiefs who dared to oppose the interests of British merchants. In 1879, Onitsha was shelled for three days by a British warship, an action which the British consul believed would have 'a most salutary effect up and down the Niger'.

It was George Goldie who saw the dangers of the situation on the oil rivers, and who responded in characteristic late-nineteenth century style. Goldie was concerned in one of the trading companies and visited the Niger in 1877. There he saw that the cut-throat competition between British companies was playing into the hands of African chiefs exacting duties from trade. He also feared the growing competition of the French and Germans, so he persuaded the main British companies to amalgamate. The new single company was known initially as the United Africa Company and a few years later became the National African Company. By 1885 he had succeeded in buying out the two main French trading companies, partly due to the fact that the French government was losing its interest in supporting merchant colonialism after various unfortunate experiences, including the death of Gambetta. Goldie's company, now with greatly augmented capital, was sufficiently powerful to persuade the rulers of Sokoto and Gando to sign monopolistic treaties with him. He was too late to prevent the Germans negotiating treaties with the chiefs in the Cameroons, where British merchants had for long been dominant, or the German government from declaring a protectorate over that territory. Nor was he able at this time to persuade the British government to grant the National Africa Company a charter which would have given its agents power to administer justice and maintain security, as Maclean had done thirty years earlier in the Gold Coast. The reputation of chartered companies as monopolistic institutions was still too tainted for Liberal free traders. It was not until they were replaced by the Conservatives in 1886 that Goldie secured his charter. In the meantime, however, the treaties he had made enabled the British government to claim at the 1884 Berlin Conference that it was the legitimate protecting power of the Fulani emirates in the northern areas.

We have seen that relations between Britain and West Africa had been uninterrupted from the early seventeenth century. British connections with the East African coast, however, were initiated much later, dating only from the nineteenth century. Moreover, the initial contact was motivated much more by concern with the British stake in India and control of the Indian Ocean than with any particular gains expected from East Africa itself. For India was Britain's major commercial and colonial concern, her wealth and her ability to absorb British products being many times greater than that of the whole of Africa. Thus the principal concern of British governments in the attention they paid to East Africa and later to Egypt was always connected with a paramount interest in keeping open their routes to India.

Before the years of 'the scramble', British interest in East Africa was almost entirely concentrated on the island of Zanzibar. From early in the eighteenth century, the Portuguese hold on East Africa had disappeared, being replaced by a return to the dominance of the Arabs, particularly of those from Oman. From the time of the Napoleonic Wars, with the accession of Sultan Imam Seyyid Said in 1804, Zanzibar became the centre of East African trade. At the end of the wars with Napoleon, as British trade and shipping interests in India grew, it was considered politic to enter into relations with Seyyid Said. There were three objectives in this approach. The humanitarian interest was as strong in East as in West Africa. The slave trade from East and Central Africa to the Arab world, though never as numerous as from the West, was nevertheless persistent and more difficult to control, so those humanitarians who had persuaded the British government to station their anti-slave trade patrol on the West African coast, urged equally strongly that it was Britain's duty to attack the Arab trade in the East. Later in the century, this impulse was greatly strengthened by the exposures of Livingstone and others of the way in which the trade was conducted and the social havoc which it caused. Zanzibar was not only the centre of legitimate commerce in East Africa; it was also the main slave market.

Secondly, in the East, as in the West, the British desire to abolish the slave trade had commercial motives mixed with these humanitarian ones. Although there was virtually no tradition of British trade with the East coast, similar hopes were entertained as in West Africa that the abolition of the slave trade would open the way to legitimate commerce. The third objective consisted of a desire to safeguard the Indian Ocean as a British lake, particularly as the French were showing signs of revival from their bases in Madagascar and Réunion. It was largely in order to offset this danger that Britain had retained Mauritius at the end of the Napoleonic wars.

The Moresby Treaty of 1822 was supposed to end the export of slaves from all the Sultan's territories. It also provided for the British government to base an agent in Zanzibar to watch over the abolition of the slave trade. It was this indirect form of influence that appealed most to the British government at this time in its relations with East Africa. However, all Britons were not so meticulous. Captain Owen, on an expedition charting the coasts of Africa, tried to intervene on behalf of the ruling family of Mombasa, which was at war with the Oman and Muscat navy. He not only supported the Mazrui family, but was able to deploy a number of British naval officers to protect

5

Mombasa against the Sultan's naval forces. Owen hoped for the direct intervention of the British government in the affairs of this region. He was disappointed. The government of British India was concerned to maintain peace on the East African coast and thought the Sultan most likely to comply. So Owen had to abandon his venture and the naval officers were withdrawn.

This left the Sultan as overlord, though not direct ruler, of virtually the whole of the East African coast. He was able to reduce the pretensions of Mombasa and to occupy its fort. By 1841, Said decided to transfer his own residence from Muscat to Zanzibar, where he believed the opportunities for trade to be particularly good. His rule did, in fact, greatly increase the importance of Zanzibar as a centre for finance and as a market for the East African coast. The clove trees, which the French had introduced from the Far East via Mauritius, were cultivated by the Arabs, and the Sultan himself encouraged the production of cloves to considerable personal advantage. Before long, Zanzibar had come to rely on clove exports almost exclusively for its revenues.

By 1841 the British Resident in Zanzibar had become not only vital to the maintenance of the Sultan's power but also an adviser who expected British advice to be taken. At the same time, British objectives in Zanzibar appeared to be contradictory. On the one hand they wished to destroy the slave trade, Palmerston in typically sanctimonious language describing Britain as 'the main instrument in the hand of Providence for the accomplishment of this purpose', but on the other they supported the Sultan. Yet their efforts to maintain the Sultan as the major force for peace in the area were weakened by their very attempt to end the slave trade. For the Sultan himself largely depended both on slaves for the cultivation of Zanzibar's cloves and on the slave trade to bolster his revenues and to maintain prosperity along the coast. British policy was thus weakening the Sultan's power over his subjects, whilst, at the same time, keeping him in office.

On the death of Seyyid Said in 1856 British influence became even more powerful. Said had divided his patrimony between two sons, effectively splitting Oman from Zanzibar. When the older son tried to conquer Zanzibar and reunite the two territories, the British prevented him, and when a third son, Bargash, supported by the French, attempted to overthrow his brother in Zanzibar, British marines arrested him and sent him to Bombay.

A few years later, however, on the death of the Sultan in 1870, Bargash was installed by the British as his successor on condition that he would abolish the slave trade which had survived all attempts to destroy it. Like his predecessors, the new Sultan realized the danger to his economy and political position involved in the abolition of slavery. He tried to resist the British, but by this time Britain was virtually ruling Zanzibar. Bargash was coerced by Sir Bartle Frere, sent as a special envoy with the backing of the Royal Navy. The consul, Dr John Kirk, threatened to blockade the island and under this pressure Bargash agreed to sign a new treaty closing the public slave market and accepting British dictation. Kirk became virtually the Sultan's prime minister, and used the Royal Navy to suppress those revolts which inevitably followed the prohibition of the slave trade. Zanzibar even had an army under the authority of British officers to support the regime of the Sultan who was thus able to impose his authority on the mainland and to resist any challenge from those sheikhs refusing to accept it.

Yet, throughout this period, British governments steadfastly refused to assume responsibility for governing or even for protecting any territory in East Africa. Even when the Sultan offered Sir William Mackinnon a trading concession under which an East African Company would have taken over political and economic control of his mainland territories, no encouragement was offered by the government to the project and it quickly collapsed. The British government was content to influence the Sultan's policies, pursue its efforts to destroy the slave trade, preserve its dominance in the Indian Ocean and offer what protection it could to British commerce in the East from this base. It did not want embarrassing and perhaps expensive entanglements. The time had not yet come when serious commercial opportunities in East Africa itself were perceived.

Large numbers of Indians were coming to the East African coast during this period and they acquired financial control of internal trade, usually acting as intermediaries between European merchants and Africans and also indulging in moneylending and becoming small-scale capitalists. Many of the Arab estates were mortgaged to them. They often financed the journeys of Arab traders into the interior from where large quantities of ivory were brought to the coast and they also played a part in maintaining the slave trade.

The Germans came to Zanzibar in 1844 when the first German commercial firm was established there. In 1859 the Sultan signed a commercial treaty with the Hanse. There were also a number of German missionaries and at one time in the 1870s there was a proposal to place Zanzibar under the protection of Germany, but Bismarck did not favour the idea.

In 1875, the Khedive Ismail, in his expansionist policy southwards, sent an expedition under General Gordon up the Nile towards Lake Victoria. An Egyptian naval contingent was sent to the coast to open a supply route for Gordon's army and then the Upper Nile was annexed by the Khedive. The Egyptians were thus approaching the mainland territories of the Sultan, and it was partly to forestall this advance that the proposal was made to Mackinnon to form his company so as to take control of the mainland territories as far as the Lakes.

Some idea of the kind of life in East Africa can be gained from the observations of the explorer Richard Burton who visited the Great Lakes in 1858: 'The African rises with the dawn from his couch of cowhide. The hut is cool and comfortable during the day, but the barred door impeding ventilation at night causes it to be close and disagreeable. The hour before sunrise being the coldest time, he usually kindles a fire, and addresses himself to his constant companion, the pipe. When the sun becomes sufficiently powerful, he removes the reed screen from the entrance, and issues forth to bask in the morning beams. The villages are populous, and the houses touching one another enable the occupants, when squatting outside and fronting the central square, to chat and chatter without moving. About 7 a.m., when the dew has partially disappeared from the grass, the elder boys drive the flocks and herds to pasture with loud shouts and sound applications of the quarter-staff. They return only when the sun is sinking behind the western horizon. At 8 a.m. those who have provisions at home enter the hut for refection with ugali or holcus-porridge; those who have not, join a friend. Pombe (beer), when procurable, is drunk from the earliest dawn. After breaking his fast the African repairs, pipe in hand, to the iwanza, the village 'public', previously described. Here, in the society of his own sex, he will spend the greater part of the day talking and laughing, smoking or torpid with sleep. Occasionally he sits down to play. . . . Towards sunset all issue forth to enjoy the coolness: the men sit outside the iwanza, whilst the women and girls, after fetching water for household wants from the well, collecting in a group upon their little stools, indulge in the pleasures of gossip and the pipe. This hour in the most favoured parts of the country is replete with enjoyment, which even the barbarian feels, though not yet indoctrinated into aesthetics. As the hours of darkness draw nigh, the village doors are carefully closed, and, after milking his cows, each peasant retires to his hut, or passes his time in the iwanza.'

Burton's may be a somewhat romantic picture and he does not seem to have observed much of the peasants' work in fields, pasture or building; but he conveys something of the atmosphere of the region as he observed it.

It was concern with safeguarding the route to India which also led to British intervention in North and North-East Africa. British investment in India during the second half of the nineteenth century was second only to that in the United States of America and British imports and exports to India were equally important. The French were established in Algeria and their influence was strong in Tunisia and Morocco; the Germans had also begun to expand their activities towards the Nile; there was constant fear of Russian advance in the eastern end of the Mediterranean. Most British moves in this area, therefore, were dictated by fears of the British government, or the government of India, that interference might develop in the free passage of British commerce to and from its rich Indian emporium.

For this reason Aden had been occupied in 1839. In the following year, the East India Company signed treaties with two rulers in Somaliland, who guaranteed the exclusion of all other nations and allowed the establishment of strategic bases. It was also partly at the instigation of the Bombay government, concerned with an affront to the imperial image in India, that, in 1868, Sir Robert Napier marched into Ethiopia to punish Emperor Theodorus for imprisoning British officials.

But it was in Egypt that the importance of this part of Africa to the Indian Empire was most transparent. The British had, of course, their own financial and commercial stake in Egypt: throughout the nineteenth century Egyptian cotton was a vital import for the British textile industry and also provided the revenues to pay foreign investors, a sum which equalled half the total value of exports and more than half the Egyptian budget. Yet this was but small change compared

with investment in India and the income it provided to Britain, particularly in supplying her essential balance of payments surplus. With
the opening of the Suez Canal in 1869, and Disraeli's purchase of the
Khedive's shares six years later, Egypt became the vital strategic hinge
of the Indian route. It was Charles Dilke who explained this most
clearly when he told the House of Commons, 'as regards the Suez
Canal, England has a double interest; it has a predominant commercial
interest, because eighty-two per cent of the trade passing through the
Canal is British trade, and it has a predominant political interest caused
by the fact that the Canal is the principal highway to India, Ceylon,
the Straits and British Burmah, where 250 million people live under
our rule.'

Thus it was not simply an imperialist interest in Egypt itself which
finally led Britain to her intervention in the early 1880s. Indeed, despite
the system of dual control with France which had succeeded the
Khedive's bankruptcy, the French themselves would not agree to
participate in direct intervention. Nor was it simply an extension of the
Disraeli type of imperialism which activated British policy, for Gladstone had replaced Disraeli in 1880. Yet, despite Gladstone's own public
commitment to peace and his belief in the Concert of Europe, his
Liberal government unilaterally bombarded Alexandria, sent troops
to occupy Cairo and brought Egypt directly under British influence.
It is true that the Gladstone government ensured continued payment
to British investors and that its military action destroyed the nationalist
revolt of the Arabs against the Khedive's rule, the feudal landowners
and foreign interference. But Gladstone's action can only be explained
rationally from strategic motives, maintaining, against the dangers of
French, German or Russian interference, control of the Nile Valley,
the canal route to India and secure channels for British commerce and
finance to seek profits in every part of the world.

Although, as it turned out, Britain did not become directly concerned
with South Africa until the end of the eighteenth century, it was only
by an accident of history that the Cape did not become English early
in the seventeenth century. Once the trade winds were charted, the
Cape became the obvious half-way refuge on the voyage from Europe
to the Indies. The Portuguese used St Helena and Mozambique as
their two berths and were, in any case, frightened of the Cape of

Storms. But the Dutch and English sailed southwards to the West African bulge, then across to the Brazilian coast and on the westerly winds round the Cape, before crossing the Indian Ocean towards Australia and using the south-easterly winds to the East Indies. On their return they also doubled the Cape. In the days of rudimentary methods of food preservation a regular place of landfall was as welcome as an oasis. The Cape provided this most conveniently.

In 1615 Sir Thomas Roe of the English East India Company put into Table Bay, apparently carrying some home-bound Japanese and eight criminals. The malefactors were put ashore and, although five of them lost their lives whilst the other three were taken back to England the following year, three more prisoners were landed for a time. In 1620 two more company servants took possession of the Bay and offered it to James I, who, however, refused the offer. Yet English and Dutch ships continued to use Table Bay to replenish their fresh water stocks. As the Dutch East India Company increased its commercial interest in the East Indies, the need for a maritime refreshment station steadily increased.

In 1652 Johan van Riebeeck, a ship's surgeon, was sent by the Dutch Company with three ships to build a fort bearing 'the name Good Hope', to plant a garden and to establish good relations with the native population in order to trade for cattle. The original Dutch settlers in 1652 encountered only Hottentots and Bushmen, the former of whom soon became partially assimilated as servants, the latter retiring inland from the Cape. It was not until the mid-eighteenth century that the colonists in the Cape came into regular contact with Bantu Africans, in the region of the Great Fish River to the East of the Cape. Nevertheless, as various Portuguese sailors wrecked on the southern coast and trekking across the eastern region to Portuguese settlements in Mozambique attested, there were already a number of African communities settled in what is now Natal, Pondoland and the Transkei before the Dutch arrived. The Cape remained in Dutch possession until captured by the British at the end of the eighteenth century.

At this time the Dutch settlement consisted of about 16,000 Europeans and slightly more slaves. Already its European population had begun to develop distinct characteristics, separated not only by a different environment from their Dutch ancestors, but also by the admixture of other Europeans, in particular French Huguenots and Germans. Their religion and their social outlook remained rooted in the mid-seventeenth century, based on the Old Testament obsessions of the Calvinists. Some of them, seeking land outside the settlement, had already begun to encounter the much larger communities of African tribes who were spreading westward and southward in search of land as the Europeans moved in the opposite direction towards them. During the eighteenth century a rough frontier society had developed, loosely associated with the banks of the Great Fish River, with all the characteristics of cattle raiding, looting and insecurity common to frontier societies.

In 1795, during the Napoleonic Wars, Britain for the first time took over the Cape, in order to prevent the French from gaining a control there potentially as menacing to the Indian route as would have been their conquest of Egypt. Although the colony was returned to the Dutch by the Treaty of Amiens, it was reoccupied in 1806, after war was renewed, and confirmed as British in the peace settlement at the end of the wars. The British negotiators considered it an invaluable naval base protecting the route to the east; its possession in fact would lead Britain into a series of complicated political and military manœuvres with Europeans and Africans that was to last for a century and a half.

Apart from its strategic importance, the first use of the Cape by Britain was for the purpose of emigration. After the Napoleonic Wars, unemployment and poverty became serious issues in British society. One of the remedies was emigration, particularly to the colonies. A small group went to the Cape in 1817, but it was in 1820 that the main scheme of settlement was initiated. It only consisted of 5,000 people and was not a success, yet this was the first serious British settlement scheme in the African continent and it introduced a British element into the South African European community.

By this time Britain had discovered that she had inherited complex and dangerous problems amongst both the European and African sections of South African society. The Boers did not take kindly to any form of authority, still less to the type of government directed by a country imbued with anti-slave fervour and emerging into a scientific, humanitarian age. The African tribal structure had already been disturbed by the incursion of the Boer farmers and the consequent limitation of African expansion. As elsewhere, the restriction of movement and land opportunities to growing native populations and their increasing herds led to political and military unrest. Inevitably, this resulted in the organization of military regimes, as it had done in Europe. In particular, the Zulu clan under the ruthless military leaders Tshaka, and, from 1828, Dingane, emerged dominant in the east.

The effects of Zulu military conquests spread like ripples from their homeland in Natal. Other tribes, along with schismatic branches of the Zulus, emulated the military prowess of Tshaka and Dingane and conquered neighbouring lands and peoples. Their expansion extended north as far as the Zambesi, west to Bechuanaland, north into Swaziland, and southwest to the mountain fastnesses of Basutoland. In some cases they resulted in the formation of new African nations, as Sobhuza's Swazis, Moshesh's Basuto, and Mzilikazi's Matebele.

The Africans and the Boers had one element in common: both were inefficient farmers. Whereas the Africans usually held their land in common under the ownership of the tribe, the Boers were looking continually for individual and, preferably, isolated farms. But in both cases large acreages were needed to support relatively few people. The African tribesmen needed large areas to maintain subsistence crops and big herds. The Boers, with their large extended families, including many idle hangers-on, also required a great deal of land to sustain their unscientific methods of production. Inevitably, therefore, a great deal of the conflict between Boer and Bantu during the eighteenth and nineteenth centuries stemmed from land hunger arising from archaic farming techniques.

There was another common element between black and white. Both sought new land, not only because neither had learnt intensive methods of farming, but also to escape from authority. The Africans might be fleeing from the Zulus and their imitators; among the Boers a long tradition had been established of moving away from the centre of government in the Cape and this movement was greatly increased when the British replaced the Dutch as governmental authority.

The British government at this time was influenced by the same humanitarian groups which had brought about the abolition of the slave trade and which were continually lobbying Westminster to use naval power for its extirpation. The impact of this pressure on the Boer society of the Cape greatly intensified the established tradition

5*

of escape. Moreover, when Christian missions followed the Union Jack to the Cape, and, in particular, when the London Missionary Society and its superintendent in South Africa, Dr John Philip, began to bring pressure on the Cape government in pursuit of African rights, the Boers were outraged. By an ordinance passed in 1828 the Hottentots were given equality in law and the right to choose whether to offer their labour instead of being compelled to accept employment. Five years later, slavery itself was abolished in all British territories. It was estimated that the Boers owned 39,000 slaves, valued at over £2 million. They were given £1¼ million in compensation. Three years later, in 1836, the British decided to return land in the Eastern Cape to Africans in order to provide a buffer frontier area.

As a result of these psychological, financial and territorial shocks, many of the Boer farmers decided to leave the Cape in a more organized and purposeful manner than previously. As before, this large-scale movement was bound to clash with the African societies beyond the frontier.

Most of the trekkers made for Natal, where fertile land had been depopulated by the expansion of the Zulus, but the appearance of the Boers caused consternation in the Zulu nation. It fought to expel them, but was defeated by the superior power of the Boers' guns, and Dingane himself was killed in action.

The Boers, however, found that they had not escaped from the authority of Britain. Before they could fully establish themselves in Natal, British troops had followed them to the coast and Natal itself was annexed.

Eventually, the Boers moved even farther afield, establishing their two republics, the Transvaal and the Orange Free State. By this time, in the middle of the century, the British government was tired of the expense and trouble of trying to govern the unruly Boers. The independence of these two republics was recognized, provided that no slavery was practised within them. By the middle of the century, therefore, South Africa had been divided into two British colonies, the Cape and Natal, and two Boer republics, the Transvaal and the Orange Free State, but the latter two were surrounded by a ring of African communities, Basuto, Zulu, Matabele, Bechuana and Griqua.

The two new Boer republics were quite unable to maintain themselves as prosperous, law-abiding communities. Their people tended still to shy away from authority or government and to set up small communities almost entirely outside the control of central governments. One of the consequences of this absence of order was once more the upsetting of African societies. Both republics tried to admit within their frontiers only those Africans whom they needed as servants. As their farmers were continually expanding their holdings and taking African lands, movement amongst the African tribal communities to seek fresh land was frequent and many African families were continually being pushed out of the republics into what were coming to be overcrowded tribal lands. British policy in this situation was to try and leave the Boer republics relatively independent whilst maintaining the frontiers of African society. In particular, the British created a buffer bloc between Natal and the Cape, known as British Kaffraria, to be considered tribal land for the Africans and ruled from the Cape. Already, despite the influence of humanitarians – indeed, sometimes because of it – the British, anxious to avoid responsibility or conflict, had begun to establish a form of racial apartheid. The racial communities were to be kept separate as far as possible, this being, so some humanitarians believed, for the good of the 'noble savage', who should be insulated against the evil effects of sophisticated white society. In the meantime, the effects of Lord Durham's 1839 report were seen in South Africa, as in other white-settled colonies. The British government approved of the self-governing principles laid down by Durham, if only because they would serve to reduce British responsibility both for colonial defence and for administrative costs. The first Cape Colony parliament was established in 1854. It consisted of a two-house legislature, both elected on a non-racial franchise based on monetary qualifications, though obviously far more Europeans could qualify than non-Europeans. The constitutions of the two Boer republics had been openly racial, renouncing any concept of equality between white and black in church or state. Natal too, separated from the Cape in 1856 and having its own legislative council, had elected members who soon found ways of excluding the Africans from what was nominally a non-racial franchise.

During the next twenty years the Cape Colony slowly developed, through the production of wool and ostrich feathers, whilst Natal gained some prosperity from its sugar planting, undertaken with the assistance of indentured labourers from India. The opening of the Suez

Canal in 1869 reduced the naval importance of the Cape, and enabled Gladstone to prepare for withdrawal of the garrison. Britain's belief in *laissez-faire* still persisted, leading the government to relinquish colonial control wherever possible. Responsibility for British Kaffraria was undertaken by the Cape in 1865, and for Basutoland, which had been annexed by Britain to halt its wars with the Orange Free State, in 1872. By now it was felt that the Colony was sufficiently prosperous and self-confident to be given responsible self-government. This was granted in 1872, still with a non-racial franchise and with the hope that it might lead to a federation of South African territories. It was anticipated that under the leadership of the Cape Colony, black and white, Briton, Boer and Bantu, might come together to solve their mutual problems of insecurity, particularly those which had developed so powerfully outside the Cape itself.

These hopes were soon dashed. During the 1870s the Transvaal moved rapidly towards bankruptcy. When in 1877 a British envoy from the Colonial Secretary, Lord Caernarvon, was sent to investigate the troubles of the Transvaal Republic, he precipitately raised the flag in Pretoria and announced that the Transvaal was annexed. The Governor, Sir Bartle Frere, had no option but to accept the *fait accompli*, though this action inevitably destroyed any immediate chance of either the Transvaal or the Orange Free State seriously considering federation. What is more, Britian immediately became involved in warfare with the Zulus on the republic's frontiers. Defeat of a British army by Zulu impis encouraged those Boers who refused to accept annexation to prepare a trial of their own strength. Disappointed by Gladstone's failure to honour his election pledge of independence for the Transvaal, or even to grant responsible government under pressure from the humanitarian element in his party which was convinced that the Boers should not again be entrusted with authority over the Africans, the Transvaalers took up arms. Under the leadership of Paul Kruger, they attacked the small British forces stationed in their country and defeated them at Majuba Hill. The short-lived annexation was brought to a sudden end in 1881.

By now, however, the whole character of the British relationship with South Africa had radically changed. The discovery of diamonds in Griqualand West and the annexation of that territory by Britain despite the claims of the Free State, introduced a new element into the relationship. For the first time South Africa was seen to be harbouring specific wealth which could be used to further British interests. Suddenly, from being a backward, neglected, outpost of Empire, South Africa became a major investment opportunity. Whereas in 1870 British investments in South Africa were negligible, fifteen years later they had leapt to £34 million, while South Africa's meagre exports doubled and her imports trebled in her trade with Britain. This was simply seed corn compared with the harvest to be reaped in the future. But though at first this applied almost exclusively to the Cape Colony within which the diamonds were located, it was significant of an entirely changed relationship between Britain and South Africa. Though the full effects of the change were only to be seen in the following decade, with the discovery of methods of raising Witwatersrand gold to the surface, nevertheless, from 1870 onwards, South Africa was viewed in a totally new light in London, and particularly in the City.

Chapter 6

From the Abolition of the Slave Trade to the 'Scramble' : 2

Throughout the three hundred years between the sixteenth and the early nineteenth centuries during which Britain and Africa had known each other, personal contact had rarely taken place more than a few miles from the African coast. It had been confined to commercial transactions, largely in slaves and payment for them in firearms, cloth, implements and trinkets, conducted beside the forts along the beaches of West Africa. Thus cultural encounters between the two peoples were minimal, affecting few other than the African and British merchants concerned.

Before the middle of the nineteenth century this situation began to change. The early explorers had broken the trail for many successors; they were followed by missionaries and the communities based on mission stations; traders soon took the same paths, especially in West Africa where they decided to circumvent African middlemen and seek the sources of their supplies. For the first time substantial numbers of British people came into personal contact with Africans, some sinking British roots within the continent and setting up their homes there. By the time that actual colonial rule spread across the continent during the last two decades of the century, many more Africans and British had already confronted each other, influencing each others' attitudes and ideas, creating a new set of relationships.

Although direct confrontation between British and African cultures only arose substantially in the second half of the century, a few preliminary encounters had taken place as early as the eighteenth century, and these had some little influence on future relations. Many West

Indian plantation owners took slaves back to Britain to act as servants in their homes. Africans were also employed as seamen, were therefore known in the ports and sometimes skipped ship to seek jobs ashore. Some slaves escaped or bought their freedom, often eventually finding their way to Britain. The Mansfield judgement of 1772, declaring slavery unconstitutional in England, both automatically released all slaves resident in the country and increased the attractions of Britain as a haven for those who could escape. From these sources a small Negro community had been created in Britain during the latter part of the eighteenth century. They were generally known as the 'black poor' for, inevitably, they lived amongst the poorest of the British working class, mostly in the London slums. It was partly in order to repatriate and rehabilitate members of this community that the first expedition was formed to establish a settlement in Sierra Leone. And even at this early stage, as quoted earlier, public discussion had started in the press on the merits and demerits of the Negro character.

Amongst the Africans in Britain at this time were a number of distinguished men. Ottobah Cugoano and Olaudah Equiano both contributed significantly to the anti-slavery crusade by writing books describing their personal experiences as slaves. Cugoano had been taken into slavery from his Gold Coast home as a child, was fortunate in being enabled to read and write whilst still under his master, and then came to Britain as a servant where he gained his freedom. In his book *Thoughts and Sentiments on the Evil and Wicked Traffic of the Slavery and Commerce of the Human Species* he adopted a style and Christian arguments well suited to appeal to the burgeoning humanitarian feelings of late eighteenth century Britain. Equiano was also kidnapped into slavery when a child, taken down the Niger and shipped across to the West Indies. He came into the possession of a ship owner and consequently made many exotic voyages, spiced with the kind of thrilling adventures beloved by readers. Consequently, when, after buying his freedom, he wrote his autobiography, *The Interesting Narrative of the Life of Olaudah Equiano, or Gustavus Vassa the African, written by himself*, it immediately appealed to the public. Its sales were increased by public lectures given by the author around the country where he supplemented the written word with graphic descriptions of his experiences as a slave. But Equiano's work did more than simply contribute to the anti-slavery campaign. His descriptions of life in the

Ibo area provided British audiences and readers with a first-hand account of one African society.

There were other Africans of intellectual distinction in Britain during this period. Ignatius Sancho published his collected letters in 1782, Anton Amp from the Gold Coast was not only a linguist with mastery of six languages, but went to lectures on philosophy in German universities. Nor was the traffic in cultural knowledge only one way. Whilst British people were learning a little about Africa and its societies from the Africans in their midst, a few Africans were able to secure a British education and return to teach something of British culture to their own people. Philip Quacoe was one example; he gained entrance to Oxford from Cape Coast as early as the 1760s, was trained for the priesthood and returned home to establish his own school. For over half a century he was the chaplain for the Society for the Propagation of the Gospel in Cape Coast Castle.

These men were naturally regarded as exceptional, but there was a certain amount of contact between Africans and British at lower levels. Not only were Africans known to the poor of the towns and ports, but a few came to be accepted in other strata of society. Dr Johnson's servant, Francis Barber, is the best-known example. He was actually born in Jamaica of slave parents, taken back to Britain by his master, Colonel Bathurst, freed under the Colonel's will and entered Johnson's service in 1752. The learned doctor sent his servant to school and thought so highly of him that when Barber left him to join the navy he secured his discharge. He then worked for Johnson until his master's death and was left money and goods in his will.

On the West African coast, too, British and African merchants had some acquaintance with each other. As we have seen above, a few Africans were sent to Britain by British trading companies to be trained in clerical skills, whilst British merchants on the coast itself were accustomed to use African clerks. Thus a small group of coastal Africans learned English and even began to adopt European dress.

Yet, in total, these eighteenth century contacts were minimal. The general view of those Africans who had any experience of the British was dominated by their role as slave traders and slave owners. Most Africans remained in total ignorance of British ways, customs and manners. On the other side, the general British concept of Africans was drawn from the slave stereotypes, reinforced by the lurid stories told by slaving merchants of the barbarous habits of the slaving middle-men around the forts. With very few exceptions Africans and British alike remained in ignorance of each others' societies until well into the nineteenth century.

During the nineteenth century various factors combined to break through the walls of ignorance – though by no means always replacing mythology with enlightenment. The growing force of the British industrial revolution, the rapid increase in Christian missionary zeal, the desire for wider geographical knowledge, more efficient transport techniques, stronger trading impulses, all took Britain deeper into African society than ever before. Finally, the burst of imperialist fever at the end of the century paved the way for political, military and administrative dominance which imposed the stronger, aggressive British technical culture on African society. Few developments in Africa itself led Africans to Britain; yet some elements of British expansion, particularly in the mission field, brought a handful of Africans to British institutions for training. There can be no doubt, however, that by far the heavier weight of cultural impact was from Britain to Africa, rather than in the reverse direction.

Both the agents of cultural export and their impact varied in character in different regions of the continent. In the west traders had preceded missionaries, but when the mission societies arrived they were able to build on a higher degree of literacy than elsewhere, training Africans both in Britain and locally to become the chief evangelists for the Gospel. The longer experience of commerce with Europeans and the higher level of economic development enabled European education and techniques to be accepted more readily than in other parts of the continent. The fact that palm oil provided a substance in great demand for British industrial society resulted in a wider commercial interest in West Africa. This was reinforced by the concentration of the British share of the slave trade in the west, with a consequent greater necessity for anti-slavery action there.

In the east and centre of the continent exploration came later than in the west and at first was promoted more from Christian than from commercial motives. Here the slave trade had been conducted mainly by the Arabs and Portuguese. Consequently there had never been much modernizing influence compared with the impact of so many European merchants in the west. Societies had remained comparatively

remote, little disturbed in their social or economic life by extra-
African influences.

In spite of these significant differences, certain general British assumptions guided Britain in the expansion of her influence to all parts of
the continent. These assumptions were always vague and often contradictory, sometimes to the degree that they appear close to self-
justification for actions taken basically for motives of commercial
self-interest. Nevertheless, they did affect the British people engaged
as well as the public view of Britain's impact on Africa.

The eighteenth century in Europe was the Age of Reason, the
Enlightenment. Its corollary, the potential perfectibility of man, aided
the rising power of humanitarians to support their campaigns –
including that for the abolition of slavery – by adding rational argument
to emotion. It therefore helped to wean the public away from their
view of the African as a natural slave and to enlist support for such
ventures as the founding of Sierra Leone as a colony where slaves
could work out their own rehabilitation. By the end of the century
these attitudes had induced a wave of evangelism within the churches,
Protestants particularly recognizing for the first time a responsibility
for converting peoples outside Britain.

The nineteenth century was a period of expansion. Yet there were
contradictions in its rationale. Mercantilism, with its concentration
on acquiring empire in order to strengthen the national economy, gave
way to *laissez-faire,* in which colonies were seen as a wasteful hindrance
to economic activity. Social Darwinism was held at one and the same
time to prove the superiority of the powerful race and yet to establish
the inevitability of evolution. And when traders sought protection
from unscrupulous African merchants or missionaries begged the
government to suppress the slave trade, halt tribal wars and protect
mission stations, how could such intervention be reconciled with
Adam Smith's doctrines?

The fact is, of course, that philosophic theories were no more allowed
to handicap immediate interests than in any other century. Governments interfered with foreigners when it seemed necessary to do so in
the interests of those whom they represented and refrained from doing
so if the pressure was not sufficiently powerful to compel action; which
explains the apparently inconsistent policies followed by British
governments during the nineteenth century in both East and West

Africa. Yet general theories did have some effect on the way in which British people regarded Africans. There was an assumption of superiority, whether it was accompanied by the belief that Africans were retarded and would eventually catch up with Europeans if given the opportunities, or by the concept of innate racial inequality. There was also a general assumption of the inevitability of evolutionary progress, shared alike by liberals, Darwinists and Marxists, if with different emphases. The conclusion was identical under mercantilism, *laissez-faire* and imperialism; it was Britain's duty or self-interest to spread her religion and techniques as widely as possible, opening up the world to Christianity and commerce. Missionaries, traders, manufacturers and politicians needed no philosophy to convince them of this, but philosophic theories were always useful to justify the forms it took.

In West Africa it was thought that an excellent opportunity presented itself to combine all these interests in the founding of Sierra Leone. Here freed ex-slaves, who had already been influenced by British life, were to be encouraged to build an extension of British, Christian, middle-class life, founded on the church, education and expanding commerce, designed to transform society throughout the slave areas. The fact that the early attempts ended in failure did not deter the enthusiasts. Even the necessity of persuading the government to take over control from private enterprise was not allowed to destroy the vision. Moreover, the composition of the Sierra Leonean community had one important natural advantage for this purpose which was to prove of considerable significance during this century. Amongst the released slaves were a number of Yoruba who not only maintained their language and cohesion in Freetown but were later to send some of their number back to Yorubaland, there to spread both the Gospel and European ideas.

As a bridgehead of British, Christian culture in West Africa, Sierra Leone, then, played a crucial role throughout the nineteenth century. To the early settlers, the Negroes from Britain, released slaves from Nova Scotia and Jamaica, was added a steady stream of captives from various parts of West Africa, freed from slave ships intercepted by the anti-slavery naval patrols. In one way or another, therefore, the population of Freetown and of the villages which grew up on its outskirts, owed gratitude to Britain. It expressed this by adopting British ways so that a community grew up which resembled an African extension of typical nineteenth century British society. Missionary societies were prominent from the start, providing a strong Protestant base to the community. Trade, workshops and farms supplied the main economic activities, with newly released slaves finding work as labourers and apprentices. Some prospered sufficiently to build large houses and to import furniture and decorations from Britain. English became the common language, young men were trained for the church, in law, medicine or as teachers. A local civil service was developed, and when the first legislative council was instituted in 1863, an African merchant and Weslyan lay preacher, John Ezzidio, was immediately appointed to it. Well before that event, in 1845, another African, the army doctor William Fergusson, qualified at Edinburgh University, had actually served as governor for a year. Above all, the community of Freetown and its environs adopted the Protestant ethic of virtuous labour and material advancement. As Fergusson himself once wrote, '. . . . a leading feature in the character of the liberated Africans is their great love of money . . . their whole surplus means are devoted to the increase of their domestic comforts and their improvement of their outward appearance of respectability. A comfortable house is the first great object of their desire. . . . their outward observance of the Sabbath-day is most exemplary. . . . the whole body of the people are to be found at one or other of the churches or chapels, which abound in the colony' – a description which would also have fitted a score of provincial British towns of the period!

Yet, although Fergusson did make some attempt to stamp out the slave trade which still continued amongst tribal communities of the interior and to open up trade routes, the influence of this Anglicized community never seriously penetrated to the indigenous Africans of the hinterland. Indeed, so unsuccessful were both missionaries and traders in extending their communications inland that by 1875 three hundred Freetown merchants were petitioning the Colonial Office to extend its jurisdiction to the interior tribes in order to promote commerce and spread Christianity.

Amongst the coastal community, though, the standards and outlook of Britain were widely accepted. This was assisted by the general British missionary assumption of the time that the object of evangelical work was to produce not only converts but local African clergy. The

Church of England's Church Missionary Society deliberately aimed to produce a self-sufficient Sierra Leone church which would train its own clergy and initiate its own missionary activities in other parts of West Africa. One major result of this policy was the foundation of a number of schools in the country, culminating in the Freetown Grammar School in 1845 and the establishment of Fourah Bay, which was to become the focus of African higher education throughout West Africa. The independence of the church was actually achieved in 1862. This independence was not always welcomed by British missionaries, however, and friction between white and black clergy was not uncommon, marked on the one side by fears of rejection and on the other by suspicions of racial prejudice.

Sierra Leone was more than a crucible for experimental grafting of British culture on to emancipated Africans. Of even greater significance was its role as a base for the dissemination of that culture to other West African countries.

From 1839, when the first voyage was made from Freetown to Badagri, a steady stream of emigrants left Sierra Leone for the east. Some of them were unhappy with life in their adopted country, though they knew that they risked re-enslavement in the unsettled conditions of their former homeland. But once the first emigrants showed that it could be done, their example was bound to be followed.

It will be recalled that during this period various conflicts were shaking the fabric of society throughout the Slave Coast and its hinterland. There was fratricidal strife in Yorubaland as different factions fought for control of the Oyo empire. Benin was in decline, whilst Iboland had been cut off from the coast by the power of the delta merchants. Tension was continually high between the Ashanti and the coastal Fante tribes. Over all loomed the continual pressure of Dahomey, still a centre of the slave trade and always ambitious to extend her rapacious power over neighbouring peoples. Meanwhile, the nineteenth century merchants from Britain, unlike their predecessor slavers, sought their profits in making direct contact with the source of oil or groundnut production in the interior and in seeking to establish markets amongst the tribal communities of the hinterland. It might take many years to overcome the obstacles to such trade, but the new techniques of transport and medicine made it increasingly feasible.

These insecure conditions made it easier for the Sierra Leone emigrants, with their adopted British habits and beliefs, to be accepted in their homelands and to influence their relatives and neighbours. Many of them tended to settle together in Badagri, Old Calabar, Lagos, and inland at Abeokuta. They kept in touch with each other, usually following the educational, social and economic customs they had acquired in Sierra Leone. Their European ways were perhaps more acceptable in mid-nineteenth century conditions than they would have been a century earlier, during the days of strong, settled African communities. Certainly they provided a firm base on which Christian missionary efforts could be built, despite the widening appeal of Islam at this time; and missionary activity brought an extension of British cultural influences.

This export of British habits was not simply the result of the co-incidence of emigration from Sierra Leone. It was the deliberate policy of leading British missionary officials. In particular, Thomas Fowel Buxton and Henry Venn laid down the attitude which was later to be widely publicized by David Livingstone. The only way to destroy the slave trade was to introduce simultaneously Christian values and legitimate commerce. To achieve this in West Africa required communications with the interior so as to provide the means for tribal societies there to produce and sell goods which the European needed and which would produce higher profits than the sale of slaves. For this purpose an African middle-class must be created, instilled with Christian moral and ethical values, convinced of the virtue of labour, imbued with all the certainties of Victorian Britain. Then West Africa could follow Britain's lead, producing industrialists, merchants and modern farmers, though perhaps concentrating on the production of those commodities needed by British industry – like cotton.

The British view of Africa's future found its exponents amongst Africans who had been exposed to British cultural influences. The well-known case of Bishop Crowther is a typical example of the mental and emotional attitude, if exceptional in achievement. Crowther became the first African bishop of the Church of England. He was another who had been taken into slavery as a child, but had been fortunate to be on a slaver intercepted by a British patrol and had been released in Freetown. There he was educated by the C.M.S., sent to England and then to Fourah Bay, after which he became a teacher. He so impressed the missionaries that he was chosen to take part in the 1841 expedition up the Niger and wrote an excellent account of it. He was then ordained in England and joined the Sierra Leone Yoruba emigrants at the mission station in Abeokuta. He sailed up the Niger twice more, establishing new missions, became a noted scholar in African languages, and, when it was decided to create a new diocese of West Africa, was the obvious choice as its first bishop.

Crowther was a close friend and disciple of Henry Venn. He shared his patron's view of the beneficent combination between Christianity and economic development. Inevitably, therefore, he had so deeply accepted British attitudes that he abhorred many Islamic practices and deplored most of the tribal customs he encountered on his journey, together with the materialism he found around the delta. His remedy for African 'backwardness' was to introduce more British habits, to bring Britain into greater participation in African affairs. He it was, for instance, who in 1861 played a leading role in persuading the King to cede Lagos to the British government. His attitude to his search for the regeneration of Africa may be summed up in words from one of his journals; 'The country abounds with produce; labour is cheap: if the youths are only taught to prepare them for European markets our work is done. . . . When trade and agriculture engage the attention of the people, and with the gentle and peaceful teaching of Christianity, the minds of the people will gradually be won from war and marauding expeditions to peaceful trade and commerce.'

Crowther and his colleagues represented a natural reaction to the succour and kindness they had received from Britishers. It was based on gratitude for their rescue from slavery and the offer of a new way of life – clearly of higher techniques – at a time when they had been torn from the stability of their own communities. But their almost total acceptance of British superiority – they were sufficiently perceptive to recognize and condemn European racialism – was never unchallenged amongst Africans.

The challenge came not from those who rejected British influence *in toto*; apart from those engaged in commercial conflicts, like the Ashanti, few Africans at this stage refused to accept that Britain might offer them some benefits. But an important section of those who took the opportunities for a Europeanized education considered that it should be employed to strengthen rather than supplant African society.

Africanus Horton was one remarkable man who pointed this way. His father was another who owed his freedom to the British anti-slavery patrol. Africanus was born in 1835 in Sierra Leone, attended the Grammar School and Fourah Bay, before graduating in medicine at Edinburgh. Most of the rest of his life was spent in the army in various West African countries. But he was also an important writer on the politics of West Africa, in his books making specific proposals for the political development of the various West African societies. He combatted those European anthropologists who were trying to establish the inferiority of the Negro, exposing their irrationality by a combination of logic, biology and first-hand evidence. He then concentrated on an insistence that Africa must develop her own independent communities to an equal status with those of Europe. But he did not reject British assistance in this task. Indeed, he welcomed the influence of the missionaries and defended the British presence in Lagos. His recipe for progress was much the same as that of Crowther and Venn, British influence extended into the interior, education and economic development. But his object was to achieve fully independent African government. He believed that education was the crucial key – and urged that a university be established in West Africa – supported the proposed Fante Confederation of 1871, and prepared blue-prints of constitutions, usually based on a monarchy, for all the communities down the coast. At first under British suzerainty, with education and economic advance these would eventually be ready for complete independence.

It is easy to suggest that Horton was a prophet before his time. Yet, recalling the report of the House of Commons special committee of 1865, which urged that Britain withdraw totally from West Africa, it can equally be argued that he was meeting the challenge of his day. As it turned out, with Britain increasing instead of diminishing her involvement in West African affairs, most of Horton's proposals remained printed dreams. Yet his significance should not be under-estimated; he had posed an African alternative to the acceptance of an imitative response to the British impact. He was one of the first African nationalists, using the new methods offered by Europe, but for the purpose of strengthening Africa's own societies.

A still stronger challenge to British domination came from George Johnson, the leader of the Egba of Abeokuta. Johnson was yet another of the emigrés from Sierra Leone, but he did not share the educational privileges of his contemporary fellow-leaders. Nevertheless, he had been to England – taken there by Prince Alfred who had been captivated by his playing of the local flute!

The Egba were recent arrivals in Abeokuta, driven there after suffering from the Yoruba civil wars. They continued to feel continually insecure as the wars progressed, always with the added danger of attacks from Dahomey. Moreover, the Europeans, who were partly responsible for the troubles of the Yoruba through their continued demand for slaves, had now appeared both in Abeokuta and in Lagos. Many Egba scarcely differentiated between European slave traders, British missionaries, and the British merchants and officials now in Lagos. What they saw was the mission station teaching strange ways whilst the missionaries' fellow countrymen were annexing Lagos and using their position there to interfere with the commercially strategic position of Abeokuta in the internal trade of Yorubaland.

When Johnson arrived in Abeokuta in 1865 the Egba's overriding need, if they were to survive these perils, was political cohesion and central direction. Through a variety of unconventional measures Johnson secured for himself an influential position as chief adviser to the local ruler. From this vantage point he challenged the British administrator of Lagos, met his tariff and blockade policy, designed to undermine the Egba commercial position, with counter-tariffs, and eventually succeeded in having the Lagos government repudiated by the Colonial Office. In 1867 the anti-European fury of the Egba was turned against the Abeokuta missionaries, churches and missionary homes were destroyed and the missionaries left the town.

It might seem on the surface that the Egba revolt against British authority was simply the reaction of an African community against European influence, whether it came from Lagos or from the missionaries. This would be to miss the significance of Johnson's influence. The Egba were trying to maintain their economic position which depended on their control of the road from Abeokuta to Lagos. They were harassed by the British authorities in Lagos who used constables on the road to molest Egba, sent arms to Ibadan, traditionally hostile to the Egba, armed local villages against Abeokuta and tried to force the road into the interior for their commerce – as well as for undermining the slave trade. Johnson saw that political unity and centralized government were essential for Egba survival. He had learnt this from his experience of European power. In the end he failed, for the Egba continued to allow centrifugal influences to weaken their strength. In any case, British interests increasingly came to demand government intervention in the area, ultimately resulting in the declaration of a protectorate over Yoruba territory. But Johnson was applying Horton's ideas in practice, employing British methods to defend African society against British domination.

There were many prominent Africans in West Africa who took intermediate positions between these contrasting reactions to the impact of British culture on African society; men like Bishop James Johnson, Crowther's successor as Christian leader in Nigeria, Sir Samuel Lewis, the noted Wesleyan lawyer and member of Sierra Leone's legislative council, John Mensah Sarbah, the first Gold Coast African to be called to the bar, and his fellow lawyer and journalist, J. E. Caseley Hayford; and many others. All made their contribution to the turbulent theoretical and practical debate as to the best way of meeting the challenge of British influence. But one man above all came to see the issue with stark clarity, to recognize the basic elements of the new situation and to argue a case rationally based on all the evidence of cultural contact between the two societies; this man was Edward Blyden.

Blyden was born in the West Indies of African parents, was refused admission to American higher education because of racial prejudice, and so was sent by the New York Colonization Society to Liberia where he attended the Presbyterian High school. He was a brilliant linguist, learning Spanish, Greek, Latin and Hebrew. He recruited settlers for Liberia in America, corresponded with Gladstone on Negro conditions in the United States and became a minister in the Liberian government. He was ordained, but also visited the Middle East where he learnt something of Islam and gained a knowledge of Arabic. In 1871 he went to live in Sierra Leone and henceforth addressed himself to Africans as a race rather than to any particular nationality.

Blyden's views can be studied from his books and from articles he wrote in the press which, both in West Africa and in London, was becoming an important vehicle of African ideas. To the theory of racial superiority he posed the alternative of varied contributions from each race to God's nature. To the assumption of European cultural superiority he counter-claimed the unique virtues of African civilization. He challenged the dogma of Christian exclusiveness by pointing out the advantages of Mohammedanism. In short, he threw down the gauntlet to the champions of European universalism, met them as equals on their own ground, and presented an equally convincing alternative cosmic perspective.

Undoubtedly Blyden's greatest contribution to Africans was to restore to those who read him or heard him a sense of pride in their own culture. And this was particularly important to those in societies which had felt the heaviest impact of British influence, which had seen the power of Europe to alter and upset their life, and which had been reared in the belief that they and their societies were inferior to those of Europeans, that they should imitate if they were to rise. It was especially important towards the end of the century when Europe became more aggressive, when white missionaries took the leading roles back from the African clergy, and when social and political progress amongst Africans was halted as Europeans began to rule instead of to guide.

Blyden taught his African cousins to be proud of their community, their family relations, even their polygamy (the bane of European missionaries). He praised their system of mutal aid, their communal attitude to work and wealth. He contrasted their communion with nature, their natural spiritualism, their awareness of God, with the Europeans' Sabbath-mindedness. He taught them that Africa had made great contributions to man's history and would make many more. He contrasted those African societies which were developing un-affected by European influences with those which had come under the effects of Europe's assumed superiority. '. . . they are growing up gradually and normally to take their place in the great family of nations – a distinct but integral part of the great human body, who will neither be spurious Europeans, bastard Americans nor savage Africans, but men developed upon the base of their own idiosyncracies, and accord-ing to the exigencies of their climate and country.' 'From the lessons he every day receives, the Negro unconsciously imbibes the conviction that to be a great man he must be like the white man. He is not brought up. . . . to be the companion, the equal, the comrade of the white man, but his imitator, his ape, his parasite.'

This line of thought took Blyden into some dangerous paths. He openly advocated the separation of races, opposed miscegenation and urged American Negroes to recognize that their only hope for the future lay in returning to Africa. Much of his description of African life was romantic, with the warts of cruelty, tribal warfare, slavery ignored. But what Blyden did supremely well was to restore to Africans a sense of cultural pride, to recreate a feeling of security in their heritage and traditions. And in doing so he was reasserting human dignity, a concept of humanity universally based on charity and compassion, a perspective often lost in the clash of European industrialized values on African communities.

If the British were hardly known before the nineteenth century to West Africans beyond the coast, they were completely unknown to Africans in the east and centre of the continent. At least there had been communication between West African and British merchants for several hundred years before Britain began to penetrate the interior. Many of them knew each other personally and some of the Africans certainly came from the hinterland. As we have seen, released slaves had come into contact with British life before their return to West Africa where they accelerated knowledge about British ways. Some Africans were also literate in English from slave trading days onward, many more became so during the nineteenth century, and therefore we have ample records of Africans' own reactions to the impact of British culture.

East and central Africa shared none of these circumstances. The only Europeans known to these areas were the Portuguese and they only along a short strip of coastline. Here it was the Arab and sometimes the Indian who was the foreigner, although many Arabs had been absorbed into the Swahili population of the coast. But Arab culture and particularly the Moslem religion had a long historical impact on the coastal peoples, who had also been accustomed to see ships from India and China in their harbours. Amongst the people of the interior, trade was almost entirely confined to an exchange of ivory and slaves for beads, cloth and firearms, conducted by Arabs, Swahili and Nyamwezi, with Indians on the coast often acting as financiers.

Yet the expansionist impulses which dominated British life in the nineteenth century took her explorers, missionaries, traders and consuls to east-central, as to West Africa. They travelled there in very different circumstances and their relations with African societies also differed radically. They had to follow the devious paths of the slaving caravans, for there were no established or maintained roads, paddle up rivers or sail on lakes. Before the imperial period the British visitors travelled and lived in societies neither they nor their government controlled, entirely dependent on the good will of local rulers. This perhaps brought them into closer intimacy with Africans in tribal societies than their fellows in the west, for they relied for all their needs on them; but it also made them much more vulnerable. The roll of mortality, injury and disaster was much longer. On the other hand, such risks attracted many more adventurous characters, attracted by the solitariness, the isolation from industrial life, the lure of the exotic and unexpected. Those who aspired to leadership and mastery over other men were particularly attracted. And although the missionaries had to resist temptation, others could pay less attention to status. Drink and African women became the accepted entertainment of most early hunters, traders, prospectors and settlers – not least of the Rhodesian pioneers at the end of the century. Whether these were the best characters to offer Africans their first glimpse of British culture may be questioned; but in societies where celibacy was odd and suspicious, they perhaps provided a more realistic reflection of British life than the more puritanical missionaries.

In one respect the environment into which the British penetrated during the nineteenth century was similar on both sides of the continent. Just as most of West Africa was deeply disturbed from the effects of inter-state and inter-communal wars, partly provoked by the consequences of the slave trade, so the east and centre were also torn by internecine strife. Here again the slave trade played a part, although the roots of the disturbances lay in South Africa. There the ruthlessness of the Zulus under Tshaka and his successors, together with the land struggle between Afrikaner and African, prompted waves of migrations northward. Sections of the Zulu tribal association hived off, collecting small weaker groups on their way, and sought new lands. The Ndebele, or Matabele, moving into what was to become Southern Rhodesia, and the Ngoni in Nyasaland and Tanganyika, were two notable examples of this migration. But they initiated movement throughout east-central Africa, further affected by invaders from the north. In such circumstances brigandage became common, offering perfect opportunities for an extension of the Arab slave trade. As the demand for slaves to the Middle East, India and for the east coast plantations continued to mount, the inducements were two-fold.

And the slavers brought more deadly firearms to intensify the barbarity of the warfare.

It was these conditions of chaotic inhumanity that the Europeans encountered on their first expeditions into the interior. They assumed that these were the normal African ways of life and reacted accordingly. Their reports to the missionary journals or geographical magazines of Britain described the African as savage and barbarous, ignorant and undisciplined. They knew nothing of his past achievements, could understand little of his cultures and, even when they encountered highly organized societies such as that in Buganda, tended to judge them only by their approximation to that of Britain. It was rather as though a visitor to Europe in the Dark Ages had regarded conditions there as typical of European civilization.

Official British policy towards this area throughout almost the whole of the nineteenth century hinged on influencing the Sultan in Zanzibar. Before the age of imperial partition there was a strong disinclination to annex or rule east or central African territory. It was considered that the Sultan could be induced to use his authority on the mainland to abolish the slave trade and to protect legitimate traders from molestation. At the same time, he would be in a position to ensure that no unfriendly power gained control of the east coast, or threatened Britain in the Indian Ocean. The fact that this policy involved supporting the power of a Moslem ruler did not disturb Whitehall; nor did the anomaly that British consuls in Zanzibar were demanding that the Sultan use power which he largely derived from the slave trade to secure its abolition.

But these factors did concern the missionaries, for they recognized that Islam was their most formidable opponent and that this rival religion drew much of its attraction from its involvement with slavery. Yet at first the missionaries had no choice but to accept the situation. They were not operating in conjuction with government policy as in the west, for the government saw little economic or strategic potential in the east. Nor had it any power to protect missionaries or traders from the hazards of their journey. The paths they took were the trails of the slave caravans, the only means of transporting goods was by the use of porters, virtually nothing was known of even the elementary geography of the region.

Missionary activity began with the arrival at Mombasa in 1844 of

Johann Krapf on behalf of the C M S. The travels of Krapf and his colleague Rebmann into the interior did not make many converts to Christianity, but they greatly added to the existing store of knowledge about the physical features and languages of the area. Kilimanjaro was seen in May 1848, Mount Kenya eighteen months later. The work of tracing the basic geography of the region was completed over the next twenty years by Livingstone, Speke, Burton, Grant, Baker and – later – by Thomson. Their published discoveries informed the British public for the first time of what east-central Africa looked like and something of how the Africans lived. These stories gave Victorian Britain some of its greatest vicarious thrills. Livingstone's writings in particular inspired British churches to equip missionary expeditions answering his call for Christian influence. The Universities Mission to Central Africa and the extension of the work of the London Missionary Society from Bechuanaland, together with the Methodists on the east coast all responded to Livingstone's appeal. But the missionaries themselves suffered terribly, many of them, including wives and children, losing their lives from tropical conditions. Even such sufferings, partly due to ignorance and poor preparation, were turned to good account by the churches. The Bishop of Oxford, commenting on the death of Bishop Mackenzie from fever after losing his stock of quinine in the River Shire when his canoe overturned, could say, 'mankind is raised, humanity is exalted, the church is purified by the examples of great heroic self-devotion, when God accepts the offering, and takes the man at once to his breast.' Of course, this was a selective interpretation of death; deaths in similar circumstances of slave dealers, liquor pedlars and fornicators were described as 'a series of most marvellous tragedies', in which 'God's hand is very plainly visible.'

The heroic-tragic romanticism of these experiences had two effects. In the first place, it induced a concept in Britain of Africa as the 'Dark Continent', where deeds of unique hideousness could be expected, and unnatural evils beset the body. In the second, it ensured that the missionaries, hunters and traders who were attracted to venture into this cauldron of danger and wickedness were of a particular character. The missionaries were usually ascetic and fanatical; the profit-seekers were generally men who could not come to terms with the new sophisticated life of industrial society. The former made few converts, but were often a source of amusement or suspicion to Africans; the latter usually made much closer contacts, drank with African men and copulated with the women, but were also regarded with suspicion for their methods of seeking wealth.

In fact, few missionaries in the early days had much time for saving souls or achieving conversion. In East and Central Africa the first task was self-preservation, the second maintenance of racial or cultural superiority. Shelter and food presented the initial problem. Houses at least approximating to British custom had to be erected on land sought from the local chief. Grain and vegetables had to be planted and their growth depended on chance. Almost always the mission station had to depend on gifts of food from the chief – often accompanied by demands for firearms or ammunition. Labour was always a cause of misunderstanding. Domestic slavery was understood by Africans, contractual employment virtually unknown. Celibacy was often regarded with suspicion if not hostility, some chiefs teasing the solitary missionary by sending him a succession of girls to tempt him. Contracts also brought misunderstanding. As in other parts of the continent, the African and European concept of contract fundamentally differed. Land believed bought by Europeans was considered as no more than leased by Africans; treaties signed implied retention of sovereignty to the African, whereas the European assumed that it involved a transfer of power to the protecting authority.

Then there was racial superiority to be preserved. Missionaries might be sent to follow Livingstone's conviction that superiority should be regarded as a trust, to improve the quality of African life. But Europeans were not trained or fitted for the hard labour of tropical life and, in any case, had to demonstrate the higher status of the white man. There was no particular arrogance shown by the missionaries on this issue, but, having been sent out from Britain to improve the lot of heathen savages, they could hardly avoid assuming that they represented a higher form of humanity than their pupils. Yet some missionaries perceived the anomalies into which this led. One of them described the situation in pungent terms: 'The first thing on arriving in camp is, for us, who have carried nothing heavier than an umbrella and a montrous hat, to rest – for the men, who have carried a load of 50lb to 60lb (sometimes more), generally on their heads, to fetch firewood and water. . . . The contrast will have struck you already. The people, to whom we have come to preach, lie on the ground or in a reed or grass hut, eat rice and a bit of dried fish. . . . carry a load under a burning sun for ten to twelve miles which I should be sorry to carry for a mile in England, walk barefoot on the scorching ground while we live in grand houses or tents (palaces to these people), sleep on beds as comfortable as any at home, eat chickens (carried in a box alive), preserved meat, green peas (preserved), tea, cocoa, biscuits, bread, butter, jam.'[1] Some found the power exercised over the less fortunate in such circumstances particularly satisfying; it reflected the social hierarchy of Britain and offered those who could never have aspired to social power at home an imitative substitute in remote Africa. A minority recognized the paradox; no one bridged the social gap. And to the British public the ideal relationship between the intelligent Christian leader and his faithful, strong heathen servants – usually the explorer's porters – recreated the secure social patterns of feudal days.

In reality, a substantial degree of the 'faithfulness' which so captivated British audiences was extracted by violence. Flogging was the accepted method of keeping porters obedient on expeditions, and missionaries seem to have been no more reluctant to follow Lugard's recipe of 'thrash them first, conciliate afterwards' than other travellers. Indeed, there would probably have been few mission stations if they had exercised any greater gentleness, for the porters on trek and the servants in the compounds owed no loyalty to the Christian church or its agents. Livingstone may be held to have shown how a relation- ship between Christian white and heathen black could be based on mutual trust; but Livingstone was exceptional. It was easier and more immediately practical for the ordinary missionary to follow the example of explorer or hunter, accept a parent-child metaphor and so justify brutality with the excuse of not sparing the rod. But this widespread feature of missionary life was little publicized in British journals; nor would it have embellished the romantic pictures of British life in Africa told to so many fund-raising gatherings.

Yet the missionaries did make some constructive contribution to the culture contact of Britain and east-central Africa. Perhaps their greatest achievement was in translating and writing African languages. If the missionaries were ever to establish the kind of relationship with

[1] C. F. Harford-Battersby, *Pilkington of Uganda*, quoted in H. A. C. Cairns, *Prelude to Imperialism*.

6

Africans which would allow genuine conversion, they could not be content with the few words of pidgin English which served the hunter and trader. The missionary needed real communication, with language providing clarity of meaning. In the slow, painstaking task of codifying hitherto non-written languages, thus opening the way to greater cultural understanding, the missionaries made a vital contribution to British-African relations in this area. The fact that the missionary was necessarily resident, often with wife and children, also deepened the relationship compared with the transient impact of the itinerant trader or hunter. Rudimentary medical treatments, elementary carpentry, some agricultural pursuits and new foods, later education in literacy, were passed on to some tribal communities where mission stations were established.

Conversion to Christianity was infrequent and often superficial. It was usually confined to the weak and insecure, to those who had become detribalized for some reason, and, of course, to released or escaped slaves. The one major exception was the case of Buganda where, during the last twenty years of the century, a battle was waged between the CMS Protestants, the White Father Catholics and Islam for religious domination. Buganda was one of the most strongly organized of African communities, but the readiest to ponder alien faiths. Religious strategy was often intermixed with political considerations, but Buganda demonstrated that Christian martyrdom could be endured by African as well as European.

Missionary activities themselves could do little to carry out Livingstone's exhortation to ally commerce with Christianity. The original UMCA expedition took a few craftsmen with it, as well as a cotton gin, but it failed within a few years. The knowledge disseminated by the mission societies provided information which could be used for commercial ventures, but there was a little to attract the trader until late in the century. Ivory became a vogue in Britain, used for billiard balls and piano keys as well as for ornament. This encouraged the hunters, as did the fashionable demand for exotic evidence of African interest like ostrich feathers, animal skins, and horns. But this was really peripheral to serious economic activity. The fact was that at this stage Britain was producing little of use to east-central Africans, whilst their territories could offer few goods of value to Britain. The high costs of transport – almost entirely on the human head – deterred any determined economic penetration. Most trade was left to the Arabs, Swahili, Indians and Nyamwezi.

There were certain areas, however, where traders did gradually bring a regular influence from the outside world, even if it still only affected comparatively few people. Matabeleland and Mashonaland were more easily accessible than most of east-central Africa. They could be reached by ox-wagon from South Africa and began to receive a growing number of trading wagons annually. Some of these penetrated farther north into Barotseland. The commercial attractions of future Rhodesia were increased when, in 1867, rumours spread that gold was to be found in Mashonaland. The consequent rush of British and South African speculators, though they were disappointed with their strikes, stimulated trade for a time and helped to develop transport routes.

Despite its drawbacks, the Zambezi also facilitated commercial communication, leading to the founding of the African Lakes Corporation in 1878 and a growth of trade in the Lake Nyasa region. The Corporation was mainly intended to supply the Scottish missions of the area and certainly helped to provide that region with a British commercial and missionary influence that was sustained well into the twentieth century.

On the east coast trade was of much greater proportions, even when efforts to abolish the slave trade began to have effect in the 1870s. Rubber, cloves and ivory provided the main exports and, although the British took little part in internal commerce, their shipping interests in Zanzibar grew very rapidly. The new Suez Canal provided an enormous stimulant by reducing distance, whilst the laying of a cable from Aden to Zanzibar in 1877 also strengthened communication. Sir William Mackinnon, a Scottish churchman and shipowner, became the principal agent in promoting the Livingstone concept. He sent his British India ships to Zanzibar monthly from 1872, began to construct roads from the coast to Lake Nyasa and Lake Victoria in 1876, and, the following year, obtained the Sultan's consent to form a trading company. It was Lord Salisbury, Foreign Secretary at the time, who sabotaged the company project, probably because of the government's reluctance to become involved with the administration of East Africa, preferring to leave it to the Sultan acting under its guidance. Scottish interests were based on Lake Nyasa where Glasgow merchants had introduced a steamship in 1874. The 1878 company was designed to increase the number of ships and stimulate local trade.

By this time Zanzibar and the east coast trade was attracting international attention, particularly that of the Germans. The Sultan was taken to England to be shown her industrial might. When, in 1875, Khedive Ismail, with the help of British officers, laid claim to the east coast on behalf of Egypt, the British government, after some hesitation, backed the Sultan and forced the Khedive to withdraw his troops from the coast. So Zanzibar remained Britain's principal agent of influence in East Africa, but, despite the government's reluctance to become directly involved, international pressures were building up to the point where withdrawal or imperial intervention was becoming an inevitable choice.

The cultural aggression which took the British into the heart of the African continent during the nineteenth century bore a lighter, more superficial touch in east-central than in West Africa. Because the societies there were less well organized or technically equipped, the gap between them and the representatives of industrialized Britain was so much the greater. This also allowed a wider degree of cultural variety as the Africans, without the deep involvement in British values seen in parts of the west, and protected by extensive, insecure communications from any massive invasion of their societies, could choose which British offerings to accept and which to reject. They could improve their life to the extent of purchasing the goods of European traders or accept those techniques brought by missionaries which did not disturb tribal tradition. But neither trader nor missionary had the power to undermine tribal life to the degree that was evident in the west. Only the arrival of imperial power could accomplish that task, desperately though the missionaries wished to do so. The only important exception to this generality was in the case of Uganda where the highly organized and strategically situated Baganda found themselves riven by schism between rival factions of Christianity and Islam marked by murder and massacre, in the vortex of politico-commercial ambitions. Yet through almost all of east-central Africa the cultural expansion of Britain had failed against the resistance of African traditionalism before the arrival of imperialism. No Fourah Bay, no British grammar schools, no clerical, medical or legal training in Britain brought British ways to the African youth of this region. If the weaker culture was to be broken by the stronger, if modern science, technology and capitalism were to be introduced to east and central Africa, it would need the forces of imperial government. And few Africans could foresee that their casual relations with alien missionaries, hunters and traders would be transformed into the master-servant relationship of colonial rule.

Chapter 7

Partition –
The Relationship Changes

From the time of the first serious contact between Europeans and Africans during the fifteenth century until the last twenty years of the nineteenth century, the vast majority of African peoples continued to govern themselves. The business of trade conducted by all the nations of Atlantic Europe, whether in materials or in human beings, took place almost entirely on the beaches. It was there that Africans and Europeans exchanged their wares. Even when, in the nineteenth century, explorers, missionaries and then traders penetrated into the interior of the continent, their object was not to plant national flags or to institute alien governments: it was again to give and take, whether the commodities were palm oil, geographical knowledge or the lessons of the Bible.

There were a number of exceptions to this general rule. The French had governed Algerians and some Senegalese since early in the nineteenth century. The British had set up a slight colonial administration in the Gold Coast and exercised a degree of political control in the Gambia, Sierra Leone and Lagos. There were also a number of small enclaves, like the French naval station in Gabon, a few Portuguese coastal towns in Angola and Mozambique, the French base on the Somali coast, where Europeans exercised some political control. Influence from Europe could also be seen in Egypt, Tunis, Zanzibar and Madagascar. But, with one exception, this still left the vast majority of Africans, even in these areas, outside European control. The one exception was South Africa, where the influence of Britain, married to increasing political responsibility by European settlers, penetrated more deeply into African society than elsewhere in the continent. Here, even though many African communities continued to live

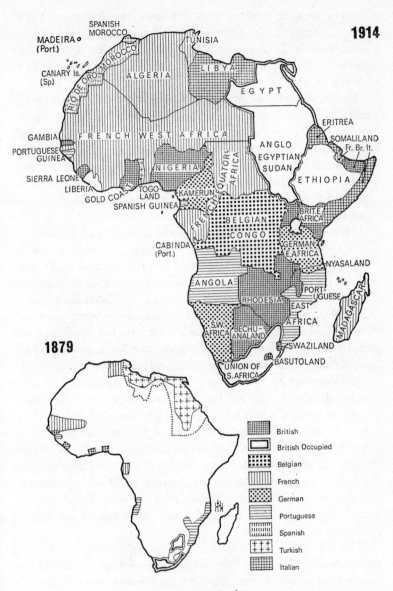

1914

SPANISH MOROCCO
MADEIRA ○
(Port.)
TUNISIA
CANARY Is.
(Sp.)
RIO DE ORO
MOROCCO
ALGERIA
LIBYA
EGYPT
GAMBIA
PORTUGUESE
GUINEA
FRENCH WEST AFRICA
ANGLO
EGYPTIAN
SUDAN
ERITREA
SOMALILAND
Fr. Br. It.
SIERRA LEONE
LIBERIA
GOLD COAST
TOGO-
LAND
SPANISH GUINEA
NIGERIA
KAMERUN
FRENCH EQUATORIAL AFRICA
ETHIOPIA
CABINDA
(Port.)
BELGIAN
CONGO
BRIT. E.
AFRICA
GERMAN
E.AFRICA
NYASALAND
ANGOLA
RHODESIA
PORT-
UGUESE
EAST
AFRICA
MADAGASCAR
S.W.
AFRICA
BECHU-
ANALAND
SWAZILAND
BASUTOLAND
UNION OF
S.AFRICA

1879

	British
	British Occupied
	Belgian
	French
	German
	Portuguese
	Spanish
	Turkish
	Italian

4 European encroachment

according to their own customs and laws, the Europeans, under British authority in the Cape and Natal and through independent governments in the two Afrikaner republics, steadily imposed their institutional structures, their culture and their authority into the heart of Southern Africa.

This was the only exception. In 1880 more than ninety per cent of African territory and its inhabitants remained under indigenous government. Yet, by the time the nations of Europe began to hurl their armaments and bodies at each other in 1914, only two political units in Africa, Liberia and Ethiopia, remained under the rule of their own people. All the rest of the continent was now governed from the capitals of Europe – London, Paris, Berlin, Rome, Madrid, Lisbon and Brussels.

Britain, of course, was only one of the seven European nations to participate in this partition. Nevertheless, she and the French were the major participants, and the impact of her rule affected many more Africans than that of any other colonial power. During these last two decades of the nineteenth century, Britain consolidated her power in the Gambia, Sierra Leone, the Gold Coast and the communities which were to become Nigeria in West Africa, extended her rule from South Africa northwards into Bechuanaland, the two Rhodesias and Nyasaland, carved out her future states of Uganda and Kenya, established a protectorate over Zanzibar in East Africa and set up an administration over her share of Somaliland. Immediately after the turn of the century she was to annex the two Afrikaner republics and declare her protection over Swaziland. Perhaps even more significant than these official acquisitions was the British occupation of Egypt in 1882, followed in the next decade by the creation with Egypt of a condominium over the Sudan. Certainly, so far as the concern of British governments and diplomats was evident, British relations with Egypt were of greater importance than those with any other part of the African continent.

Why was it then that Britain, which during the first four-fifths of the nineteenth century had apparently been reluctant to establish her rule or even accept administrative responsibilities in those parts of the African continent where her citizens were trading, now suddenly asserted her suzerainty over many thousands of square miles in East, Central, South and West Africa? Why, indeed, did this mood of imperial aggrandizement simultaneously take possession of the chanceries of so many European states? After all, it was not only the British who had been reluctant to incur further expenses or provide the personnel for administrations in Africa. Bismarck had professed himself sceptical of the advantage to be gained by colonization, whilst the French had thought so little of their colonies that they offered them all to Germany in 1871 on condition that the Germans would resist the temptation of annexing Alsace-Lorraine; significantly, the Germans chose Alsace-Lorraine. This change of attitude has been explained in terms of the natural development of the capitalist system to a monopolist phase; as the consequence of over-production and under-consumption in domestic economies; as an outlet for surplus European populations; as the extension of missionary evangelical efforts to take the Bible and other elements of European civilization to ignorant savages; by popular Darwinists, as arising from the survival of the strongest nations through the subjugation of the weaker; as the outcome of widespread literacy in industrial Europe, inviting mob emotions through the appeal of the popular press and the development of national jingoism; as the by-product of European politico-diplomatic manœuvres; as the inevitable consequence of a new technical age, providing swifter communications and mechanical means of transport; as an outlet for the investment of surplus profits made through newly-maturing industrial and commercial systems; as the natural result of growing international commerce, based in the trading capitals of Western Europe. Each of these theories has been examined and re-examined by its critics. None of them in isolation stands the test of analysis.

Hobson may argue that the investors were attracted overseas because of diminishing returns at home; but the bulk of overseas investment from all the imperialist countries went to nations in the process of industrialization rather than to the new African colonies. Lenin's description of the monopoly stage of capitalist development might fit some aspects of the German situation in the late nineteenth century, but it certainly did not mirror that of Britain or France. He also followed Hobson's fallacy regarding capital investment in the new colonies, whilst his proposition that finance capital was concerned with the development of resources in the new colonial territories was hardly borne out by subsequent experience. Schumpeter seems to have been

6*

so frustrated in failing to find causes for national expansion that he was reduced to the argument that annexation is an object in itself. Yet his 'social atavism' fails to explain why certain states should build colonial empires whilst other equally powerful states did not do so, or why colonial expansion should develop at one particular period rather than another. Mansergh provides us with a clear picture of the part played by African partition in the diplomatic manœuvres of European governments; where he fails is in explaining why such governments should be activated by these particular motives at this moment in history. Those who argue that popular jingoism or bowdlerized anthropology caused governments to pursue expansionist policies are surely putting effect before cause. Various popular ideas and emotions were certainly used by all European governments to secure support for their imperial objectives, but there is no evidence that a popular appetite for colonial possessions suddenly developed and then thrust its will on the ministers in power. Even John Strachey, with the benefit of fifty years' hindsight, partially accepted the theory that colonial expansion arose from domestic underconsumption and used this explanation to support his assertion that imperialism had been ended by the creation of the welfare state after the second world war. There seems as little justification for the deduction as there is for the original assumption.[1]

What happened, then, from about 1880 onwards to change the whole character of British relations with Africans, after they had remained broadly constant for over three hundred years? It might be that the nineteenth century had seen the replacement of human cargoes from Africa by such material commodities as palm oil. Yet throughout these three centuries the concern of those British people who had made direct and deliberate contact with the peoples of Africa had been almost entirely confined to the exchange of goods, or, later, the export of ideas. Within this relationship there had been virtually no appetite amongst British people for the acquisition of African land or for political suzerainty over African peoples – with the one exception of South Africa.

[1] J. A. Hobson *Imperialism – a Study*, London 1902, V. I. Lenin *Imperialism – The Highest Stage of Capitalism*, 1916, Joseph A. Schumpeter *Imperialism and Social Classes*, 1919, Nicholas Mansergh *The Coming of the First World War – A Study in the European Balance 1878–1914*, London 1949, John Strachey *The End of Empire*, London 1959.

Moreover, the prosperity of Britain and the international power which flowed from it had been based for most of the nineteenth century on the principle of free trade. In the earlier days of industrialization and during her agrarian revolution, Britain had, of course, followed a policy of protection, behind the walls of which she could develop her new productive methods free from outside interference. But from the 1840s onwards Britain, with her new industrial power and as the first major state to wield such power, sought to ensure that markets and resources throughout the world were open to all traders. She did not use her strength to raise protective barriers around those areas where her merchants operated. For she knew that at this stage, in open competition, she could defeat any competitor. It was neither altruism nor coincidence that during this period British policy was directed towards giving greater political responsibility to her old colonies like Canada, Australasia and the Cape. Having learnt a lesson in failing to maintain control over their American empire, the British now turned against the whole concept of ruling vast overseas possessions. Reinforced by the Durham Report of 1839, which advised offering increased self-government for the Canadian community, British governments hoped that their colonial subjects would take progressive degrees of responsibility for their own affairs. At the same time, governments at Westminster were reluctant to accept any further imperial commitments. Their attitude was that, whilst they would do all in their power to assist the trading activities of the influential merchant class, this effort could only be handicapped by any attempts to impose British political control over the areas where trade was conducted. Moreover, the maintenance of overseas administration would make financial demands which in themselves would handicap the commercial prosperity of the country. So long as restrictions on trade were avoided in all parts of the world, the British outlook in the mid-nineteenth century was that her prosperity and power were assured from the strength of her industrial techniques and commercial skills, rendering colonial rule or possession both unnecessary and restrictive.

But these circumstances, so happy for Britain, did not continue indefinitely. After 1870 British supremacy in industrial production was increasingly challenged by America, Germany, France and other European nations. After her civil war, the United States doubled industrial production within a decade. Between 1880 and 1890 her steel output overtook that of Britain and Germany's did the same in the following decade. British foreign investment had certainly created many new markets for her manufacturers; but the time came when the effects of the export of capital goods began to gather their own momentum. Those who bought British machines put them to work, and, in doing so, developed their own competition to British manufactures. British exports to the United States steadily declined from twenty per cent to ten per cent of her total export trade during the third quarter of the century.

Moreover, Britain's new industrial competitors recognized the same needs as their British mentors had in their early days. In order to develop their new manufacturing systems they had to raise tariff walls within which their infant industries could grow to maturity. To this was added the incentive of protecting their productive systems against older established British competitors, and so the growth of competition limited the expansion of British exports. The deployment of tariff barriers only increased this trend. And, just as expansion in British export markets resulting from capital investment overseas had stimulated domestic growth within Britain, thus providing increasing supplies of consumer goods, so the decline of the export markets correspondingly hit the internal market.

Once the peak of manufacturing exports which followed the Franco-Prussian War had been passed, Britain suffered during the rest of the 1870s from a deep depression. Towards the end of this decade Britain's European competitors in Germany, Russia, France and Austro-Hungary increased their discrimination against British exports and thus deepened the crisis. It is true that the critical situation of British industry was partially hidden by the impact of falling import prices and increased productivity, allowing some rise in living standards. Nevertheless, that important section of industry and commerce engaged in continuing to sell abroad coal, iron and textiles found itself exposed to the increasingly cold winds of foreign competition.

The fact was that Britain, at the latter end of her industrial revolution, was now competing with countries which, because they had entered the industrial processes late, had been able to adopt newer and more modern methods. The small scale of British firms and the inflexible structure into which manufacturing business had ossified in Britain were now exposed. Having exhausted her earlier initiatives, the economy of Britain remained comparatively stagnant, the eyes of the sons and grandsons of her former industrial innovators being largely closed to the new opportunities open to them. Industrial processes which could have been developed in such new fields as electricity, chemicals or the use of the internal combustion engine were ignored in favour of continuing to rest on the dividends of former achievements. Likewise, the educational system, founded on the classics, failed to recognize the growing need for technical and scientific training. The Germans in particular demonstrated what advantage could be taken of a new educational outlook. Moreover, when profits began to fall the fragmented small-scale industrial enterprises in Britain had not accumulated the resources to branch out into new developments to offset the consequences of increased competition in traditional exports. Conservatism and the lure of security prevailed, even though growing failures amongst domestic companies exposed the critical decline into which British industry was sinking.

The initial reaction of the British merchant class to this challenge to their power was to seek neither imperial expansion nor counter-protection. Indeed, governments under their influence continued dogmatically to adhere to what they considered as the sacred principle of *laissez faire*. But a number of complementary influences pointed to increased foreign investment as at least some palliative for the crisis. The London capital market was in any case oriented towards foreign investment, which still seemed to offer better returns and greater security than that in domestic industry. Government policies strengthened this trend by offering protection to overseas investment, including the guarantee of loans to India. Significantly, German governments adopted the opposite policy of home investment, but the whole tradition of Britain was to look overseas for investment, especially in trade. Even the T.U.C. in 1879 passed a resolution calling on the trade unions to invest in a projected African Corporation in order to help to extricate the economy from its depression. Trade unionists did not appear to appreciate that concentration on exports, particularly of iron and textiles, was retarding the development of new industries in Britain which might have solved the problem of un-employment and offered better wage prospects.

An obsession with foreign investment led Hobson and Lenin to exaggerate the connection between investment and imperial expansion.

It is true that, as their international markets contracted as a result of growing industrial competition and protection, the British often turned to seek opportunities within the Empire. But by far the largest proportion of both investment and exports continued to flow to industrial countries outside the Empire. Within the Empire itself the only serious interest shown was towards the opportunities in those older colonies, soon to become dominions, which were themselves in the process of industrialization. During the 1860s, for instance, only thirty-two per cent of exports and thirty-six per cent of investments found their way to the Empire. Of these only one per cent of exports and a negligible amount of investments were sent to Africa outside South Africa. During the 1880s, exports to the Empire had merely risen by two per cent, but investment had now increased to forty-seven per cent of the total. Exports to colonial Africa, however, remained at the previous level and investment was only recorded as one-half of one per cent. The big increase had come in investment to the dominions, which had risen during this period from twelve to twenty-nine per cent.

It was only after the turn of the century that any substantial increase in either exports or investment to colonial Africa could be observed. Even then, up to the time of the first world war, the figures remained but a minute proportion of Britain's overseas economy, reaching no more than two per cent of her exports and two and a half per cent of her overseas investments.[1]

Throughout this period Britain was regularly sending more exports to Europe than to the whole of the Empire combined. British investment in Europe did sharply decline from the 1870s onwards, at the same time as it rose steeply in the dominions and South America, but in the United States it diminished much more slowly, falling from twenty-seven per cent in the 1860s to only nineteen per cent by 1914. The picture is quite clear: the capitalist in Britain sought his profits and interest, not in the undeveloped tropical colonies, but wherever industrialization was taking place. Nor did the sharp increase of investment in Australasia, Canada and South Africa lead to a policy of imperial protection. Britain still considered herself sufficiently powerful as a commercial-industrial nation to be able to defeat her competitors

[1] Michael Barratt Brown *After Imperialism*, p. 110.

in free markets, even though she might have to divert a part of her marketing into the dominions as a result of increasing competition and protectionist policies in America and Europe.

What, then, does the evidence suggest as the basic cause of British colonial expansion during the 1880s and 1890s? It was clearly not so much from a search for new markets and fields of investment that British governments were led to annexe or 'protect' so many thousands of square miles in Africa and Asia during this period; the need rather was to defend established markets and territories already economically or politically controlled against the dangers which suddenly arose from rivals to Britain's commercial and military supremacy. The central British interest was to defend the freedom of her merchants to trade with all parts of the world, and much more importantly with the industrialized countries than to the largely under-populated, primitive societies of Africa.

Within this concern, of course, the channels between Britain and the dominions were highly valued. Already the British stake in the development of the dominions was large. They provided sure markets, cheap foods and raw materials. The re-export of many of their products greatly assisted Britain's trade surplus. Situated in three continents and both hemispheres, they greatly added to the power, prestige and security of British world influence, particularly in the interest of international free trade. But, though important, they were only a part of British concern for her freedom to trade throughout world markets. And, indeed, British encouragement to dominion self-government showed that political control over them was not considered essential to a preservation of their place in the British economy.

As the dangers of nationalism in newly-unified Italy and Germany were added to traditional French rivalry and the growing power of the United States, it seemed as though British control over the trade routes of the world was seriously threatened. Once this supremacy began to diminish, it would become impossible for Britain to insist on international free trade. To the merchants of the British Isles, accustomed for half a century to an unchallenged belief that free trade was synonymous with prosperity, it seemed that the Ark of the Covenant was menaced. Their reaction was not to raise counter-tariff barriers against their rivals, for this would have seemed to be participating in a heresy doomed to lead to disaster. They responded by using their influence in persuading their successive governments to take control of lands either essential for the protection of commercial channels or which their rivals coveted, even if these appeared to possess no immediate commercial attraction. From such reactions to the new international challenges to British commercial supremacy stemmed the policy of colonial expansion.

Within this general sense of threat to the lifelines of Britain's international commercial power, one issue was constantly paramount. India was the keystone to the British imperial arch. In the eighteenth century conquest there had provided the East India Company and its servants with tremendous plunder. In the nineteenth century India became perhaps the main factor providing Britain with a surplus in her balance of payments. Britain found ready markets, particularly for her textiles and steel, in India, whilst the Indians were selling their cotton and jute to the Americans, Europeans and Japanese. So, although India had a trade surplus, she was in considerable commercial deficit with Britain, buying British exports with the proceeds of her sales to the rest of the world. In addition, the Indians were taxed to provide the expense of the British administration there and the interest on their government's debt. All this helped to provide Britain with a surplus balance of payments with India, helping to offset her general adverse balance of trade.

During the second half of the nineteenth century, this deficit in trading balance increased from £27m to £161m, yet the balance on current account increased from £5m to £40m at the end of the century, and it had been more than double this ten years earlier. The difference was supplied by ever-growing surpluses on services and from interest and dividends. The latter rose during this half century from an average of £9m a year to about £100m. These were the returns on overseas investments all over the world, but by far the greatest jewel in the imperial crown was India. Not only did she provide Britain with markets for eleven per cent of her exports during the latter part of the century, but the thirty-six per cent of British investment which flowed during the 1860s to the Empire included twenty-one per cent to India alone. Although this proportion of investment tended to fall during the rest of the century, not only did it remain substantial but the interest on investment already in India remained a vital element in the British balance of payments and provided funds for further investment abroad, which allowed Britain's credit balance to increase from £209m in mid-century to £2,397m by its end and about £4,000m by 1914.[1]

Control of this vast storehouse of wealth was always accepted to be the one exception in anti-colonial campaigns, even by the most fervent opponents of colonial rule. For no one could doubt that the expenses incurred in British administration of India were many times repaid from the value of her market and the returns on investment – particularly as the Indians were called on to pay for their own governmental services.

Thus, when British world power began to be challenged towards the end of the nineteenth century, the defence of all routes to India took priority. British commercial interests were determined to preserve their ability to trade across the oceans, but the routes through Suez, and round the Cape were considered sacrosanct. With this uppermost in their minds Disraeli bought Egyptian shares in the Suez Canal in 1876 and Gladstone occupied Egypt in 1882. Subsequently, it became essential for British governments to so order their diplomatic policies as to retain at least the connivance of the Germans in continued British occupation of Egypt.

Concern with the same route persuaded Britain to look to its position in the whole Nile valley, from Uganda through the Sudan, once European rivals appeared anxious to seize these lands. Indeed, Britain's whole policy towards East Africa, from Zanzibar along the coast to Mombasa and into the hinterland towards Uganda, was activated by the same motive. It was essential to keep naval control of the Indian Ocean, of the Mediterranean, the Red Sea and Suez. Eventually the French were allowed to establish a dominant position in North Africa, but only at the price of accepting Britain's paramountcy in Egypt.

It is in this context that we should regard Britain's reactions to the outburst of colonial expansion by France, Germany and Italy during the 1880s and 1890s. As the French were already established in Algeria, showed signs of extending their North African empire, had taken control of Madagascar and were expanding in Asia, the threat was obvious. Meanwhile, the Germans had begun to develop an influence on

[1] Brown *op. cit.*, pp. 84–5, 75 and 110.

the mainland opposite Zanzibar and the Italians were looking at the Red Sea coast and into the heartland of Ethiopia.

The evidence thus suggests that British colonial expansion at this time was caused by a desire to defend what she already possessed – the power to enforce free trade and safeguard certain vital imperial possessions – rather than by any change in attitudes towards the relations between colonial policy and economic prosperity.

Amongst those European powers who were challenging the might of Britain a variety of motives led to their imperialist expansion and partitioning of the African continent. Yet, in one way or another, the imperialism of each was part of the fundamental commercial diplomacy of the age, through various tactics challenging the supremacy of Britain. If there was one general attitude common to all, it was the mistaken belief that British commercial and industrial power was a consequence of the existence of a British Empire. This was to reverse the order of cause and effect. In practice, the Empire had been acquired as a result of the commercial and industrial enterprise of Britain, rather than the reverse. But based on this misconception, in their search for means to compete with British economic prosperity, the merchants and bankers of Europe decided that they must seek colonial possessions in order to secure markets for their industrial goods and investments, supplies of raw materials for their factories and naval or military bases to protect their commercial enterprise.

Leopold of Belgium, with the assistance of Stanley, made the first move when he staked a claim to control of the Congo basin through the establishment of a commercial company. Leopold, however, simply sought products in the Congo which he could sell at a profit and so accumulate personal wealth. Yet his initiative encouraged the French and Germans in particular to seek colonial possessions in Africa, and the activities of these two states were much more profoundly important to partition than those of Leopold himself.

It is significant that Bismarck was initially opposed to accepting colonial expansion as part of his German national policy. He had declared in the early 1870s that Germany would confine its interests to the continent of Europe, that projects for German colonization 'would be just like the silken sables of Polish noble families who have no shirts'. Yet, by the mid-1880s, he went so far to contradict this dictum as to declare that, 'Colonies would mean the winning of new markets for German industries, the expansion of trade and a new field for German activity, civilization and capital.'

The French also radically changed their attitudes toward colonization between the early 1870s and the beginning of the 1880s. Prepared to sacrifice all their colonial possessions to the Germans in 1871, by the beginning of the 1880s, Jules Ferry was asking, 'must we, in the name of an excessive and short-sighted chauvinism, drive French policy into an impasse and, with our eyes fixed on the blue line of the Vosges, let everything be done, everything be undertaken, everything be decided – without us, around us, against us?' By this time Gambetta, Ferry and Saint-Hilaire had convinced the French that their survival as a great power and their ability to compete in the increasingly cut-throat age of international commerce depended upon colonial expansion.

The significant feature of this political conversion to imperialist expansion in both Germany and France was the economic influence behind it. In Germany a variety of Hanseatic firms had begun serious overseas trading during this period. They were financed by bankers like Bleichröder and Hansemann, O'Swalds in East Africa, Woermanns in West Africa and Godeffroys in Asia, who bore witness to the new German merchant interest in the potential of colonial areas. Indeed, by the beginning of the 1880s, the Germans were exporting a considerable volume of goods to West Africa, and also importing even greater quantities of African products, particularly through Hamburg. It is significant that the bankers, Hansemann and Bleichröder, were both friends of Bismarck, the latter being Bismarck's financial adviser. As the Chancellor himself was anxious to secure support from the merchants in applying his protectionist policies, the outlines of a bargain can be discerned. Moreover, Bismarck himself was soon to realize that, with the increase of protectionism around the world, his own policy was only likely to succeed if he could secure colonies to guarantee trade for Germany. The activities of German financial-commercial interests, anxious to convert their government to imperial policies, were exposed in the words of one publicist advising a pro-colonialist association: 'Make yourself a focus for the wishes and interests of our traders on unappropriated coastlands (of Africa). . . . undismayed by occasional failure of endeavour. . . . and I am convinced that the day will come when suddenly and unawares a German warship will produce a *fait accompli* there, where the Association shall have prepared the ground.'[1]

Similarly, in France, Jules Ferry, supported by overseas merchant groups, was talking of the need for French investment opportunities abroad, for trade outlets to encourage the development of French industry, for coaling stations to enable the French navy and mercantile marine to maintain France as a first-rank nation.

By this time a favourable international context for imperial expansion had developed. After the defeat by Germany in 1871, most French leaders were anxious to restore national pride through some kind of achievement which would appeal to their humiliated citizens. The Germans, under Bismarck, hoped to encourage the French to seek national adventures overseas in order to forget the loss of Alsace-Lorraine and to be diverted from *revanchiste* ideas. Bismarck also found it useful to bargain with Britain: for British support for his overseas policies he would use his influence on the *Caisse de la Dette*, the international organization of Egypt's creditors, to back British rule in Egypt. Moreover, he saw that he could gain diplomatic advantages for Germany by setting France against Britain in West Africa, Italy against France in Tunisia and by using Leopold against both French and British interests in Central Africa.

By this time the industries of Europe were thirsty for every kind of raw material which could be poured into them. Cotton from Egypt, rubber from the Congo, palm oil from West Africa, were all eagerly sought by European industrialists, while their working classes could be fed from the sugar cane, coffee, cocoa, tea, bananas and dates to be found in tropical lands. Not only the lure of diamonds and gold attracted Europeans to South, West and Central Africa, but for a time a myth was given credence that the continent itself might be a new El Dorado. Meanwhile, as protectionist policies multiplied, so the temptation to take political control over areas which could then be brought under imperial economic direction grew until it appeared as a national compulsion. France, although for a period she allowed merchants from other nations to trade with her colonies, generally pursued a protectionist policy, keeping trade in Senegal, Guinea, the Ivory

[1] Gustav Freytag, quoted in Leonard Woolf, *Empire and commerce in Africa: A Study in Economic Imperialism*, p. 34.

Coast, Dahomey, Gabon and Madagascar, in the hands of her own merchants and maintaining naval forces to exclude foreigners. To her industrial merchants, still some way behind the manufacturing strength and skills of their counterparts in Britain, this appeared essential.

The outlook of such industrialists and merchants was expressed by a whole series of publicists. Lothar Bucher, an associate of Bismarck, was writing as early as 1867, 'Companies should be founded in the German seaports to buy lands in foreign countries and settle them with German colonies; also companies for commerce and navigation whose object would be to open new markets abroad for German manufacturers and to establish steamship lines. . . . Colonies are the best means of developing manufactures, export and import trade, and finally a respectable navy.' Less than twenty years later, Bismarck himself had been sufficiently converted to this view to declare to the Reichstag, 'Colonies would mean the winning of new markets for German industries, the expansion of trade, and a new field for German activity, civilization, and capital.' In Britain, Sir Charles Dilke took up the imperialist cudgels in his famous book, *Greater Britain*, and Froude followed with articles praising the glories of imperialism. Ten years later John Seeley saw his Cambridge lectures, *Expansion of England*, become a bestseller. Freidrich Fabri argued that the German surplus population should be able to emigrate and still live within the orbit of German civilization, whilst the historian Treitschke was teaching his students that 'every virile people has established colonial power.' In France Professor Leroy-Beaulieu was leading the political economists in advocacy of colonization, declaring that 'colonization is for France a question of life and death; either France will become a great African power, or in a century or two she will be no more than a secondary European power; she will count for about as much in the world as Greece and Rumania in Europe.'

Organizations and associations were formed with the object of promoting the concept of imperialism. In Britain the two most noteworthy were the Tory Primrose League and the Liberal Imperial Federation League. The efforts of various lobbies succeeded in persuading some leading politicians to espouse the cause of colonial expansion. Disraeli led the way in Britain, committing the Conservatives to a programme of imperialism and social reform, believing that this combination would not only further his conception of British progress but also appeal to the electorate, now rapidly increased in numbers, becoming ever more literate and thus progressively sensitive to persuasion from popular newspapers.

It should not be thought, however, that the entire capitalist system was united behind the drive to expand the empire. Pressure came mainly from the exporters and the manufacturers of cheap goods for exchange, like calico, alcohol or trinkets; from the importers of those raw materials to be found mainly in the tropics, rubber, cotton, coffee, tea, copra, palm oil and tin; from those engaged in the various branches of the shipping industry; from certain sections of the banking and insurance community; from the manufacturers of armaments and uniforms, of telegraph and railway equipment. There were still some sections of industry which believed that investment should be con-centrated at home, but the weight, not least the political weight, of the overseas lobby, was beginning to prove the heavier.

There were other factors in this era especially favourable to imperial expansion. During the preceding ninety years or so explorers had greatly increased Europeans' knowledge of the geography of Africa's interior. Mungo Park in West, Livingstone in Central, Speke and Burton in East Africa, have all been mentioned previously. Joseph Thomson, as late as 1879, led an exploration party to open up to Europeans Lakes Nyasa and Tanganyika, travelled inland from Mombasa, brought back knowledge of Kilimanjaro and Mount Kenya, penetrated to Victoria-Nyanza and later explored the area from the Benue to Lake Chad and the White Nile. These adventure tales excited the British and European populace; this was the age of Rider Haggard as well as of explorers. As we have seen, these explorers were supported by the business community or by geographical societies and Christian missions. But their revelations were of particular value to the traders who wished to buy and sell goods, to commanders who were sent to establish a military presence, and to statesmen attracted by the vision of controlling such areas and preventing them from falling into the hands of rivals.

Now scientific progress, including the invention of various mechani-cal appliances capable of overcoming the natural hazards of tropical areas, provided the physical means of travelling to parts of the continent hitherto inaccessible. The steamship greatly speeded communication across the oceans and, as we have seen in the case of the Niger, could be used to penetrate inland up certain rivers. The locomotive could in some regions overcome natural hazards, carrying heavy goods and equipment over vast distances. Electricity provided new forms of power, medical knowledge and drugs protection against disease. The repeating rifle could be employed to conquer native armies larger in numbers but equipped with far less deadly weapons.

Imperial expansion was also useful to politicians anxious to excite national enthusiasm and mobilize nationalist feelings to divert attention from social inequalities and class consciousness. The Christian missions, although often engaged in valuable educational and agricultural endeavours in addition to proselytizing, frequently became victims of persecution which could be used to arouse passions at home. Personality cults, such as that surrounding David Livingstone, also played a part in stimulating the vicarious excitement of newspaper readers in Britain. The ceremonial return of Livingstone's body from central Africa via Zanzibar under naval escort to Britain to be buried amongst the national heroes of Westminster Abbey, played no small part in enlisting a popular following for Disraeli's imperial policies. The growth of social Darwinism, based on distorted ideas of superior races and their civilizing duty to their inferiors, added yet another element to the popularization of imperial emotions. Moreover, there was a deep military connotation to every aspect of imperialism. Many of the later explorers themselves had a military background – Goldie and Lugard from Britain, Faidherbe, the explorer of Upper Egypt and De Brazza of Central Africa in France, Nachtigal, the German investigator of the Sudan. This military aspect of the imperialist ethic could be usefully exploited to stimulate jingoistic patriotism which politicians of the European states considered valuable in the increasingly nationalistic fervour of the late nineteenth century. The long experience of empire in British history had already greatly strengthened British nationalism by the time that the era of European colonial expansion opened. It was emotionally stimulated by the events of the thirty years before the first world war. This imperialist excitement was used to counter the increasing pressures of class consciousness as industrialism rose to maturity. The chauvinism which it instilled in the newly literate populace was to rise to a climax when, in 1914, the appeal for loyalty towards international working class solidarity found virtually no response.

All this may seem a very complex set of motives and there were certainly many diverse elements within the drive towards imperial expansion. Nevertheless, the controlling influence is clear and comparatively simple: Britain, enjoying industrial domination, was concerned to preserve the principle and practice of free trade throughout the world, knowing that she could sell her goods against any competitor. She believed that her continued prosperity depended on their preservation. Thus she exported machinery and capital goods as well as manufactures and by so doing she encouraged the growth of industrialism in Europe, America and, later, in other parts of the world. As these countries began to develop their industrial systems they did as Britain had done in her early days, raising protective tariff barriers to safeguard their infant industries. Britain therefore found it progressively more difficult to export goods into these markets and had to seek other outlets. Meanwhile, during this process, techniques were improving, industry, particularly in the newer countries, became more concentrated and productivity rose rapidly. There were thus increasing incentives for all industrial nations to seek new markets, whilst the development of better methods of transport and the exploration of new lands, as in the continent of Africa, provided ever-increasing opportunities to do so. Britain saw here a challenge to her economic prosperity, fearing that as the European powers began to enter the field of colonialism they would exclude her trade from their colonial markets. She was therefore induced to follow parallel paths: firstly, she must take possession of those lands, islands and strategic enclaves which safeguarded her world trade, especially those which protected her trading routes to India, the most lucrative of her possessions; secondly, she must forestall those of her competitors who were employing the same tactics and thus threatening British world power.

So far as Africa was concerned, this threat began in 1876 with the formation of the International African Association under the honorary presidency of King Leopold of Belgium. Despite the fact that at the time it was no more than a small cloud on the horizon, it was this event which initiated the scramble of European powers to seize their share of the African continent. It was under the auspices of the

Association that Stanley, having been rebuffed by the British government, returned to Africa in order to open up the Congo basin and organize it as the Congo Free State. Leopold quickly realized that the development of roads and of communications along the river would enable him personally to monopolize the trade of the basin provided that he could supply a railway system to the coast and steamers for river transport. His objectives were quickly challenged by the French under the leadership of De Brazza. The French interest appeared to threaten the position of British traders long active around the Congo, particularly when it extended westwards and included the annexation of parts of the Nigerian coast. Faced with this rivalry, Leopold sought recognition of his rights in the Congo, bribing the French with a secret guarantee that if he should not himself succeed in governing the Congo, it would revert to France. Bismarck also supported Leopold, in the hope of further embarrassing the British. When the British government tried to forestall Leopold's plans by supporting Portuguese claims over the river's mouth, it met opposition from some of its own merchants, who had been bribed by Leopold with the offer of commercial contracts.

By 1882 Britain had occupied Egypt, the most important strategic area of the whole continent. This unilateral action infuriated the French, who sought counter-measures by intensifying their development of West Africa in competition with the British merchants there. It was now suddenly revealed that Bismarck had reversed his former antagonism towards German colonial expansion, and during 1884–85 he declared protectorates over Togoland, the Cameroons and South-West Africa. With the Germans in East Africa opposite Zanzibar and the French in Madagascar, having stepped over the heads of the long-standing British missionary connections there, the British commercial position throughout the African continent had now come under severe challenge.

The meeting of the Berlin Conference called by Bismarck in 1884–85, ostensibly to discuss the affairs of the Congo, only increased British harassment. One of the Conference decisions was to declare that there should be free navigation on both the Niger and the Congo, thus frustrating attempts by British merchants to monopolize the former against their French competitors and by Leopold to dominate the latter.

Britain therefore had to react against these new challenges if she was to preserve, let alone extend, her position in Africa. George Goldie had already demonstrated one commercial method by which this could be done, when his new amalgamation trading up the Niger undercut its French competitors and forced them to sell out to his companies. Yet, if the British position was to be maintained in Egypt, it seemed politically essential for the British government to pay the price of allowing both French and German expansion in West Africa. The French had already begun to penetrate into the valley of the Senegal and had contemplated linking their position there by rail to the Upper Niger, where they could hope to channel off most of the trade from the West African hinterland. They were now allowed, virtually unchallenged, to lay claims to great areas of West Africa, although most of these were sparsely populated and of doubtful commercial value. Yet, with this French expansion and with the Germans declaring their two protectorates, the British position was confined to four comparatively well-defined territories, the Gambia, Sierra Leone, the Gold Coast and the Nigerian areas.

Following the Berlin Conference, therefore, the British government, now under the leadership of Lord Salisbury, turned its attention to the south, central and eastern areas of the continent. It declared a protectorate over Bechuanaland, thus frustrating any idea of linking German South-West Africa to the Boers in the Transvaal. Bechuanaland might not appear to be commercially attractive, yet it was the high road to the north and might lead to another Witwatersrand, rich in gold. Three years later, in 1888, Salisbury pursued the logic of the Bechuanaland protection and declared the area between the protectorate and the Zambesi a sphere of British interest. It was through Bechuanaland that in 1890 Cecil Rhodes's pioneer column of white settlers travelled to establish their camp in what became Southern Rhodesia. Not only was there by now some hope of mining in this area, but by declaring a British interest over it Salisbury prevented any chance of the Portuguese linking their East and West African colonies. Claims over Northern Rhodesia and Nyasaland followed naturally in 1889–90: the British had opened their road from the Cape into the heart of the continent.

In the east a quiet but significant series of manœuvres had taken place around the Horn immediately preceding the Berlin Conference of 1884–85. The importance to trade routes to Asia of the narrow straits at the southern end of the Red Sea is self-evident. Britain had established herself in Aden in 1839, and this was now matched by the French base across the waters at Obok on the Somali coast. In 1883 the Italians claimed nearby Assab and in the following year the French established themselves at Djibuti. Britain answered by declaring a protectorate over British Somaliland. Each power could therefore feel reasonably confident of its ability to oversee its commercial routes to Asia. But with Britain's control of the Suez Canal to the north it was clear that she, though prepared to allow certain concessions to her rivals, remained in firm control of this vital lifeline.

Further south Salisbury lost no time in meeting the potential threat to the Indian Ocean and the Nile Valley of the German presence on the mainland opposite Zanzibar. In 1886 he came to an agreement with Bismarck, dividing the main area of the Sultan's East African dominions between their two countries. This allowed for a British sphere of influence over what came to be called Kenya, with an option on its extension into Uganda, thus foreshadowing the reconquest of the Sudan, protecting the Upper Nile and opening the possibility of developing trade with the well-organized societies of Uganda.

Salisbury completed his African dispositions when, in 1890, he negotiated a comprehensive agreement with Bismarck by which Britain ceded to Germany the island of Heligoland in exchange for German recognition of the British position in Zanzibar, Kenya, Uganda, Northern Rhodesia and Bechuanaland, and of the boundary between Nigeria and the Cameroons. In the same year, agreement was reached with the French on the frontier between Nigeria and Dahomey, whilst Britain recognized the French protectorate over Madagascar. In the following year agreement was negotiated with the Portuguese establishing the frontiers between the Rhodesias, Nyasaland and Portugal's territories.

Within these few years, therefore, nine-tenths of the African continent had been divided between the European powers. Yet, it should be noted that this partition was so far little more than a series of paper transactions. Vast areas were claimed as colonies, protectorates or spheres of influence, with somewhat vague lines dividing them from their neighbours. But at this stage there was very little actual occupation of the new dependencies by European forces or administrators. Indeed, for some years to come, the actual demarcation of frontier lines, particularly between the French and British in West Africa, continued to be either negotiated or established by a military presence.

For the time being, the most active agents of the European powers were commercial companies rather than military forces. The United Africa Company had been established in the 1870s and by 1886 this had become the Royal Niger Company. Two years later the British East Africa Company was formed and the following year the British South Africa Company. As the European governments had only a tenuous control over the vast areas won by diplomacy, they were very willing to allow these new colonial companies both to pursue their trading interests and to exercise some degree of administrative supervision, and granted them charters accordingly. When in difficulties, of course, the companies could call for national military support. Thus, for the first twenty years or so after partition it was they who were mainly responsible for confronting Africans with European people and European culture.

It is significant to note that all these arrangements, political, diplomatic, commercial and military, were made in Europe by Europeans. The partition of Africa took place without reference to and without consideration of those factors important to Africans. The geography, economics, tribal habitation within the continent, African kingdoms, religions, languages and social structures were ignored. The continent was divided solely according to the interests, will and balance of power of the European imperial states. They divided Africa into a mosaic of European possessions, irrespective of the interests of the Africans living within them.

Salisbury gained for Britain a substantial share from the division of the African continent, though his main concern was to expand British imperial possessions only in so far as they were important to essential British national interests. Yet, despite this vast expansion of the British Empire in Africa and elsewhere, no substantial increase in the proportion of British investment or trade to the colonies seems to have followed. During the years succeeding Salisbury's settlements, the larger part of British investment continued to flow to North America, Oceania and Europe, whilst overseas investment, attracted by higher rates of return, continued to rise. After the turn of the century there was a considerable investment boom, and just before the first world war overseas investment actually exceeded that in the domestic field.

This was a period in which earlier British investment overseas was yielding major profits within the national economy. From 1870 onwards the large balance of payments had been swollen by increasing income from previous investments. After the turn of the century this was further increased by funds accruing from the Indian settlements. By 1913 nearly one-tenth of the national income derived from payments on investment overseas, but only one-sixth of these came from the colonies. Indeed, during the boom in overseas investment which continued from the turn of the century until 1914, two-thirds of new investment went to the American continent. As another tenth flowed to Europe, the whole of Africa and Asia was left with only a combined total of one-quarter. The pattern continued as before. It was the industrial nations which attracted capital; the only industrialized countries within the Empire were the dominions, Canada being included in the American total and South Africa in the African. Thus the new colonial territories in Africa and Asia barely participated at all in this new flow of British capital.

Nevertheless, despite the focal importance of world-wide free trade, leading in consequence to a policy of protecting trade routes' by expanding the Empire, there were those within the British political scene who would have liked to use the new imperial possessions to establish a form of British *zollverein*. During the last decade of the century British overseas trade seriously declined, partly through increased competition, so it seemed natural to some that the nation's merchants should turn to the Empire in order to replace the losses suffered in trading relations with others.

As mentioned above, this was a period of widespread popular excitement over imperialism. The deeds of adventurers like Stanley and Cecil Rhodes supplied numerous themes for the literature of the popular press. The jingoism often associated with some of the explorers was reinforced by the knowledge that vast areas on school atlases were now coloured British red. The African continent as a land of exotic savagery, spectacular pictures and exciting wild animals seized the public imagination. The fact that Britain had advanced in all directions across the continent, taking possession of a new African Empire, appealed to the public mind. Added titillation was induced by melodramatic military adventures such as the Matabele Wars, the Jameson Raid and, finally, the Boer War itself. The fact that the Royal Jubilee in 1887 had been celebrated by the first assembly of Empire prime ministers contributed a more serious content to the imperial mood. Behind the calling of the conference was the Imperial Federation League, combining initiatives from the main imperial publicists of the time, Seeley, Froude, Rosebery and Bryce.

This new movement towards an imperial focus produced its own champion. Joseph Chamberlain had thrown down the gauntlet in 1894 when he addressed his Birmingham followers in social imperialist terms strongly reminiscent of Disraeli: 'Give me the demand for more goods and then I will undertake to give plenty of employment in making the goods; and the only thing, in my opinion, that the Government can do in order to meet this great difficulty that we are considering is so to arrange its policy that every inducement shall be given to the demand; that new markets shall be created, and that old markets shall be effectually developed. You are aware that some of my opponents please themselves occasionally by finding names for me and among other names lately they have been calling me a Jingo. I am no more a Jingo than you are. But for the reasons and arguments I have put before you to-night, I am convinced that it is a necessity, as well as a duty, for us to uphold the Dominion and Empire which we now possess. For these reasons among others I would never lose the hold which we now have over our great Indian dependency – by far the greatest and most valuable of all the customers we have or shall ever have in this country. For the same reasons I approve of the continued occupation of Egypt; and for the same reasons I have urged upon this Government, and upon previous Governments, the necessity for using every legitimate opportunity to extend our influence and control in that great African continent which is now being opened up to civilization and to commerce.'[1] Imperial fervour played no small part in the return of the Tories in the 1895 election.

Together with Salisbury and Balfour, Joseph Chamberlain was one of the three most powerful figures in the Conservative party. When

[1] Quoted in Woolf, *op. cit.*

he chose to take the office of Colonial Secretary, the significance allocated to the new Empire was clearly revealed. Chamberlain, who had been one of the original subscribers to the Royal Niger Company, again made his outlook perfectly clear in the year of the election by declaring, 'I regard many of our colonies as being in the condition of undeveloped estates, and estates which can never be developed without imperial assistance,'[1] and when he told an Imperial Conference in London, 'I believe that the toast of Empire would have carried with it all that is meant by Commerce and Empire, because, gentlemen, the Empire, to parody a celebrated expression, is commerce.'[2]

For the next ten years Chamberlain was to use all his political influence and powers of persuasion with the industrial and commercial communities to guide British policy into imperial channels. His object was to build the Empire into a kind of modified federation, with Britain at the centre, commanding combined military forces and controlling a vast trading organization based on a policy of preferential imperial tariffs. His Tariff Reform League deliberately aimed to supersede the traditional British commercial principle of free trade with a system of protection which would give a privileged position to the countries of the Empire. Thus, in the person of Joseph Chamberlain, the concepts of imperial consolidation and tariff protection against Britain's new industrial and commercial rivals were combined.

But, although Chamberlain was the personality, his influence would have been minimal if his ideas had not represented the interests of a considerable section of those directly concerned with the control of the British economy. The landlords supported him because they hoped to find protection for their agricultural products against competitors now pouring cheap food into Britain. The steel barons and other producers of heavy industrial goods sought tariff defences against the competition of Germans and Americans, now offering cheaper steel. Yet the textile manufacturers still wanted cheap cotton, engineering and shipbuilding enjoyed the advantages of cheap imported steel, the working and middle-classes were reluctant to sacrifice their cheap food, and exporters in general feared reprisals against tariffs in overseas markets.

---

[1] Quoted in Brown, *op. cit.* p. 103.
[2] Quoted in Woolf *op. cit.*

Chamberlain eventually failed in all his objectives. Although the type of monopoly which could most profit from protection had not yet become a major force in Britain's politico-economic world, he was not defeated so much by his industrial opponents as by others. His domestic background was based in the field of Midland manufacturing, but Britain's economic power at this time derived far more from the merchant bankers than from commercial industry and manufacturing. Chamberlain was defeated by the City, which now controlled the dominant section of Britain's overseas economic wealth. It gained its profits from loans, brokerage, insurance and bills of exchange, the financial paraphernalia which smoothed the channels of world trade. London had become the financial capital of the world so it was still in the City's interest to maintain free trade throughout the globe, together with British overseas' positions of strength from which to defend it. The City was concerned to see that British exports made their way freely to the four quarters of the globe, there to compete on terms which were still largely advantageous with those of other nations; to keep trade flowing around the world because a large part of it still brought financial returns to London; perhaps above all, to ensure that the interest on earlier loans, now rapidly growing and providing capital for further investment, was maintained. In order to ensure this, it was essential to maintain British domination of the economic policies of foreign governments throughout the world. In maintaining such international political strength the merchant bankers were in a very influential position inside and on the fringes of British governments and their establishments. America and Germany would seem to be presenting new threats to this position, both through their challenge in world markets and by their national expansionist policies. So it might seem necessary to the City for Britain to increase her colonial possessions in order to protect her world power; but this power was still to be exercised essentially in the preservation of free trade, not in its supersession by the restrictive effects of protection.

There was one exception to the general rule that the British were not interested in the investment prospects of Africa and it may be that it was this exception which misled Hobson into exaggerating the link between the drive for overseas investment and the growth of imperial expansion. That exception was South Africa. Here, prompted by Cecil Rhodes, the diamonds and gold king, direct investment grew to be of such importance to the City that it became worthwhile, not only for the British government to extend its imperial possessions, but eventually to fight a war in its defence. As we have already seen, British investment in South Africa rose from negligible proportions to £34 million in 1885. By the end of the century this figure approximated to £200 million and by 1911 to £351 million, a sum equal to the investment in India though still much lower than that in the American continent and somewhat below investment in Australasia.[1] This tremendous increase in investment was followed by some expansion of trade, but this was by no means the main concern. In the thirty years before the first world war, trade with South Africa had multiplied threefold, yet, despite the fact that investment was now equal to that in India, the trading quantities were less than one-third those with the Indians.

The central interest amongst investors in South Africa was in the mining of diamonds and gold, an activity which raised the country to international importance from 1870 onward. Before this date South Africa was a backward, rural, half-forgotten colony, of virtually no interest to British investors and of little more to her traders. There was some small commercial enterprise, including some amongst the Africans, mainly supplying the Cape settlement with certain of its needs, or assisting the settlers in Natal – with the aid of Indian labour – to grow and market their sugar. One example is noteworthy. In the second half of the nineteenth century certain African communities were persuaded to substitute blankets for their traditional leather clothes, made from animal skins. The production of these blankets provided employment in the wool mills of the West Riding of Yorkshire, where the 'traditional tribal' blanket designs were invented. Incidentally, the sale of these blankets provides an instance of how the need for money was created amongst Africans, helping to induce them to enter the wage-labour market.[2]

But it was not until the discovery of diamonds in 1867 that the outside world became seriously aware of, let alone interested in, South Africa. The rush to stake claims in Griqualand was only one part of the economic expansion which followed from this discovery. Before long, Cecil Rhodes and his associates had bought up the concessions and

[1] Robinson and Gallagher, *Africa and the Victorians*, p. 6.
[2] H. M. Robertson *South Africa – Economic and Political Aspects*.

7

established the De Beers' monopoly. The capital accumulated from diamonds was applied to opening the country more thoroughly by the building of railways. It was this capital also which made possible the mining of gold along the Witwatersrand from 1885 onwards. The presence of gold in this area had been known for some years, but, unlike diamond mining, the extraction of gold required large-scale capital and a high degree of organization. This now became available for the first time as a result of the investment flowing into the diamond industry and the returns which it commanded. Deep-level mining of gold on the Witwatersrand attracted even greater investment and, by the end of the century, an African labour force of about a hundred thousand was being employed.

Cecil Rhodes set himself to exploit these dramatic windfalls to the full. He had shown through his De Beers' company how a monopoly could capture the market. He followed this achievement by the establishment of his British South Africa Company, which set out to establish a similar monopoly of mining concessions throughout southern Africa. His agents raced rival French and Portuguese prospectors to obtain treaties with scores of chiefs, who conceded sole rights over minerals found in their territory in return for money, trinkets, firearms or liquor. Rhodes enlisted the support of British governments to pursue the same policy, in their case gaining the mineral rights as the price of British protection. He was thereby successful both in attracting the capital he required from the City of London and the support he needed from the British government to pursue the political expansion essential for the protection of his investments and commercial interests. He persuaded some people in Britain that his adventures could provide a solution for the problem of the increasing British population, offering emigration as an alternative to class civil war, and as we have seen, this argument convinced even the Trade Union Congress at the end of the 1870s, illustrating one aspect of the attractions offered by Disraeli's prescription of imperialism and social reform.

The outlook of Rhodes also largely coincided with that of Joseph Chamberlain. Rhodes's belief in the expansion of the British Empire in Africa and British control of its mining potential, investment and markets, complemented Chamberlain's attack on free trade and his efforts both to expand and to integrate the Empire. The Jameson Raid of 1895 may have led to the fall of Rhodes as a politician; it did not divert his collaborator, Chamberlain, from pursuing the policies on which they both agreed. As a consequence the British Empire went to war in 1899 largely in order to protect the huge stake of the City in South African gold. Once the war was won the needs of the gold mines were given a higher priority than Britain's diplomatic reputation, and Chinese labour, despite international protests, was brought in to supplement that of the Africans. In the decade before the first world war capital was attracted to the lucrative mines on an even larger scale; accompanied now by an ever-increasing number of British immigrants. South Africa had, indeed, become a classic example of the extension of Empire for the purpose of investing high interest overseas capital, but it remained the unique exception in British imperial Africa.

So far in this chapter we have confined ourselves almost exclusively to the manœuvres and objectives of European states in their partition of the African continent. This is warranted because virtually the entire initiative came from Europe. Indeed, with the exception of South Africans and Egyptians, the partition of the continent owed nothing to the activities of the Africans themselves.

It is difficult to assess the depth and unwise to generalize on the extent of the impact produced by this new British relation to African society. It varied from region to region. In the commercial areas near the West African coast, for instance, trading conflicts were simply intensified. In the north of both Nigeria and the Gold Coast, rivalry with French ambitions brought British military and administrative forces into contact with certain African societies for the first time. In South Africa, as we have already seen, the impact on white Africans – the Afrikaners – was catastrophic, as their old rural society was uprooted by the twin forces of mining and imperial military intervention. In Rhodesia and, to a lesser extent, Nyasaland, many Africans lost their land to the new European settlers and this pattern was to be followed a little later in Kenya. In Uganda local religious and political conflicts were exploited and intensified by the British in the course of their colonization. Control over Egypt was used for the reconquest of the Sudan, involving large-scale loss of life and an extension of the imperial fiat.

Three general effects can be isolated in this variegated picture. First, despite the expansion of colonial possessions, the British politico-economic establishment remained hostile to the expenditure of public money on the administration of colonies. The economic outlook did not change with the altered colonial perspective. Reluctance to incur expense on colonial peoples survived Britain's participation in the carve-up of Africa; any expenditure was still held to be wasteful, contrary to national economic interests. Consequently, the new colonies were themselves expected to raise the expenses of administration. Where these attempts were unsuccessful, or where the activities of the traders and administrators invoked increased imperial military operations, grants-in-aid were only provided with extreme reluctance by British governments. In order to raise these administrative expenses some form of taxation became essential, and as a result, from the early days of colonization, the new imperial presence was directly associated by Africans with demands for taxes from alien rulers.

The collection of taxes led to a second general effect. Taxation could only be imposed where some form of cash economy either already existed or could be created. In the trading and mining areas this was comparatively simple, but these were very few. Elsewhere, the first necessity was to build roads, railways and harbours in order to provide the elementary infrastructure of an exchange economy. At the same time, mines were being sunk and plantations cleared. All this led to a growing demand for labour. The combination of a taxation system, and the building of an economy to support it, thus led to many Africans being virtually forced out of their settled communal life into selling a part of their labour to the colonial government, to the mining companies or to European farmers. Sometimes they received no direct payment at all, their work being taken as commutation of tax liability. Often, too, the recruitment of labour was conducted by chiefs, prepared to work with the colonial government's officers. This process, therefore, provided many chiefs with new authoritarian powers, not least to rid themselves of opponents by conscripting them for labour.

The third effect arose out of the situation outlined above. African communities had to decide whether it was in their interest to work with the new colonial administrators or to resist them. Particularly at the beginning of the colonial period, only a handful of government officials or company agents appeared in the new colonies, perhaps together with a few soldiers, but in some cases wishing to raise local armies of Africans. Their power to administer, tax or trade depended very largely on their ability to secure local allies. Thus conflicts between rival African societies, which we have already seen develop earlier in parts of West Africa, were exacerbated throughout most of the new colonies. The colonial powers bought cooperation by offering assistance to one community in rivalry with its neighbours. The alternative for the Africans was either to cooperate with the colonial authorities or to risk military attack, the deposition and exile of their chief, loss of their land and the destruction of their community. Yet, even when it became apparent that the small initial military forces would be supplemented by the imperial power whenever serious resistance was offered, many African societies in British and French colonies continued to resist until well into the twentieth century. The general effect of this imperial impact, therefore, was to aggravate fragmentation within African society and to exacerbate hostility between communities.

The new claims for British political control over African territories had been invoked in order to protect British freedom to trade, and were used by British trading communities in Africa to defend their interests against both European and African rivals. Thus when, in 1886, Goldie's Niger Company was given its Royal Charter, the mutual interest of the British government and the traders became apparent. The Company accepted the responsibility for administering the Niger area, and in exchange it received governmental approval for a virtual monopoly of trade, despite the fact that under the Berlin Treaty trade on the Niger was supposed to be free.

These powers gave Goldie and his Company a strong lever against their French, German and rival British competitors, and moreover, it left the Company free to deal with those African merchants who were inclined to obstruct its activities. The famous Nigerian trader, Ja Ja for instance, had established almost a monopoly in the supplies of palm oil from the interior. When attempts were made to bypass the routes he controlled, he retaliated by interfering with the new trading communications, thus provoking British merchants to form an African Association to reduce the price they paid for the oil. When Ja Ja circumvented this manœuvre the British traders appealed to the government in London, who instructed Sir Harry Johnston, Vice-Consul in the Cameroons, to free the obstructed trade routes. Ja Ja was captured, tried and deported to the West Indies. The outlook in London could not have been more clearly expressed than by the words of Lord

Salisbury, 'We need not discuss the principles, . . . they amount to this, that when a merchant differs from a native chief as to their respective rights, the native chief is to be deported.'

Similar commercial considerations led to the subjugation of the city states in Yorubaland. Again there was interference in the trading routes, partly deliberate and partly caused by conflicts between the Yoruba themselves. British traders also feared the competition of the French, particularly through neighbouring Porto Novo in Dahomey, which France was in the process of conquering, but by 1895, with the conquest of Oyo by British troops, this important oil-producing area of the Yoruba people had been brought under British control.

With the deposition of Nana of the Jekri, a chief similar to Ja Ja who had tried to establish his own monopoly, and with the submission of Brass, whose warriors had attacked a company depot and paid the price of seeing their town destroyed by British gunfire, only Benin remained outside the control of the British government-merchant alliance. The ruler of Benin tried to resist British expansion and to restrict the trading routes into his country, whilst continuing to allow slave trading from his territory, but when a British consul and his party were ambushed and massacred a military and naval force invaded Benin State, occupied it and deported its Oba.

This completed the conquest of the southern areas of Nigeria. In the meantime, Goldie had made an important treaty with the Sultan of Sokoto in 1885. By this move he guaranteed friendly relations with most of Hausaland in the north, though the Company's armed forces, the West African Frontier Force, had to be used to conquer Nupe and Ilorin on the borders of Yorubaland. In this area, however, Goldie and his supporters were confronted with French forces advancing from Dahomey. The strategic town of Borgu could only be occupied in 1894 after a French expedition had been forced to withdraw. By now, however, the threat of open conflict with the French induced the British government to abandon its principle of non-interference. It was persuaded to provide both finance and officers for the West African Frontier Force in 1897, and two years later the Company's charter was revoked, compensation was paid and the British government itself accepted responsibility for the administration and military defence of Nigeria.

In the Gold Coast the kingdom of Ashanti remained the largest stumbling block to British control over commercial development. Unrest in Ashanti itself aggravated the dislocation of trade, for during the 1880s and early 1890s agitation gained momentum within the kingdom for a reconquest of the former tributary states between Ashanti and the coast. At the same time, British merchants along the coast were pressing for further intervention in Ashanti itself. When Prempeh won the Stool as Asantehene, after a number of his predecessors had been destooled for not adopting a more aggressive policy, it was clear that further conflict was imminent. In 1895 the British authorities accused the Ashanti of breaking their former treaty agreements and demanded that they accept a British protectorate. When the demand was ignored, British forces marched on Kumasi. Prempeh, together with some of his family and entourage, was exiled to the Seychelles, a British protectorate was imposed and a Resident installed in Kumasi. Five years later, in 1900, when the Governor demanded that the Ashanti surrender their golden Stool, a nine months' war ensued, culminating in Britain annexing the kingdom as a Crown Colony.

Having conquered the Ashanti stronghold it was now possible for the British to extend their authority to the northern territories whose trade previously had been controlled by Ashanti merchants. Protectorate treaties were now negotiated with the chiefs of the north, thus stemming the advances of the French from the Ivory Coast and of the Germans from Togoland. An incidental consequence of the subsequent agreement with the Germans over the boundary with Togoland and the French in the Ivory Coast was to split the tribes on the frontiers, the Ewes being divided between the Gold Coast and Togoland and the Twi-speaking peoples between the Gold Coast and the Ivory Coast.

In East Africa, opposition to the arrival of British administration was more scattered and less organized. The Sultan of Zanzibar, in his exposed island position, had to accept the protectorate which Britain imposed in 1890. Already before this date his mainland territories had been taken from him and were being partitioned between the British East Africa Company and its German counterpart. He was left with a strip only ten miles wide along the coastline, part of which was bought by the Germans and the rest leased by the British company. It was the Arabs, who had been accustomed to trade in slaves and ivory throughout east-central Africa, who objected most strongly to the incursion of the British. From 1887, for ten years, spasmodic conflicts continued between Arabs and British, from Lake Nyasa northwards into Uganda. In Uganda itself this conflict coalesced with local rivalries. Here the kingdom of Buganda, where Christian groups had overcome Moslem opposition, supported the British occupation. It was in Bunyoro, already a rival of Buganda, that the principal resistance was centred. There the Arabs and the local Moslems mounted a joint opposition, which was only finally defeated in the last year of the century with the help of the Baganda. Buganda was rewarded for its assistance by being given slices of the rival Bunyoro kingdom.

By this time, learning that the East Africa Company intended to withdraw, the British government had established a protectorate over Uganda, and shortly afterwards set up the East African Protectorate, which was to become Kenya. Indian troops were introduced to meet the resistance of those East African tribes, like the Kikuyu, Kamba and Nandi, who opposed the European incursion. By 1901 a railway had been completed from Mombasa to Kisumu, the upper reaches of the Nile had been safeguarded from German and French interference, the often illicit trade of the Arabs had been suppressed, and the fertile uplands of East Africa were lying open to settlement by farmers from Britain. Meanwhile Kitchener had taken his Anglo–Egyptian troops into the Sudan. Although this was now an orderly state run by the Mahdiyya, Kitchener conquered the country and occupied Khartoum, in the face of fanatical resistance by the Mahdist armies. It seemed to the British that yet another threat to the Nile, this time from possible Italian or French invasion, had been thwarted – although not before Britain and France had nearly gone to war over it.

British expansion into Rhodesia provided examples of almost every facet of the new imperialist perspective. Here was the opportunity to forestall the expansion of Germans and Portuguese; here, too, were the prospects of investment in mining, a growth in trade and the settlement of white farmers; and in Rhodesia the resistance of the African population was as strong as anywhere in the continent.

Having blocked any German pretensions to penetrate into Central Africa from South-West Africa by the declaration of a protectorate over Bechuanaland, Cecil Rhodes set his sights on what he hoped would be the mineral wealth of the Rhodesias. He made a powerful effort through his agents to capture what was thought to be the wealthy Katanga kingdom of Msiri, but eventually had to be content with its partition between Leopold's Congo and what later came to be the Copper Belt of Northern Rhodesia. He also found that the Portuguese in Mozambique were trying to impose their authority over Nyasaland and the Zambezi Basin. Meanwhile, Kruger's Afrikaners in the Transvaal were persuading the Paramount Chief of the Ndebele, Lobengula, to accept a treaty of friendship with them. Such an alliance might well frustrate all Rhodes's schemes for securing mining rights in what he hoped would be the mineral-rich areas of Matabeleland and Mashonaland.

Rhodes was prepared to pay for the support of the British government. Salisbury secured him a Charter for his British South Africa Company, giving it power to govern the Rhodesias. In exchange, Rhodes gave his financial support to the government of Nyasaland, soon to become a protectorate, and promised to extend rail and telegraph communications as far as the Zambezi. Sir Harry Johnston went out to Nyasaland to forestall the Portuguese by declaring a British protectorate and to supervise the negotiation of agreements with the chiefs. By 1890, under threat of naval action, the Portuguese had been coerced into withdrawing their troops from Central Africa and retiring into Mozambique. In the same year, Lewanika, the Litunga of Barotseland, signed a treaty with one of Rhodes's agents, though he seems to have had no idea that this gave the Company control over his land and minerals.

In 1890, also, a pioneer column, led by Colonel Starr Jameson and including five hundred white policemen, trekked from Bechuanaland into Matabeleland and on to establish Fort Salisbury in Mashonaland. There, land was taken from the Africans, farms given to white settlers and military forts built. But the early settlers were disappointed. Little gold was found and the land did not seem suitable for European-type farming. They began to think enviously of Matabeleland, where rumour had it that the soil was better and gold more plentiful. Raiding from both sides across the rough border between the two territories began to resemble conditions on the eighteenth century frontier further south beside the Great Fish River. Following a large raid by the Ndebele warriors in 1893, Lobengula's capital at Bulawayo was attacked by the Company's mounted police with cannons and machine guns. European firearms proved that in central as in South Africa the lands and peoples of African societies were to be subject to the will of the white man. Lobengula fled and the Ndebele followed the Shona into servitude under the white invaders. They lost their lands and cattle, were confined to reserves, forced to work on white men's farms and to pay taxes to the Company governor.

Both the Ndebele and the Shona had been tricked by false promises and deceived by smooth words, but their spirit of resistance was not yet shattered. In 1896, the Ndebele rose against the settler government and killed a number of white farming families. They were followed by the Shona, so that the two communities were fighting a war for their lands simultaneously against the new white settlers and the Company which had imposed its rule. Rhodes himself, showing great courage, personally persuaded the Ndebele chiefs to submit and accept Company rule. The following year the Shona had to bow to the superior power of the white man's machine guns. Rhodesia had been conquered by the white invaders, who were now left in virtually unfettered control of the colony.

If the Africans in west, east and central Africa were able to offer no more than a valiant but futile resistance to the imposition of British rule across their territories, the white Africans of the south proved to have a great deal more power in their defiance. The political issue involved was whether the Afrikaner nation, led by its national stereotype, Paul Kruger, was to establish hegemony over South Africa; or whether the wider concept of Cecil Rhodes, linking Boer and Briton in joint exploitation of southern-central Africa under the British crown and flag, was to prevail. The central economic issue was simply who was to control mineral mining, particularly in the Transvaal, but possibly in the future in Rhodesia also. Rhodes was convinced that the Kruger-style political economy must be removed if his imperial schemes were to be successful. After the ignominious failure of Jameson's Raid in 1895, Rhodes had to leave political life, but by this time Chamberlain and his followers in the British government, together with the City financiers, had accepted Rhodes's thesis. The agent chosen to represent this policy and to succeed Rhodes in implementing it was Sir Alfred Milner, the High Commissioner. He succeeded in provoking Kruger and his Afrikaners into war by 1899.

To Milner the issue between Britain and Kruger was of crucial importance to the British Empire. He believed that unless the Afrikaners were brought under complete British imperial control, they would gain power over the whole of South Africa, which would then be lost to the British Empire. Chamberlain himself shared this view, as he illustrated in declaring once that, 'Our supremacy in South Africa and our existence as a great power in the world is involved.'

The Afrikaners, however, were much more strongly organized than the Africans who resisted British imperialism. The sixty thousand of them who fought in the name of Afrikaner nationalism challenged the whole British Empire, which had to call on four hundred thousand troops to effect their defeat. In the process of this bitter war, Afrikaner farms were laid waste across the republics, whilst one hundred thousand women and children were herded into camps, where thousands of them died. By 1902 the Afrikaners had to sue for peace. British supremacy was assured and the heavy investment of the City of London in the Witwatersrand was protected by the imperial government under conditions so favourable that it was almost doubled by the time of the first world war. But the bitterness of the Boer War lingered on. In the end it was not to be the ideas of Rhodes, Chamberlain or Milner which prevailed in South Africa; Paul Kruger finally had his revenge, although he did not live to see it.

During the last quarter of the nineteenth century, therefore, the relationship between Africans and British was fundamentally altered. Elements of that change had been visible, particularly in West and South Africa, earlier in the century, but the last twenty-five years saw a dramatic set of new relations established throughout the continent. On the maps, what had been represented as vast unbroken areas were now criss-crossed by frontier lines; whereas the British had been content to indicate their presence in a few coastal regions – Gambia, Sierra Leone, Gold Coast, Lagos, Cape Colony and Natal – now British ownership and political rule was claimed over thousands of square miles and millions of their African inhabitants. Administrators, soldiers and company agents from Britain were seen in thousands of African villages for the first time; they brought with them the power to give orders and enforce obedience. For the relationship between Britons and Africans, which, for three hundred years had been one of merchants trading with merchants, had suddenly been transformed into that between master and subject.

Chapter 8

Masters and Subjects

At first it was usually the agents of companies who came into personal contact with the African people. But from the time that imperial rule was first imposed, the authority of the British government was always present in the new relationship between Britons and Africans. Whenever there were trading disputes, differences over taxation, opposition to conscription into armies or labour battalions, the power of Whitehall lying behind the dictat of British officials, agents or settlers, gave the relationship its unequal character. Wherever the interests of Britons came under pressure, the British government could be called on to tilt the scales. For it was now recognized by governments of both parties at Westminster that if colonial authority was to be maintained British forces would have to be deployed wherever British citizens encountered opposition.

As we have seen, the power of London had been increasingly thrown into relations between British and Africans in South and West Africa during the course of the nineteenth century; but at that time it could never be taken for granted. British governments were still reluctant to intervene in African situations, even when their citizens were in danger. Cape governments often had their request for intervention rejected and when their pleas were heeded, it was only after serious debate in London. British merchants on the West African coast were expected to handle their own affairs to an even greater degree, finding most Whitehall administrations unsympathetic to their demands for imperial protection.

The most dramatic occasion on which a British government withheld assistance was, of course, when Gordon lost his life in Khartoum. By this time – 1885 – imperial sentiments had begun to mount, and although Gordon was in Egyptian, not British, employ, many people in Britain thought that Gladstone's government ought to have rescued him. That it did not do so was largely because of hesitation over the expense involved. It was still felt by many of Gladstone's ministers that public money should not be spent on an issue which was not directly related to the national interest. The Gordon incident, however, marked the end of this *laissez-faire* attitude. Public outcry over Gordon's fate taught British politicians that they could no longer blindly follow the precepts of Adam Smith. Even thirteen years later it was felt necessary to appease popular emotions over Gordon's death by reconquering the Sudan and collectively punishing the Sudanese in a most uncivilized 'civilizing mission'. It can be argued that by this time imperial expansion was now acceptable to the economic theorists, that rivalry with other expanionsist European states now took precedence over reluctance to spend public funds on imperial crises. Yet, whatever the motivation of British policy, the lesson for Africans was unmistakeable: whenever and wherever they found themselves in conflict with Britons they could now expect to be opposed by British imperial forces.

This superior power based on the metropolitan country was to remain the essential element in the new, unequal relationship between Africans and Britons down to the last days of colonial rule in the late 1950s and early 1960s. This was the vital influence in the changed relationship, but there were other effects which arose out of colonial government. The period from partition to 1914 was mainly taken up with establishing various forms of imperial administration in each territory. Although all the European imperial powers claimed large areas as part of their new colonial empires and agreed between themselves on their frontiers, few regions were actually occupied by European authorities. Even after the various army manœuvres were completed and boundaries delimited, the European powers had still to discover how to impose their authority on their new colonial subjects. This had usually to be achieved through trial and error for, although Britain and France had some experience of colonial government, no state had ever before tried to rule such large areas or such widely diffused communities.

Britain had the most extensive experience of ruling colonial subjects, but her history in America, the West Indies, India, Australasia or South Africa provided her with few lessons relevant to the government of her new African territories. In all the colonies except India she had been accustomed to see her own people setting up their homes, planting their own culture, taking with them familiar economic activities and political institutions. And when she tried to adopt a similar policy to that used earlier in India by entrusting administration to chartered companies, she quickly found that this was now anachronistic and inadequate. The companies in West and East Africa had surrendered their charters before the end of the nineteenth century, unable to cope with the complexities of the colonial relationship. Only in Rhodesia, where Rhodes's British South Africa Company reigned until 1923, was the earlier model of the East Indies Company effective, and only there because of the conquest of Africans by South African forces and reliance on white settlers.

But if Britain, like the other European imperial powers, had few precedents on which to base her infant administration in Africa, those responsible for her colonial government soon discovered that one factor of administration was crucial. Whitehall might modify its traditional antipathy towards spending public funds on colonial expansion; it might even be willing to send imperial troops to suppress the African rebellions which persisted into the world war years; but governments had no intention of dipping into their treasuries to finance the adminstration of the colonies they had acquired. It was the first duty of the administrator to raise his revenues from his own subjects, as had been customary in the older colonies.

The early governors all had to find some means by which to extract money to pay for administrative expenses. Almost all the new colonial subjects were peasants living a subsistence life, cattle-herders, or nomads. Few were engaged in any cash transactions or used money for any purpose. So, if revenue was to be raised, methods had to be devised to introduce cash economies. In other words, the lives and work of many Africans had to be changed by direct conscious action on the part of the colonial administrators.

It was from the various methods devised by governors and commissioners to secure these funds that arose some of the most important economic changes experienced by Africans from the new colonial impact. One of the most important was certainly railway-building. Often the railway was of greater value than the road, for roads in tropical areas could frequently become impassable. Railways were also much more useful, particularly at this early stage of internal combustion development, for carrying large and heavy loads.

The development of Africa's railway systems had a multi-purpose. South Africa had shown the way. From the building of the first Cape Colony line at the end of the 1850s, through the rest of the century, the two colonies and the two republics were criss-crossed with lines as their economies developed exchange potentials. After the discovery of Kimberley's diamonds and the gold of Witwatersrand, the incentives for railway-building quickly soared. At the same time the railways became subject to political dispute. Their direction and their control became a major factor in both the security and the economic development of those areas through which they passed. Whether the rapidly rising imports and exports of the Rand were to be routed to Lourenço Marques or to Cape Town, Durban, Port Elizabeth and East London became one of the vital issues of international relations in Southern Africa during the late nineteenth century. And when Rhodes decided to extend his empire northward into Rhodesia, his venture was based on building the rail from Salisbury to Umtali, later extended to the port of Beira, together with the linking of Bulawayo to the Cape system through Bechuanaland. A few years afterwards this was pushed through into Northern Rhodesia, to Livingstone, Lusaka, Broken Hill and Ndola, and eventually into the Congo.

The earlier lessons of the south were not lost on the new administrators nor on the army officers. They saw that railways had been invaluable not only to the economic development of Southern Africa, but to the imposition of imperial rule. They had been essential for the successful prosecution of the Boer War, for suppressing the Ndebele and Shona, for dealing with various African uprisings in the Cape and Natal. So Kitchener had no hesitation in basing his reconquest of the Sudan on the building of a railway from Wadi Halfa to Atbara and Khartoum; the Ashanti wars produced the line from Takoradi to Kumasi; a revolt in Sierra Leone Protectorate led to the construction of the Freetown-Bo-Kenema-Pendembu line; and the rail from Lagos to Ibadan was extended to Ilorin, Kaduna, Zaria and Kano as the British moved northwards. Meanwhile, in the east, the rail from Mombasa was being steadily constructed as far as Nairobi, and then on to Nakuru and Kisumu beside Lake Victoria.

This railway building may have originally been primarily concerned with military support for the imposition of imperial rule; but its effects were to be much more important to the economic development of the territories.

Economic opportunities were naturally seen most clearly in West Africa. On the coast, as we have already seen, trading between Africans and British had been continuous for three hundred years. Inland, internal trade had a much longer history. Its centres moved towards the coast during the period when slaving was the magnet and enterprise increased correspondingly. Nowhere else in Africa was there such a long, unbroken experience of peaceful commerce between Africans and Britain on which the new economic imperialism could build.

It was in the Gold Coast that the most dramatic impact of the railway appeared. In 1901, the year that the line to Kumasi reached Tarkwa in the centre of the mining district, the country exported gold to the value of £22,000. In 1902 the value of gold exports rose to £97,000; in 1903 to £255,000; by 1914 it had reached £1,687,000.[1]

At the same time, it should be noted that an important change had taken place in the character of gold mining. These dramatic increases in production were not mainly the consequence of expansion in the traditional operations of Africans, who had mined their gold in this area for over a thousand years. First the annexation of a part of Ashanti in 1874, and then the defeat of the whole nation, had opened the way for the entry of British companies. It was these London-based enterprises which now controlled most of the gold production; most of the Africans had become mining employees.

The railway in the Gold Coast affected more than mining. The cacao tree had been introduced in the latter part of the nineteenth century and was cultivated by both missionaries and African peasants. At the turn of the century some two hundred tons were being exported, bringing a return of about £40,000. As the railway reached Kumasi where the harvest could be collected and freighted, the figures began to rise. By 1914 they had jumped fifty-fold and represented almost half the country's total exports. Meanwhile, manganese, diamonds and timber were also reaping the benefits of railway transport, helping to make the Gold Coast the most prosperous colony in the continent.

[1] Oliver and Atmore, *Africa since 1800*, London, 1967.

Yet, although this expansion of production in the Gold Coast certainly raised the standard of living of some of its inhabitants, it did not basically change their way of life. At the beginning of the colonial era about three out of every four were engaged in subsistence farming, producing the necessities of life for their small kinship or village groups rather than selling their produce for cash. It was a minority who were occupied in trading or in the production of goods for sale. The increase in cocoa growing added cash sales by peasants to the subsistence life, for cocoa could be grown with little capital and without complicated agricultural techniques. Thus the majority of cocoa farmers simply continued to add cocoa trees to their existing plots. There was no agrarian revolution, nor were the profits of exporting directed into industrial development. Food production remained much as it had been before, the new lucrative crop being solely designed for export, as were minerals. Imports could be increased as the value of exports rose, but these tended to remain in the traditional field of unproductive goods from Britain, like alcohol, firearms, and cloth, rather than of capital goods which could have developed industry and agriculture. The mining companies imported machines, the railways their equipment, and there was some demand for road-building materials, telegraphs and the like. But the growth of Gold Coast exports saw virtually no foundations laid for a modern economy.

On the other hand, the expansion of the economy did prove valuable to the British administrators. It enabled them to levy and collect taxes with far greater facility than in other colonies. Not only were the greater numbers of goods produced and exchanged open to taxation, but imports could be subjected to customs duties, which were much easier to collect than direct taxes. Thus the economic growth of the Gold Coast provided its British administrators with the opportunity to achieve the primary task of a colonial regime, to collect its own revenue.

In the Oil Rivers area of Southern Nigeria, in Lagos and in Yorubaland, conditions approximated more closely to those of the Gold Coast than elsewhere. The trading which had developed from slaving to palm oil provided a basis of customs duties; direct taxes, like the hut tax, could be added. There might not be the same wealth per inhabitant as in the Gold Coast, but there was sufficient for the early needs of administrators. When, in 1906, Lagos and the old Oil Rivers Protectorate, which had become the Protectorate of Southern Nigeria, were amalgamated as one colony, it was considered to be self-supporting.

But the situation was quite different in the northern territories. Landlocked, with only the uncertain reaches of the Niger on which to transport its goods, and ruled by Fulani emirs, this vast area, inhabited by perhaps ten million people, presented very different problems. It could only be administered by securing the support of existing authorities, and, even then, needed subsidies from the British treasury. To obtain this support the colonial administrators gave their backing to the emirs, whom they encouraged to continue their functions of policing, taxing and judging their subjects. British Residents were installed at their courts to supervise these operations. Lugard, the first governor, hoped that these British officials might also encourage the development of economic activity and help to expand the meagre provisions for education. But essentially life in the north remained unchanged. The support given by Britain to traditional Fulani authorities allowed them to continue to rule their Hausa subjects much as before. Indeed, some of the Residents absorbed the local atmosphere to such an extent that they themselves resisted change, particularly the introduction of wider education, which they feared might raise social discontent.

Northern and Southern Nigeria thus formed two separate adminis-strative units of British Africa. But they shared common customs duties, the railway and river communications served them both, the same detachment of troops maintained security in both areas. Even the methods of government were not entirely dissimilar. Although direct rule was applied to the east and centre of the Southern Protec-torate, in Yorubaland much the same methods were used as in the north. Here, also, the chiefs were used as agents of colonial administra-tion, their positions strengthened by the support of colonial authority, their functions blended into the colonial pattern.

It therefore seemed to the British government that amalgamation of the two units would be both more efficient and less expensive. The peoples of the two areas had no common history, little common culture and some tradition of conflict, but this, if it was ever considered at all, appeared irrelevent to Whitehall. In 1912 Lugard was sent back to Nigeria from his fresh assignment in Hong Kong with the task of amalgamating Northern and Southern Nigeria. This he accomplished in 1914, though he retained separate administrations for the two sectors of the new country. Henceforth it was hoped that the British tax-payer would be relieved of the burden of supporting the north, by making it reliant on the richer south. Services and communications were linked together, with the southern ports now inviting produce from the north. But when Lugard tried to apply his principle of indirect rule to the south he met with immediate resistance. He might command his subordinates to find 'chiefs' in Iboland to carry out British policies; but the Ibo had never been governed by chiefs. They and some of the Yoruba resisted in the most effective way open to them – by refusing to pay taxes. Lugard might hope to establish law, order and a sense of discipline by replacing local judges with administrative officers and by giving his officials supervisory powers over native courts. He might encourage education in order to prevent the rise of elements subversive of authority. But the 'trousered blacks' whom he despised used their education in protest against the remodelling of their communities to suit imperial administrative convenience. They even dared to write their objections in the newspapers. For the time being the power of the new colonial masters was sufficient to remould society to its needs; but the seeds of future conflict were already being sown from the discontent felt amongst those who found themselves under the orders of aliens.

In East Africa also the railway had originally helped British forces to impose imperial rule. British and Indian troops first subdued the resistance of those coastal peoples who, from Somaliland to Mombasa, were unwilling to accept the new order. They then found that tribes inland, the Kikuyu, Kamba and Nandi, rose in opposition as the railway proceeded on its way towards Lake Victoria. They were similarly dealt with by Anglo-Indian forces. The railway reached the Lake in 1901 and, singularly, was not only paid for by the British government, but presented to East Africa as a gift.

Here, however, East Africa's development diverged from the West African model. There was no established trade in this area capable of providing taxes with which to pay for colonial administration. Ivory and slaving had formed the only considerable commercial transactions, neither suitable for the purpose of colonial taxation. Yet revenues had to be raised to pay for the administration, and the railway had to be enabled to pay its own way. Nor was it any use trying to impose taxes on the African inhabitants so long as no cash employment was open to them. They were either subsistence peasants or cattle-grazers, with no incentive to seek money wages.

So the policy of the administration had to differ from that in West Africa. It might have sought to intensify African agriculture, introducing cash crops like the coffee and cotton which were to become important to the economy of the area later. Some African products, like skins and hides, were exported, but none of the early administrators seems to have thought the African capable of participating in a modern economy. Instead, it was assumed that revenues could only be raised by taxing the Indian traders who followed their immigrant compatriots as they settled in East and Central Africa, by offering land to European and South African farmers to produce taxable cash crops, and then by using hut taxes and the like to force Africans to take wage employment on the white man's farms, in his mines or in public works.

So far as Sir Charles Eliot, the commissioner of Kenya, then called the East African Protectorate, was concerned, he never seemed to have any perception of the possibility of developing African agriculture. He appeared fascinated by the prospect of controlling large areas of virgin land which was thought to be almost uninhabited. He saw this as his opportunity to attract European farmers to the country and so to found a new colony of white settlers which might become another South Africa or Rhodesia. By 1904 he had allocated almost a million acres of fertile land to a few hundred farmers from Britain and South Africa. Although African land rights had previously been acknowledged by the Protectorate government and some of Eliot's own district commissioners showed themselves aware of their importance, African ownership was ignored in the obsession with attracting Europeans.

The result of this policy was to deprive certain African communities of their land, or of parts of their land. The Masai probably suffered most, for they were cattle-grazers, accustomed to moving their herds from area to area. The land in the Rift Valley, for instance, which the Europeans considered to be unoccupied, was part of the area where the Masai periodically grazed their cattle. Yet the Masai were moved out in order that white farmers could be offered its rich soil and some Kikuyu also lost their individual claims to tenure as a result of the partition amongst white farmers. They, together with the Embu and Meru tribes, were confined to reserves, which quickly became grossly overcrowded.

The policy of creating African reserves had unfortunate effects. Its object was to keep Africans off the farms established by white farmers, whilst, at the same time, providing a pool of labour for European farmers and an easily administered system of security and taxation. But the Africans had been accustomed to shifting cultivation and nomadic herding. The restrictions on their movement thus vitally interfered with their economic life. They immediately found that they had less land to cultivate and that it must be used continuously. In the same way, the cattle were now forced to graze constantly in the same areas. The consequence was inevitable; soil erosion spread rapidly. As soon as European medicine and cattle-raising techniques became available, much of their beneficial effects were quickly dissipated, for they produced an increase in human and animal populations still dependent on the same limited areas for their food supplies.

The reserve system was used in Kenya, Southern Rhodesia and – on a much smaller scale – in Nyasaland. In Southern Rhodesia it penetrated the social outlook so deeply that it became the foundation on which the whole racial pattern was drawn. Africans who left their reserve, whether to work on European farms, labour in the towns or go down the mines, were regarded virtually as aliens. They were compelled to carry passes, prevented from normal social intercourse with Europeans, and even prohibited from using the pavements in some towns.

In all the countries of white settlement the government or company need for tax revenue coincided with European demands for labour. Taxation of African inhabitants both raised funds and forced Africans to seek paid employment, in domestic service, on white farms, in the mines or in public work. In Nyasaland there were even cases in which government officials burnt down African huts as the penalty for non-payment of taxes, whilst physical coercion became a common practice for white employers in disciplining African workers.

All Africans in the white-settled countries did not, however, experience the effects of European contact during the early years. There were many communities in Kenya living away from the area of white settlement who barely realized that white farmers had entered their country. In neighbouring Uganda white settlement never assumed significant proportions. At first it was expected that the railway to the Lake and the fertile lands north of the Lake would attract European farmers. But the distance from the coast was considerably greater than that to the highlands of Kenya. The first and strongest attraction, therefore, was offered in Kenya, which skimmed off most of the potential European settlers.

Equally important was the different character of the African population. One of the attractions of trade to Uganda was the presence of strongly organized kingdoms in the area of the Lake. In the course of the military operations undertaken by the British to gain control of the country the Buganda kingdom proved an invaluable ally. Their chiefs were rewarded by entrenching their land rights and thus transforming them into a landed aristocracy. The Baganda continued to serve Britain by helping to administer other parts of the country, whilst their own monarchial government was allowed to continue its functions with only the lightest supervision from colonial officials. With the Buganda kingdom accorded such a status, it would have been very difficult to introduce a community of privileged white farmers. In any case, the Baganda quickly adopted cotton growing with fair success so that enough national revenue was raised to relieve Britain from the necessity of providing further grants-in-aid. Cotton in Uganda played a similar role to cocoa-growing in the Gold Coast.

The success of this cotton-growing in Uganda led to a proposal for a similar attempt to be made in the Sudan. Here military operations continued against groups of resistors until 1916, whilst in Somaliland it took the British authorities until after the first war to suppress a Mahdist rebellion. But, even before imperial security had been fully established in the Sudan, an experimental scheme for irrigating land around the Blue Nile proved successful.

It is significant to note that in both Uganda and the Sudan the expansion of cotton production was supported by the Cotton Growing Association of Britain, which persuaded the colonial government to provide roads and railways capable of facilitating a large-scale export trade. This not only provided considerable wealth for some of the African growers but also enabled the colonial administration to raise its revenues and pay for its wars against the rebels. Already, though, the Anglo-Egyptian government of the Sudan, controlled by the British with Egyptian, Lebanese and Sudanese officials, was treating the country as two units. The Arab north and the African south were governed almost as separate countries, with most attention paid to the north. Shadows of future conflict between the two communities were cast from the very early days of colonial administration.

It was perhaps in South Africa, where the imposition of colonial administration was a minor matter, that relations between Africans and the British took their most momentous turn. And this change was effected through a third party, by using British imperial power to invest South Africa's white residents with greater authority.

The British government and the public exhibited a curious conversion from jingoism to guilt in relation to the Boers after the Boer war. Boer leaders like Botha, Smuts and Reitz became imperial heroes, despite the fact that they had been fighting against the British. The Boer people were cast in the role of a small nation which had fought for its self-determination against the might of a great power, an attitude which was to become familiar in the next decade. The fact that the great power had been Britain herself was ignored, yet it seems likely that it was a subconscious recognition of this fact that stirred the guilty feelings of the British.

However this may be, Britain now presented the Boers with most of the power for which they had unsuccessfully fought. So far as their authority over the Africans in their territories were concerned, the Boer generals secured their major objective at the Vereeniging peace conference which ended the war in 1902. They were promised by Kitchener and Milner that Africans would not be given the right to vote before the two defeated republics had regained self-government. This promise provided the leaders of Afrikaner nationalism with the key to unlock the whole racial power situation throughout South Africa. For, by the time that self-government was restored in 1906 and 1907, they were able to re-establish the racial foundations of their states on the traditional principle of 'no equality in church or state'. And, when they conducted negotiations for union with the two British colonies during 1908 and 1909, they were strong enough to make the conservation of this principle a condition for joining a wider South Africa. From that time onward their central objective was to extend their own racial attitude to the rest of the Union.

The paramount British concern with the economic opportunities in South Africa which had been revealed by the war was now reflected in her post-war policies. She paid great attention to the economic reconstruction of the defeated and partially devastated Afrikaner republics. Railways, tariffs and labour supply were given immediate consideration. Help was provided to restore the destroyed farms. All these were matters of importance in rebuilding the economies of the Transvaal and the Orange River Colony on which, at least in the former case, much of the gold investment returns depended. But when it came to racial principles, on which rested the future of the large African population – supposedly one of the British reasons for fighting the war – appeasement of Afrikaner prejudices was accepted by Conservatives and Liberals alike. Apparently no lessons were learnt from the American Civil War; there was no attempt here to follow the example of the reconstruction policy; it appears to have been accepted by both British parties that the racial attitudes of the American South were appropriate for South Africa, provided that the economy could be refurbished and dividends guaranteed.

It was not least from a desire to forge a common policy towards the Africans that the white politicians of all four colonies were led to contemplate a union. There were earnest discussions amongst the more thoughtful politicians of South Africa as to what the racial policy of the new state should be. Although advice was offered by various people concerned with race relations in Britain, British politicians themselves seem to have had little interest in this aspect of union. In the Cape a colour-blind franchise had existed since the institution of an elected parliament in 1854. Voting rights were based on property qualifications, which excluded most Africans and Coloureds, but skin colour itself was no bar. Cape leaders believed that the preservation of this policy was essential to avoid conflict between the races. Merriman conducted a long correspondence with Smuts on the subject, warning that the preservation of an non-racial policy was an essential safety valve for African emotions. Sauer, a Cape leader with liberal pretensions, saw even deeper into the roots of the significance of political representation when he declared, 'I do not believe that where representative institutions exist a class that is not represented will ever receive political justice, because after all it is material interests that will eventually prevail, and therefore the class having no political power will suffer.'

The Cape liberals were supported by the leaders of what little organized African opinion had developed. Tengo Jabavu, editor of the Xhosa paper *Imvo Zabantsundu*, and John Dube, founder of the

Ohlange Institute, were noteworthy examples of moderate, gradualist leaders who worked with the liberals.

But the asp of Afrikaner racial feelings had bitten too deep for even an intelligent man like Smuts to be open to reason on this issue. Smuts hoped to postpone the reckoning, or at least to persuade himself that it was not as imminent as Merriman suggested. He wrote in one letter to the Cape leader, 'When I consider the political future of the natives in S.A. I must say that I look into shadows and darkness; and then I feel inclined to shift the intolerable burden of solving that sphinx problem to the ampler shoulders and stronger brains of the future. Sufficient unto the day, etc.'[1] And Smuts represented the more reasonable section of his people! Most Afrikaners thought only with their emotions on this issue and were determined that Africans should remain permanently the helots of the white man.

In the meantime, a commission appointed by Milner had reported mainly in favour of racial segregation as a solution to the problem. It was strongly influenced by the experience of New Zealand with her Maori population. The commission had a powerful impact on Smuts's mind for the rest of his life. Its segregation proposals were also in line with the attitude adopted by many missionaries during the nineteenth century when it was believed that the African resembled a 'noble savage' who should be protected from contamination by the white man's social evils. But at this stage, because segregation would have entailed setting aside land for African occupation, the policy was rejected by the body of Afrikaner opinion.

When the draft bill for Union came to be considered by the British parliament in 1909, Liberal and Conservative members regarded themselves as virtually bound to accept the compromises which had been agreed between white South African leaders at their National Convention. Each province was to keep its existing franchise provisions and the Cape franchise was to be entrenched behind the requirement of a two-thirds majority of both houses to change it. But one existing right of Africans, Coloureds and Indians was abolished. Henceforth only Europeans were to be allowed to sit in Parliament; no non-European had ever sat in the Cape parliament, but they had had the constitutional right to do so.

[1] W. K. Hancock *Smuts*, Vol. 1.

Whatever their personal reservations, British politicians, with the exception of a few Labour members, hid behind the skirts of the South African leaders, who had reached an agreement which seemed to offer that prospect of British-Afrikaner cooperation for which Rhodes and Hofmeyer had striven. When challenged on the racial issue Asquith's Liberal government and the Conservative opposition rationalized their complicity in racialist legislation by expressing confidence that the liberal politics of the Cape would eventually spread to the three other provinces.

W. P. Schreiner, a white liberal, and Walter Rubusana from the South African Native National Conference, Jabavu and a delegation from the African People's Organisation all descended on London to try and persuade the British government to amend the bill before approving it. Schreiner was not to be diverted from the central principle of representative democracy by claims for the overriding importance of securing Union. He enunciated this with simple clarity in his statement: 'To embody in the South African constitution a vertical line or barrier separating its people upon the ground of colour into a privileged class or caste and an unprivileged inferior proletariat is as imprudent as it would be to build a grand building upon unsound and sinking foundations. In our South African nation there must be room for many free peoples, but no room for any that are not free, and free to rise.' As with Merriman, there was to be discerned here a combination of liberal principle with the warning of potential dangers from its abrogation. But the British government was disinclined to listen. Self-determination for states identified as 'civilized' took precedence over self-determination for peoples – particularly when the former had become an important part of Britain's investment empire. The only concession which the British government was prepared to make was to reserve the transfer of the colony of Basutoland and the protectorates of Swaziland and Bechuanaland to the new Union until it saw how South Africa's racial policy progressed. But it was generally expected at the time of Union that before long these three territories and the Rhodesias would be incorporated into a wider South Africa.

Within two years of the founding of the Union politically-conscious Africans demonstrated their reactions. No longer could the gradualists like Jabuvu and Dube, who were accustomed to work with European liberals and take guidance from them, maintain their hold on the African political scene. Their failure and the inability of the liberals to secure democratic rights for Africans in the Union consititution compelled African political society to seek the means of independent action. In 1912 the African National Congress was founded to represent the interests of Africans throughout the nation across the provincial boundaries. The African congress movement was influenced by Gandhi's South African Indian Congress, founded on non-violent principles, and perhaps also by Abdurahman's peaceful leadership of the Cape Coloureds. Yet, although the A.N.C. could never be considered as a revolutionary body, it represented an important break with tradition. Henceforth the African inhabitants of South Africa had an organization which would devise policies and tactics independently of white politics. Within a year of its formation this new independent attitude was demonstrated. When the Cape liberal, Sauer, introduced his Native Land Act prohibiting Africans from acquiring land outside their reserves, the A.N.C. immediately denounced the measure. Those, like Jabavu, who continued to support the white liberals even in such policies were in the future clearly exposed as unrepresentative of African opinion.

It is also significant that within a few months of the creation of an African nationalist movement, traditionalist Afrikaners followed the same path. When Hertzog broke with Botha and Smuts and formed his National Party in 1914, the two genuine nationalisms of South Africa had each organized its own separate camp. The future of their common country lay between them; it would be moulded according to their mutual relations. Britain, and British South Africans, were already becoming irrelevant to its destiny. Some years had yet to pass before the insignificance of British influence was to become apparent; but its demise was already fore-shadowed in 1912–13. Britain's last major impact on South African politics was to give the white community power over the Africans through the Act of Union.

During this first quarter-century of British rule the effects of the new colonial relationship fell very unevenly on different sections of the African people. In some areas armies fought, in others land was taken away to be given to white farmers or to rival tribes, roads and railways appeared in certain districts, elsewhere young Africans found their way over long distances to work in mines. The district officer made an increasingly frequent appearance in most colonial localities, bringing with him new orders for the payment of taxes, supplies of labour or for keeping the peace. Many Africans throughout the colonies remained in their former villages, living much the same life as before, subject to the same headman or chief. But, as the authority of colonial administration spread, the higher courts were taken out of the chief's jurisdiction, magistrates appeared, serious offenders found themselves tried under strange laws, with alien procedures and new sentences, whilst taxes of various types began to feature in almost every community.

Perhaps the deepest disturbance caused to African social life by the imposition of colonial rule came from the growth of missionary activities. Many missions had established their first footholds in Africa before the partition of the continent. Under colonial rule they were encouraged by governments and found greater opportunities to extend their own initiatives. As the growth of Christian evangelism was paralleled by expansion in Islamic efforts, Africans on the long borderlands between the two faiths came under rival pressures. Nor did Christianity present a common front. Tacit division of parishes was sometimes accepted by rival sects; but there were also many areas where denominations openly competed with each other.

Yet, despite the confusion of mind which frequently resulted from this confused impact of various Christian teachings on the spiritual traditions of African societies, both Islam and Christianity brought one profound contribution. They both built schools and introduced formal education. It might be that in the first instance the teaching was largely confined to the lessons of the Koran or to reading, writing and arithmetic. Many of the early schools consisted of nothing more than a chair for the teacher under the shade of a tree, with the pupils sitting round it on the bare earth. (Indeed, some such 'schools' could be seen until very recent times.) Even when buildings were erected, they were of the most primitive type, as vividly portrayed by Bishop Kitching in Uganda: 'Imagine a rough shed, built of mud and wattle and thatched with grass. Very likely it is leaning sideways and is propped up with extra poles at varied angles. A few gaps left in the mud serve for windows and doorways. At one end the floor is raised a few inches by way of a chancel, and a pole or bamboo runs across as a Communion rail. At each side a mud-walled enclosure does duty as reading-desk and pulpit. On the inside of the roof hang innumerable hornet's nests, and possibly a few bats. On the walls, suspended from little pegs, are sheets displaying the alphabet, or rows of syllables, some of them nibbled by intrusive goats or fretted by the ubiquitous termites. Look in at about 8.30 in the morning, and you will see groups of readers of mixed ages and sexes, seated on the floor in front of the sheets, saying over the letters or syllables in a sing-song voice. Somehow they get the syllables memorized, and are promoted to reading consecutive print.'

Such training may seem rudimentary, though to it should be added the contributions made by missionaries in the fields of medicine, hygiene and agriculture. But it gave African young men and women an outlet from their traditionally static life. Many became teachers or clergy themselves; others found employment as clerks or craftsmen on European farms, in the mines or in stores and workshops. At first most of them welcomed their new opportunities, increased social status, the new pleasures and excitments open to them. They accepted as inevitable that they should be offered inferior positions and wages compared with Asians or Europeans. But they formed the first genera-tion of new expectations. They induced novel needs in their children. Skills were acquired which opened the door to communication with other peoples in foreign lands. Those who could read the Bible or the Koran could also read political books and newspapers. The second generation was not only to experience still higher expectations, but to question the discrimination it found in employment opportunities, civic rights and social rewards. Eventually it would query the legiti-macy of that alien authority on which the colonial system itself was based.

The colonial administrators of Europe had not fully completed the imposition of their authority over their territories when the European war broke out in 1914, which makes it all the more remarkable that so many Africans fought for their imperial masters in that conflict. In South Africa there was a rebellion of nationalist Afrikaners led by the Commander-in-Chief of the Defence Forces; but it was suppressed early in 1915. Resentment against involvement in Britain's war was also felt in Egypt, particularly after that country was officially taken from the Ottoman empire and declared a protectorate. Yet thousands of Afrikaners and Egyptians fought within British imperial armies. And thousands more Africans took part in the British war effort, both as combatants and as carriers, whilst the Cape Coloureds made a notable contribution in their Cape Corps. Meanwhile, thousands of Africans from the German colonies were fighting on the other side. What is remarkable is that no attempt was made to take advantage of the Europeans' preoccupation with their war to throw off the new imperial ties – except by the most fanatical nationalists within the Afrikaner nation.

In the course of the war more Africans than ever before travelled outside their own countries and came into contact with other peoples. West Africans fought with South Africans, Indians, Central and East Africans in East Africa. Afrikaners and British South Africans fought in Palestine and France. Nigerians, Gold Coasters and Gambians served beside West Indians and Indians in Togoland and the Cameroons.

This experience introduced many thousands of Africans from different territories to each other for the first time. It also enabled them to meet people from other continents and to observe the customs and techniques of other lands. For the first time, these African soldiers became aware that they were members of national units larger than the traditional horizons of their local communities. Moreover, in the war Africans were trained and encouraged to kill white men. They also saw common European soldiers acting as ordinary men like themselves, in contrast to the authoritarian colonial officials dressed in the panoply of imperial power whom they were accustomed to regard with awe at home. And the sight of huge armies of Europeans engaged in annihilating each other must have caused many Africans to revise their opinion of the white man's civilization.

The contribution made to the war by Africa brought a new evaluation of the continent in British eyes. Not only were the ports and harbours of East, West and South Africa clearly vital to British imperial defence, but the products of the continent were seen to have a commercial as well as a strategic value. Unfortunately for Africa, the needs of war led to a great over-production of her resources. When peace returned production levels could not be maintained, so that many Africans shared in the post-war depression to an even greater extent than Europeans. The one country which did benefit was South Africa, where the war-time shortages of imported goods stimulated local manufactures and agriculture. This enabled the South Africans to build the foundations of a modern economy which was able to sustain its growth after the war. But elsewhere, as colonial economies persisted, African ex-servicemen found themselves unemployed, forced to return to their subsistence life or to take jobs as messengers and clerks in the white man's regimes.

Yet the war had introduced more Africans than ever before to the world of international politics and political ideas. These might yet affect only a tiny minority, but the ideas were taken home to be discussed and further digested for application to local conditions. Not least important amongst these concepts was the new awakening of international responsibility for colonial peoples. It was the first world war which incubated the notion of the mandate system. At the end of the war the League of Nations instituted the first form of international protection for peoples under imperial rule. It allocated the German colonies to the victorious allies: to Britain, Tanganyika and parts of Togoland and the Cameroons; the remainder of the latter two territories to France; Ruanda-Urundi to Belgium; South-West Africa to South Africa; but each was placed under the Mandates Commission of the League, with annual reports on their administration to be supplied to the Commission. The interests of the local inhabitants were to be recognized as equally important to those of the governing state, with an indication that eventually they would be enabled to rule themselves. International supervision broke the tradition of unilateral imperial authority; it might take many years to work through the logic of this new relationship, but the path had been charted.

Chapter 9

Colonial Economics
and Administration

The effects of the first world war seriously weakened Britain's economic position. Not only had she devoted a large part of her industrial effort to war production, lost a large section of her young manhood, and diverted most of her international trading machinery to war purposes, but she had also had to sell an important sector of her overseas investments in order to pay for the war. British foreign investment fell from 9.3 per cent of her national income immediately before the war to 2.3 per cent immediately after it; gross investment income from overseas from 8.6 per cent to 4.3 per cent during the same period. In particular, investment in the United States was drastically reduced. Whereas it formed 19 per cent of total British investment before the war, this had declined to 5.5 per cent some ten years later. An idea of the type of investment which had been liquidated to pay for war materials may be gained from the fact that in 1913 16 per cent of British overseas investment was in the United States railways, whereas by 1930 the figure had fallen to one per cent.

Nevertheless, despite the weakening of the British economy, which we can now analyse through such figures, at the time this was hardly apparent to the peoples of the British colonial empire. The decline might be crucial to Britain's domestic position and to her power in the world's economy; in contrast to the colonial peoples she still appeared an all-powerful, imperial, industrialized state.

It was, indeed, the unequal economic relation between Britain and the African colonies which formed the main elements of the imperial relationship. At the end of the war, about eight hundred million people, one in three of the world's population, were ruled by colonial powers. Amongst them were to be found virtually all the peoples of the African continent. In these lands most of the natural resources were controlled by companies based either in the metropolitan country or in the capitals of other industrial states. In opening up these colonial and semi-colonial lands, the power of European industry had been used to destroy the manufactures of indigenous people. This was particularly marked in the impact of British manufactures on India and China, but it also applied to Africa. There the local industries might be on a much smaller scale than those of Asia; they consisted of textile manufacturing, the mining of minerals and some metalcraft and pottery. Nevertheless, as with India's textiles, they had been destroyed before the might of European industry, and their markets opened up to Europe's exports. It was through this process that Africans were allocated their place in that international division of labour between the primary producers and manufacturers which formed the central character of relations between Europe and the outside world in the nineteenth century. The application of the principle of free trade during the same century ossified the division. The effect of imperial expansion in the late nineteenth and early twentieth centuries was to entrench this unequal relation still deeper as European capital was employed in exploiting the mineral wealth of such lands and introducing primary crops for export.

The contrast between the power of even weakened industrialized imperial states and their colonies was well illustrated by the effects of the war and by post-war conditions. During the war an insatiable demand for primary products forced their prices upwards, leading to a wide expansion of capacity. In the post-war period demand was suddenly reduced, prices fell, frequently ruining the economies of primary-producing countries. At the same time, the industrialists in developed countries were able to maintain their price levels for manufactured goods by organizing cartels and price-fixing agreements. But the prices of primary products were determined by the operation of the free market, in which a slight excess of supply over demand led to catastrophic falls in prices. Nor could the primary-producing countries insure themselves against such adverse movements, because they had not the strength to withhold their crops until prices rose. Thus, although the colonies secured the advantage of having the London commodity market at their disposal, they were forced to accept the wild price fluctuations which it and other similar markets allowed. The only

8

people who were able to safeguard themselves against such instability were those European firms operating in the colonies which possessed the economic strength to stockpile when prices were low.

Some conception of the manner in which colonial economies were hit by the post-war conditions is revealed in the fact that the terms of trade for primary producers fell in 1921 to seventy per cent of the 1913 figure and, after some recovery in the later 1920s, fell lower still during the 1930s. It should not be assumed that the reduction in the prices of primary products necessarily benefited British industry by reducing the prices of manufactured goods so that they could be more easily sold in colonial countries. It is true that Britain gained by having to pay less for her food and raw materials. Yet, not only did she receive a lower return on her investments in primary production; the markets for her exports inevitably contracted as the primary producers found themselves with fewer resources to purchase them, particularly after the world economic crisis broke in 1929. Although the terms of trade turned sharply in favour of the industrialized nations, the total volume of trade was reduced. The primary producers, suffering from lower prices for their products, simply could not buy the goods of British industry. It was they and those thrown into unemployment in British export industries who were the real sufferers in this vicious circle. The only sections with power to protect themselves against this spiral were those British companies concerned with mining and export crops in Africa who were able to defend their profits by agreements on restricted production and controlled prices. Indeed, the large companies were able to take advantage of the embarrassment caused to their smaller brethren by buying them up and building even larger combines. These great commercial associations, like Unilever and Imperial Tobacco, were then in a position to create near-monopolies, using the low prices of raw materials to secure high profits by selling-price agreements.

Nevertheless, in national terms, the fall in prices of primary products was accompanied by a reduction in the total volume of British manufactured exports. Immediately after the war, the volume of British exports fell to seventy per cent of the 1913 figure. At the beginning of the 1930s, it fell still further to fifty-three per cent. It was clear that the lower revenues received by the primary producing countries for their exports were drastically reducing their power to buy manufactured goods. As a consequence, those areas in Britain dependent largely on exports, like Lancashire on cotton, Yorkshire on wool, the coal and steel regions and the ship-building of the Tyne and Clyde, all suffered from heavy unemployment. Yet, at the same time, the possession of a colonial empire was now seen to be cushioning British export industries from the stark realities of the post-war world. Although imports from the colonial empire actually declined after the war and, even on recovery from the mid-1920s onwards, only regained the pre-war volume until rearmament boosted them higher in the late 1930s, exports to the colonies increased considerably, despite the fall in total exports. The increasing share sent to the colonies revealed that when British exports met resistance in the world markets they found that they could turn to the Empire. Thus, instead of the reorganization of British industry demanded by post-war conditions, the British export industry found it still possible to send its traditional textiles, iron and steel to Empire markets. It is true that the Dominions and India still took most of this increase, but Africa also participated slightly in it. Africa did not, however, secure any increase in British investment. Total overseas' investment was drastically reduced, whilst capital exports fell to less than a fifth of their pre-war volume. Yet, of this latter figure, the Empire's share rose from forty-six to fifty-seven per cent between 1910–13 and 1925–29. As before the war, however, investment in Africa was almost totally confined to South Africa, the only dominion in the continent.

The value of imperial possessions became most obvious after the world economic collapse of 1931. It was at this time that Britain finally abandoned her free trade position, adopting protective measures particularly designed to safeguard the interest of British capital and industry overseas. What Joseph Chamberlain had vainly urged on British governments at the turn of the century was now adopted in the emergency conditions of the 1930s. Not only was British capital able to find a new haven from the rough waters of international retrenchment in the Empire; but within the international cartel agreements negotiated to protect industrial and financial interests across the world, the Empire played an important part. The companies engaged in producing primary materials, such as copper, rubber, lead, sugar, tea and tin, all reached agreement on commodity controls within the Empire. At the same time, the Imperial Economic Conference held in Ottawa in 1932 allowed for a preferential agreement between Britain and the Empire, based upon the introduction of import tariffs in Britain. Empire goods were given preference on entry into Britain and, in exchange, British exports to Empire markets were given special privileges. Yet, because of the structure of imperial trade, it was largely the farmers of the dominions and the British-controlled mines and plantations in the colonies which gained from this arrangement, for they dominated the export of those primary products most in demand. At a time when all countries were trying to reduce their imports and expand their exports, the primary producers as a whole suffered hardship; but the powerful interests within the Empire were again able to protect themselves from the full effects of the world economic storm. And, although the colonies only provided a tiny percentage of the raw materials produced throughout the world, they included important products like rubber, palm oil, tin and copper. Germany's exclusion from the cartels, established by those who controlled this raw material production, became the major motive for Hitler's demand that her colonies be restored.

It might also be noted that this imperial cushion, as in the 1920s, again retarded the re-deployment of British industry needed to meet her new position in world markets. There was a little structural re-deployment within the British economy; and where new industries, like those producing motor cars and chemincals, had begun to develop, they gained the benefits of imperial protection. Moreover, in a time of mass unemployment throughout the world, the fact that the Empire provided jobs for some twenty thousand administrators and armed forces was not insignificant. So the possession of a colonial empire softened some of the blows dealt by the impact of international crisis, whilst again delaying a confrontation with the long-term needs of Britain's economy.

As before the war, it was the dominions rather than the colonies which prospered in the inter-war years. In Africa, the only economy which reached a point of self-propulsion during this period was that of South Africa. It became evident that only where economic and political independence had been attained was it possible to accumulate local savings and devote them to the establishment of indigenous industrialization. Only through economic independence could sufficient wealth be retained from local production to build a modern industrial system and only political independence would enable local governments to protect their infant industries until they had reached competitive maturity.

In British Africa most of the important resources were controlled by British companies. This was so in South Africa as well as in the colonies, for the mineral mining which remained the core of South Africa's economy was always under British and American control. Yet in South Africa, two factors enabled local residents to achieve a degree of economic development impossible in any of the colonies. Because the South Africans were increasingly allowed to govern their own affairs, to the point at which they became formally independent in 1931, so they were able to use their political authority in order to secure from the profits of the mines sufficient revenues both to provide for governmental action, like the setting up of an iron and steel corporation, and to build an infra-structure encouraging the diversification of the economy. Secondly, and partially as a result of such activities, the local population was enabled to accumulate its own capital and to invest this in a variety of economic activities, including the gold industry.

These processes were never possible under colonial rule, where political life was controlled from London and much of the economic activities organized by overseas companies. In some cases, for example, in that of Unilever's United Africa Company in West Africa, companies established to collect and export raw materials actually entered the retail trade, thereby handicapping the development of an African entrepreneurial class. In Northern Rhodesia, as late as 1937, whereas £5.5 million were paid in dividends and royalties from the mines, the government only collected £0.7 million. In the same year dividends and royalties accounted for £1.3 million from the Nigerian mineral output of £2.5 million.

Thus, the main difference between the British impact on South Africa and on those parts of the continent which remained under British colonial rule was that whereas the former was able to use its connection with the British economy to build its own strength, all the latter remained in economic subservience to the metropolitan economy. One fact, in particular, illustrates this difference. By the time that the second world war broke out, South Africa was the one country in British Africa where the majority of the population was employed in other pursuits than agriculture.

Moreover, the local markets in the colonies were themselves depressed as a result of the colonial relationship. It may be that, as we have seen, many Africans were forced into the cash economy as a result of taxation. Yet, within this economy, they were almost always paid low wages, either as migrant labourers in the mines or on European farms. The normal expectation was that African workers would retain their roots in their villages or tribal societies where their families and homes remained, so that their social security in sickness, old age or unemployment did not have to be provided by their European employers. Not only was such a system inefficient from the point of view of both industrial and agricultural productivity; it also prevented the African working class from organizing demands for modern consumer goods or obtaining the resources with which to pursue them.

It might be argued that this system was applied in South Africa as well as in the British colonies. This is true, for a great deal of South African production in minerals, agriculture and manufactures was based upon cheap labour, often organized on the migrant basis. The South African gold industry, for example, recruited its labour from all over Southern Africa, on contracts lasting usually from nine to eighteen months. The average wages of African mine workers remained unchanged for fifty years, from 1890 to 1940, at two shillings a day, plus subsistence.

But in South Africa, the Africans really stood in a colonial relationship to white society. It was their labour which was exploited in building the separate white economy. The economy of the Europeans acquired its own momentum by these means and, because it became much stronger and more diversified than other African economies, it began to offer Africans a wider variety of employment and higher wages than elsewhere in the continent. Even so, the low wages of the African population and the retention of a considerable section in subsistence agriculture retarded the growth of the South African market in the same way as in the colonies.

It is also true that, because gold mining remained largely under the control of overseas companies, dividends regularly left South Africa. In the first sixty years of gold mining they amounted to nearly £500 million; after 1945 over fifty per cent of the profits were still going overseas. It is true that these mining activities were always suspect to European South Africans and particularly to traditionalist Afrikaners; and that the white working class in the mines not only fought their employers for better wages, but were also continually and bitterly opposed to the employment of Africans in any of the skilled jobs. (This hostility to African advance developed along similarly bitter lines at a slightly later date in Northern Rhodesian copper mines.) The European working class also joined Afrikaner traditionalists in criticising the expatriation of profits from the gold companies to British and American investors. Nevertheless, starting with the supply of equipment, food and services to the mines, proceeding to the accumulation of investment capital, and eventually reaching the opportunity for industrial and manufacturing development, the South African European community was able to forge its own modern economy from the activities initiated by gold mining. In the end, it was even able to satisfy critics of the alien investors by using its political strength to increase taxation, retaining a growing percentage of profit within the country. Thus the South African white community was able to imitate the example of American or Australian former colonists in its relation to Britain instead of accepting the inferior status imposed on African colonial subjects.

During the period of British colonial rule in Africa, and particularly between the two world wars, some degree of economic development was certainly achieved. Most of this was in building the infrastructure, in railways, roads, harbours, telegraphs and, later, in airports, essential for the conduct of a colonial administration and for the economic activities which accompanied it. Where Europeans settled, as in Kenya, the Rhodesias and South Africa, this investment was proportionately much greater than elsewhere. There were, however, certain minor exceptions to this rule. In parts of Uganda, for instance, where economic development was more profitable than in most colonies, an excellent system of communications was provided. Yet the main objective for building such infrastructures was always to assist the process of exporting crops and raw materials most useful to Britain and profitable to her investors. Frequently, this led to the growth of pockets of modern economic activity within unchanging subsistence economies, where the net result was to remove wealth without making any stimulating impact on the rest of the economy. This was particularly the case in areas dependent on mining, like Northern Rhodesia, or on export crops which reduced local food production, as in some parts of West Africa, Kenya and Southern Rhodesia.

One of the major differences between the colonies ruled directly by Britain and a country like South Africa, where a substantial white settler community was established, was in the degree of British investment. We have already seen that, after the partition of Africa, British investment in the colonial territories, as distinct from that in South Africa, rose only very slightly. In 1913, for instance, eight per cent of British overseas investment was concentrated in South Africa, only two and a half per cent in the whole of the rest of British Africa, and ten years later the latter percentage was actually slightly less. And, although Africans in most colonies might escape from the debilitating diseases widespread amongst mining labourers – particularly tuberculosis and pneumoconiosis, which often affected more than half of the African mineworkers and were transmitted back to their families – they were also deprived of the modern medicines and education which were often supplied to the mining areas. Little was done until after the second world war to attack the endemic tropical diseases, such as malaria, bilharzia, and those consequent on malnutrition; meanwhile the vast majority of colonial children remained illiterate.

There was, of course, some economic gain, even from the building of facilities designed for exports. Some African workers were brought into modern employment in the building of railways, roads and harbours, or in working in the mines; they acquired some skills, even when inhibited by the opposition of white workers. Towns grew up, a few young people went to school, some even to colleges or universities abroad. Though infinitesimal as a percentage of the total populations, it was from these people that African leadership was to be drawn.

Jan Smuts and Frederick Lugard, two men of similar atittudes, exercised a dominant influence over British policies in Africa between the two world wars. Each had a military background, believed in discipline, and adopted an authoritarian outlook. Although Lugard had much more experience of mixing with Africans than Smuts, he adopted the vague, paternalistic attitude of a trustee, characteristic of much of Smuts's racial approach.

Lugard's *The Dual Mandate in British Tropical Africa*, became the nearest book to a Bible for the British Colonial Office. In it he argued that it was an imperial responsibility to develop the resources of the African continent as a contribution to the world's economy and, at the same time, to assist the peoples of Africa to progress to the point at which they could participate in its benefits. This thesis provided Britain with a convenient ethical justification for her imperial position. Lugard believed that in order to fulfil these twin responsibilities British administrators would have to form an alliance with the established authorities in every locality, echoing nostalgically similar alliances with the princes of India.

Every British administrator was expected to absorb the lessons taught by Lugard. Thus, in the Gold Coast, it was the Ashanti Asantehene who received most British support; in Northern Nigeria it was the Moslem emirs who were allowed to maintain their traditional Islamic courts; in the Sudan, British authority stood behind traditionalist Islamic sheiks.

Nevertheless, despite the professed universality of the Lugard policy, some factors were undermining its success. Lugard believed in the spread of education, although he mistakenly expected it to induce obedience to authority. But, as a handful of schools and colleges were instituted, so the students learnt more than Lugard anticipated. They began to read political tracts and digest the ideas of political, social and economic thinkers of other countries. Fraser and Aggrey at Achimota in the Gold Coast encouraged their students to pursue higher studies. Fourah Bay in Sierra Leone provided a focus for study far beyond its original missionary purpose. A few privileged students began to find their way to London and the United States, led by the prominent Nigerian, Nnamdi Azikiwe. Although there was a tendency amongst West African students to concentrate on legal studies which would enable them to gain large salaries as lawyers, the anti-colonial spirit could not be kept from them. By the mid-1930s, when Azikiwe returned from Lincoln University in Pennsylvania, an independent African press began to circulate in West Africa. Inevitably it espoused the anti-colonial cause.

Nor were all the British administrators completely enamoured of the Lugard approach. In Nigeria from 1922 four Africans were elected to the legislature from Lagos and Calabar. By 1924 Freetown elected three members to Sierra Leone's council. In 1925 Governor Guggisberg introduced a new constitution for the Gold Coast. In it, he recognized that the meagre number of Africans appointed by West African governments from the mid-nineteenth century onwards to participate in the advisory functions of the governors' councils no longer sufficed

8*

to meet the rising political demands of Gold Coast Africans. Although he confined the application of the new constitutional forms to the coastal provinces, excluding Ashanti and the north, he nevertheless provided a political outlet which could only be widened by exercise. His new constitution allowed for the appearance of fourteen unofficial African members in a legislative council of twenty-nine. Nine of the fourteen were to be elected from the coastal towns, the rest representing the provincial councils of the southern colony.

Opposition to the Lugard policy also arose amongst Nigerians. The attempt to nominate government-supported chiefs in Eastern Nigeria, where such authorities had never previously existed, led to riots at Aba and Opobo in 1929. The discontent arose because, under Lugard's policy, the local chiefs had the responsibility of raising taxes, being allowed to retain a proportion of them to pay for their local administration. As the Eastern Nigerians had never been accustomed to the rule of chiefs, their imposition and the tax demands which followed aroused considerable resentment. The rioting convinced the British authorities that they could not impose this system on Eastern Nigeria and they had to revert to direct rule.

By 1938 discontent amongst the cocoa producers of the Gold Coast had also risen to the point at which they displayed a remarkable degree of organization. Here the hostility was caused by the combined activities of administrators and cocoa companies. Whilst the administration was giving its support to local chiefs, the companies were considered to be taking advantage of this policy in order to obtain their cocoa at low prices. The cocoa producers combined to challenge both the administration and the companies by refusing to sell their cocoa.

Lugard's ideas also had some influence in East and Central Africa. They had particularly applied in Uganda, where the traditional monarchies were accorded the support of the colonial authorities, and in Tanganyika, where Donald Cameron, who had served under Lugard in Nigeria, enthusiastically applied his master's ideas in seeking out local rulers amongst the many tribal communities in that country. In doing so, he could count on the support of the League of Nations Mandates Commission, which was strongly influenced by Lugard himself, who was British representative. The impact of his teachings was also to be seen in Northern Rhodesia and Nyasaland and in the three

High Commission territories, Bechuanaland, Swaziland and Basuto-land.

We must not exaggerate the degree to which indirect rule was applied in practice. Often the chiefs or other local authorities who were supposed to be given the responsibility of ruling were kept strictly under the control of district officers. In Tanganyika, for instance, Donald Cameron genuinely believed in Lugard's principles. In his first memorandum in the territory he told his subordinates, 'We must not, in fact, destroy the African atmosphere, the African mind, the whole foundation of his race. . . . (instead) we (endeavour) to purge the native system of its abuses, to graft a higher civilization upon the soundly rooted native stock.' In fact, Tanganyika was much too large to be developed by the few district officers and their Asian and Arab assistants available to Cameron, so devolution of authority was in-evitable. The British found that the small communities of the country had many headmen but few chiefs. They, therefore, tried to reduce the large number of local authorities by merging communities into single units. This policy, however, forced many unrelated groups of people without any experience of common authority to live within a single, artificial unit. In these circumstances, the native authorities were bound to be almost wholly dependent on British support, for they could count on no tradition of allegiance from their peoples. Thus the district officer had to be frequently at the side of the native ruler and by this continual presence he tended to break down African traditions, replacing them with the British customs he found more convenient and efficient. In the early days, African courts had been re-established in Tanganyika under traditional control but now they came increasingly came under the supervision of the district officer.

In other areas, too, even where the principles of indirect rule were supposed to form the basis of policy, authority tended to be concen-trated on the district officer. This was the case in Northern Rhodesia and Nyasaland, where colonial officers showed considerable reluctance to devolve their powers. The same trend was to be seen in Uganda, where the Protectorate government progressively reduced the in-dependence of the Buganda kingdom. The authority of the Kabaka and the parliament of Buganda, known as the Lukiko, had been so undermined by 1926 that an outstanding Baganda prime minister, Apolo Kagwa, resigned in protest.

But in the settler sphere of the continent, southwards to South Africa, Jan Smuts had an even stronger influence than Lugard himself. Smuts never faced up to the realities of racial policy in his own country nor in the east and central territories where Europeans had settled. He had a constant tendency to procrastinate and, on occasion, as we saw previously, said himself that this was an issue which would have to be left to future generations. On one of the few occasions when Smuts allowed himself to reveal his thoughts on racial policy in South Africa, in the course of an election speech in 1910, he exposed the fear which dominated his outlook on this problem. According to the Transvaal Leader's report, 'He personally was not against the native, but was against the policy of oppression. He would help the native in every legitimate way in accordance with his present requirements; but he could not forget that civilization had been built up in this country by the white race, and that they were the guardians of liberty, justice and all the elements of progress in South Africa. The franchise was the last argument; it was more powerful than the sword or the rifle, and the day that the white race gave away the final protection they possessed they would have to consider very carefully what they were doing. They had received a heritage of civilization from their fathers, which he hoped they would hand on intact and unspoiled to their children. If those children found an opening to extend the rule of liberty and political rights in this country, they could do so; but to his mind it would be one of the most dangerous things for the white race, constituted as it was, in South Africa, to take any such steps today.'[1]

If one can perceive any specific attitude, it would be somewhat vaguely drawn from the nineteenth century British policies in the Cape and Natal. There, both British administrators and missionaries based their policy towards Africans on a paternalistic, trusteeship outlook, designed to protect the Africans from the evil effects of contact with European society, allowing them to develop within their own areas. This inevitably led to a segregationist conclusion.

Smuts, Godfrey Huggins in Southern Rhodesia and Cavendish-Bentinck in Kenya, all espoused the concept of dividing their countries into white and black reserves, the Europeans taking the richer and often the larger part of their territories, whilst relying, like Lugard,

[1] Quoted in Hancock, *op. cit.*, pp. 319.

on the support of chiefs and elders to legitimize the division. The influence of these white leaders, under the guidance of Smuts, on the British Colonial Office was profound. There were occasions when the British government felt impelled to modify their ambitions. When the Southern Rhodesians were given powers of self-government in 1923, for instance, the electoral roll was colour blind, as it had been in the Cape. Qualifications for the vote required sufficient wealth to exclude all but a handful of Africans, but race was not mentioned in them. In Kenya, too, in the same year, the British Colonial Office, arbitrating between the rival political claims of the white settlers and of the more numerous Indians, issued its famous declaration that the interests of the African population must be considered paramount and that it was the responsibility of the British government and of the European settlers to act as trustees for them. This declaration alarmed white settlers all over East and Central Africa, but was reaffirmed by Sidney Webb on behalf of the Labour government seven years later. The reactions of the settlers were well expressed by a member of the Northern Rhodesian legislative council speaking in 1933, when he said: 'We white people have not come to this country solely and even mainly to raise the native in the scale of civilization. Our main objective is to survive ourselves, to improve our conditions if we can, and.... to raise a family and perpetuate our race.' But, in practice, British governments continued to accept the guidance of white leaders in each territory. The general outlook towards Africans throughout this period was well expressed by the comparatively liberal Hilton Young Commission of 1929, which reported that in East and Central Africa there could be no early prospect of including Africans in the legislative councils.

In his own country Smuts was less effective in preserving British influence. In 1924 he was defeated by a coalition of Afrikaner nationalists and the white trade unionists who were organized in the South African Labour Party. From this time onward the concept of Afrikaner domination steadily undermined the British connection. In 1926 Hertzog secured a definition of dominion status which led to the complete independence of South Africa under the Statute of Westminister five years later. Henceforth, dominions were recognized as sovereign states, equal in status to Britain. Meanwhile, the Afrikaner and their white working-class allies applied a policy of 'civilized labour' under which the poorer section of the white community was given preferential opportunities in employment and highest wages than its non-European competitors.

It took the financial crisis of 1931 to force Hertzog and Smuts into alliance. By 1933 they had formed a coalition government and merged their rival parties. Even a convinced Afrikaner Nationalist such as Hertzog discovered that when the cold winds of international financial collapse blew on South Africa his country still needed its British connections, particularly in the City of London. He and his followers learnt this lesson; for the next thirty years the Afrikaners concentrated on gaining increasing influence within the financial and commercial sector of their country's economy so as never again to find themselves dependent on Britain.

By the 1930s Smuts was ready to accept the basic tenets of Afrikaner national policy. The 1910 British hopes of liberalism spreading from the Cape into the other provinces were exposed as vain. In 1936 Hertzog and Smuts in alliance destroyed the Cape franchise, removing Africans from the common roll and setting up an alternative shadowy communal electoral system. Smuts half-heartedly offered as recompense a form of conciliar local government in the Transkei, again echoing nineteenth century British ideas. But, in fact, the era of qualified British liberal influence was at an end. It might be temporarily and superficially revived under the pressure of war needs after 1939 when Hertzog left Smuts on the war issue; but even then its failure was exposed, as segregationist measures continued to dominate South African political life even when Smuts was alone in the saddle. It finally came to an end in 1948.

Chapter 10

A Second Volte-Face

If the imposition of British imperial rule on Africans in the late nine-teenth century had been dramatically sudden, the dissolution of colonial governance came with even more spectacular abruptness. Within twenty years following the conclusion of the second world war virtually the entire British African empire had been dissolved. The relationship between Britons and Africans, which at the beginning of that war had appeared more deeply rooted in the soil of imperialism than ever, experienced its second violent reversal within seventy-five years. It is still too early to discern the outlines of its new character.

The most remarkable aspect of this *bouleversement* was that it took place at a time when the gap between British and African strength was wider than ever before. During the course of the war Britain had participated in the discovery of means to split the atom, providing her with a source of power never previously possessed by man. More-over, despite expenditure of her treasure, she had expanded her manu-facturing and industrial capabilities beyond her pre-war achievements even if she had yet to realize their potential. Britain had also emerged victorious from a war in which, despite the eventual participation of the United States and the Soviet Union, she had stood alone at a crucial time against the collective resources of Europe organized against her by the Nazis and Fascists. One might therefore have assumed that her imperial *élan*, backed by greater power to enforce her dictat, would have enabled Britain to reinforce her grip on the Empire.

We may be too close to the events to assess judicially the reasons for history confuting this expectation. But we must at least attempt to analyse some of the elements, however incomplete the conclu-sion.

In the twenty-year period of decolonization which followed the war the colonies certainly had neither the economic nor military power to challenge British hegemony. What they did possess, however, was the ability to force Britain to choose between progressive decolonization and a series of colonial wars. It was already clear by the end of the war that the Indian sub-continent would revolt if complete self-government were not offered quickly. Perhaps Britain could have defeated the Indians militarily, but only by involving herself in a long and costly war fought against the entire weight of international opinion. French and Dutch colonial wars in Asia revealed that even in the age of atomic bombs the nationalist forces of poor countries could cause imperial powers acute embarrassment and undermine metropolitain economies. British experience in Malaya and later in Kenya, even when fighting with some international sympathy, taught the same lesson.

It may be argued that if this rationale had been applied in the nineteenth century the British Empire in Africa would never have been built. There is some truth in this assertion, although, despite the resistance shown by some Africans, large areas of Africa were annexed without active opposition. But the more apposite fact is that Britain's strategic, economic and political interests had radically changed since the nineteenth century. Independence for India in 1947 removed the paramount strategic necessity of controlling the sea lanes which the development of air power had, in any case, reduced in importance. British concern in overseas trade and investment remained concentrated on the industrialized countries, whilst the important resources of the African colonies were already controlled by British companies which could expect to continue their operations after political control had passed into local hands. In both international and domestic fields the political atmosphere had become heavily laden with anti-imperialist elements.

In order to understand British attitudes towards decolonization, both her conscious and subconscious motives, we need to examine the country's economic and political situation in the mid-twentieth century. The central factor was that Britain had now finally lost her nineteenth century economic pre-eminence. We have already seen how, in the latter part of the nineteenth century, British industrialists had begun to lose the momentum gained in the earlier part of the century. They had failed to recognize the opportunities for new forms of production to replace traditional products in which they were being overtaken by

America and Germany. The first world war seriously dislocated British production and, although it removed German competition for a time, it also enabled the Germans to return in the 1930s with a rebuilt, modernized industrial machine. The absence of German competition and Britain's privileged imperial position obscured the harsh realities for the first half of the inter-war period, but the world crisis again exposed them. Even though imperial preferences again helped to cushion the shock and although some diversification was accomplished during the 1930s, by the outbreak of the war British had once more been overtaken by the Germans, whilst the Americans were were almost out of sight.

The consequence of the second world war to Britain's economic position were even more drastic than the first. To pay for her efforts she had to sell overseas capital assets worth a net amount of nearly £5,000 million, more than she actually held in 1939. Although this 'net sale' does not indicate that all these assets actually left British ownership, those which did not were offset by foreign debts incurred in order to pay for the war – many of them forming part of the sterling balances owed to colonial countries for goods provided to Britain on credit. And industrial production had again been diverted from constructive paths in order to supply the needs of war.

The second world war finally exposed the demise of Britain as a great power in the economic world. It is true that this fact was once again slightly disguised by the removal of Germany and, this time, of Japan, too, from international competition. But both were back in the forefront of international industry by the 1950s. They returned with modernized structures rebuilt out of the ashes. Few people deceived themselves about the reality of Britian's decline this time. Dependence on American aid during the war had prepared most observers for an inevitable continuation of assistance in rebuilding the economy after the war. Now it was to be Britain which would seek injections of external capital if her industries were to be regeared to supply her post-war needs.

Thus, in one way, Britain in the mid-twentieth century had exchanged places with the America of a century before. She might have opened up an even wider gap between the standard of life of her people and that of her African subjects, but to maintain that standard she would now need American dollars, and to gain them she possessed the enormous advantage of colonies which earned dollars. In Africa cocoa and gold from the Gold Coast, copper from Northern Rhodesia, joined Malaya's tin and rubber as the sterling area's main dollar earners. During the decade following the war the colonial share of the sterling balances rose from twelve per cent to thirty-two per cent, from £450 million to nearly £1,300 million. Their value also suffered from devaluation in 1949; whilst although they were to become available to the new states after independence, for the time being they could not be used by the colonies concerned to buy the dollar goods needed for development and earned only about three per cent interest.[1]

Some people may have been deceived into believing that Britain was back again on the road to economic power when overseas investment showed a remarkable post-war recovery. In the ten years after the war it attained the pre-war monetary figures, although the income derived from it was never to reach the percentage of national income reached in the 1920s and, of course, could not aspire to the pre-1914 heights. But two aspects of this investment boom tell another story. Whilst the monetary figures were impressive, the net figure was much smaller than the gross. For the period 1946–54, for instance, gross overseas investment produced an income which averaged 3.85 per cent of the national income; but the net income showed an average of only 1.65 per cent. The difference arose from the amount of overseas capital entering Britain.[2]

The consequences of this factor can be seen from another angle. During the same period net property income was never large enough to pay for more than fourteen per cent of British imports. In fact, that figure was only reached in 1950 and only in one other year did it attain double figures. Yet, even in 1938, after several years of disinvestment, it was nineteen per cent. Moreover, during this post-war period imports were running at a lower volume level than in 1938.[3] The conclusion is clear. Not only had Britain to rely on exports to pay her import bill to a far greater extent than ever before – ninety per cent by 1949 compared with fifty-six per cent in 1938 – but the investment of foreigners in Britain was largely offsetting the income obtained

[1] See H. M. Treasury, Balance of Payments, 1947–57, 1958–60.

[2] Brown, *op. cit.* p. 109.

[3] London and Cambridge Economic Bulletin, December 1962.

from her own overseas investments.[1] The days of *rentier* Britain, with her imports and national income substantially subsidized from earlier investment, were obviously over.

The nineteenth century positions of Britain and America had now been reversed in another direction. Not only were Americans investing in Britain, but it was now America that insisted on free international trade. The Atlantic Charter guaranteed 'access on equal terms to trade and raw materials' and, despite Churchill's concern for Empire agreements, the only qualification the British delegation could get the Americans to accept was that such free trade should be 'with due respect for existing obligations'. The Lend-Lease contract, the Keynes Loan, the General Agreement on Tariffs and Trade and Marshall Aid all undermined imperial preferences by insisting on convertibility of sterling (vainly, as it transpired), a halt to discriminatory protection and reduced restrictions on dollar imports. (This American pressure also played a part in persuading the Labour government to dismantle the war-time government economic controls which could have helped to plan the economy.) It was now American technological supremacy which stood to gain from free trade, although Americans, unlike the nineteenth century British, were not so self-confident as to abandon their own protective system; they were living not in the single world economy of the nineteenth century, but in a world divided between Communist and capitalist blocs.

The result was that America threw her weight into the anti-colonial balance, always on condition that the regimes which succeeded colonial rule could be trusted to remain in the capitalist camp, and were prepared to keep the rules now laid down by the dominant sectors of American capitalism. For, like the British in the previous century, America regarded empires as a restraint on the trade she knew she could dominate if restrictions were removed. Thus, from the declaration in the Atlantic Charter that America and Britain respect 'the right of all peoples to choose the form of government under which they will live and they wish to see sovereign rights and self-government restored to those who have been forcibly deprived of them', America took an active part in giving moral aid to anti-colonial movements and in persuading her allies that the days of imperialism were past. In vain did

[1] H.M. Treasury, *Balance of Payments*, 1946-61.

Churchill protest that colonies were not covered by this clause. Americans sought a post-war world in which imperial practices discriminating against her trading potential were abolished. Her position as the world's supermarket and credit controller gave her an irresistible power of persuasion, as Britain and France were to learn abruptly over the 1956 Suez invasion.

It might be expected that Britain and the other European imperial powers would resist American pressures to undermine their colonial empires. To some extent they did so. The Dutch and French fought particularly bitter colonial wars in Asia and the British in Malaya, while the American qualification to her anti-colonial attitude was clearly seen in the case of British Guiana. When Britain's decolonization policy provided an opportunity for a communist-socialist government to take office, the Americans fully supported British efforts to remove it.

But in Africa the situation was more ambiguous. Once the choice had been made to give India independence rather than face a costly imperial war, a strong case could be made for considering a similar policy for the Gold Coast and possibly for Nigeria. It was not simply that post-war disturbances in West Africa presaged anti-colonial conflict there; American and British overseas capital had become equivocal as to where their interests lay in the future development of British Africa.

It is important to examine the character of post-war British external investment if we are to understand its influence on the government's colonial policy. This character was already changing during the inter-war years. Instead of being largely composed, as before the first world war, of small *rentiers* investing in government stock, it was the large combines which increasingly dominated overseas capital. Moreover, it was largely from the public sector that capital sales were secured during the war. The impact of the war itself accelerated this process. Thus, during the period 1938–48 sales of private overseas capital totalled £650 million of the £3,000 million held, whereas £1,050 million of the £1,500 million public holdings were sold. And in the five years following the war £4,300 million was added to the private sector compared with only £350 million to the public. It is also significant to note that the general direction of investment remained in the same channels as before: business investors were still much more interested in the developed than the developing countries. During this five year period more private capital was invested in South Africa than in all the colonies combined. Although the opportunities in Europe had now been almost exhausted, the U.S.A., Canada, Australia and the Rhodesias, added to South Africa, still attracted the bulk of investment. The proportion invested in underdeveloped areas even declined after the war, despite the fact that Middle East oil now accounted for nearly half the total to these developing countries.[1]

So the main investing interests in the post-war period still regarded the colonial empire, and particularly the African section of it, as no more than of peripheral concern. They were more involved in restoring Britain's position in the international fields of banking, investment and trade, concentrating on those countries where development had already taken place. Often they were engaged in buying a share of international combines. They saw the importance of avoiding further expense and dislocation from unnecessary wars and of averting international hostility in a world atmosphere which had become increasingly chilly towards imperialism – and particularly cold in the most important environment, America.

The main investors directly involved in Africa were now combines, of which the Unilever subsidiary, the United Africa Company, is a good example. As we have already seen, this had become a vertically-integrated organization, collecting raw materials, processing them, and also selling consumer goods in the local market. It was therefore important for these combines to maintain control of raw material production, but equally important to remain on good terms with local leaders. Not only did they aim to increase dividends – and succeed in doing so – but, taking a longer term view, to plough back a proportion of their profits. It was from this process that an important section of increased investment was derived. This again depended on good relations with local representatives. These large corporations operated as quasi-political units. In contrast to the earlier small investors they controlled such a proportion of colonial incomes as to hold an independent position within a colony, responsible to neither imperial government nor local nationalists. As colonial power was threatened they recognized

[1] Brown, *op. cit.*, p. 282. See also W. B. Reddaway and others, *The Effects of U. K. Direct Investment Overseas: an interim report.* C.U.P. 1967.

that their future depended on sympathetic relations with anti-colonial leaders and parties; and the nationalists also had to accept the fact that it was unlikely they would be able to develop their economics without some kind of alliance with the alien economic giants.

Moreover, although immediately after 1945 the demand for African products maintained the upward curve of the wartime years, with the world seeking both minerals and agricultural goods, this increased demand flattened out in the 1950s. Britain was now growing more of her own food, substitutes for certain raw materials were introduced, whilst modern industry anyway needs less raw material than in the past. The material content of many manufactures began to decline in ratio to the labour added; meanwhile synthetics were replacing natural materials. After 1951 Britain's imports of food and raw materials showed only slight increases.[1] The consequence was that the combines operating in the African colonies began to plan more sophisticated and long-term activities than simply the collection of raw materials. They recognized the immediate post-war opportunities both to sell consumer goods and to start industries. For Africans had returned from war service with new demands, whilst the war had stimulated African cash economies and accelerated the building of infrastructures. Urbanization had greatly increased, providing modern, if low-scale, markets for the first time. In the immediate post-war years the terms of trade for primary producers varied between thirty-five and forty-five per cent above pre-war figures.[2] Vertically-integrated combines like Unilever, Dunlops, Imperial Tobacco, Bowaters, were able to restrict the consequent rise in costs by monopoly control of raw materials, holding down the wages of colonial workers and rationalizing on the use of materials; but even more important to them was the extra income received by colonial customers. When this was added to the increased volume of external aid and to the, albeit restricted, drawings on sterling balances, the market possibilities looked both inviting and stable. And when the terms of trade turned against primary producers in the 1950s, increased profits could be made through lower costs, although the companies, like British exporters, probably suffered more from loss of colonial earnings than they gained from the fall in the

[1] See *London and Cambridge Economic Bulletin*, December 1962.
[2] *U. N. Statistical Yearbook, 1961*.

cost of materials. They were caught in an insoluble dilemma; low costs diminished their markets; high costs inflated prices.

It is true that the degree of industrialization in the colonies was small – infinitesimal compared with that of South Africa – and that it was almost entirely confined to light industries. In capitalist economic terms it could be argued that Britain was a more suitable location for industrial concentration; that the only advantage of locating new industries in the colonies was the public benefit to colonial people – not an advantage calculated to appeal to shareholders. So the heavy industrial base remained in Britain, colonial industrialization being largely concerned with processing local raw materials or assembling imported products. The big corporations preferred to keep their main industrial base at home as a form of insurance against the dangers of future instability or nationalization and as a more profitable policy. But the markets thus opened, if small, represented a different type of economic interest in the African colonies from that of the past.

The changed character of post-war British capitalism raised its own dilemmas. If the objective was to be quick and large profits, was it not necessary to keep down colonial wages to a minimum and to exert every effort to depress raw material prices? Yet, if this policy was followed, would the colonial market not inevitably grow more slowly as fewer resources were obtained from the export of primary products and wage-earners found their pay packets insufficient to purchase consumer goods? On the wider level, was there not a conflict of interest between the City, now inextricably inter-linked with the great combines and giving first priority to maintaining the value of sterling, to borrowing short to lend long, and the industrial-trading sector concerned with expanded markets?

British capitalists, moreover, never resolved the central predicament in their post-war relations with the colonial countries outlined above. If they were to concentrate on the colonial markets it was essential that modernized industrial systems be built in the colonies to generate that degree of economic activity which would expand market resources. This might be slow, but it would bring inestimable long-term rewards for a trading nation like Britain. But the British were always reluctant to build genuine industrial complexes, preferring to sell consumer goods and to leave the industrial base in the already-developed countries. They contented themselves with providing infrastructures and never faced the focal choice between domestic and overseas investment. As a result, although the colonial proportion of British trade increased immediately after 1945 – exports by six per cent over the first post-war decade compared with pre-war figures – the increase could not be sustained beyond the mid-fifties. Colonial countries remained economically dependent, unable, without their own strong industrial systems, to develop self-sustaining economies capable of growing into equal trading relations with Britain. (The British economy as well as the colonies suffered from this failure. In the choice between concentrating on building virile economic structures in the colonies and ex-colonies or competing within the cut-throat, rich, industrialized world, where re-equipped Germany, Italy and Japan again resumed an advantageous position, British capitalists shied away from both. Consequently there were frequent balance of trade crises as rising import costs could not be matched by exports. They contented themselves in the colonial field with a timid partial development which left colonial peoples exposed to the wild fluctuations of primary prices, severely handicapped from buying Britain's exports.)

The dilemmas of the concentrated British capitalist system, engaged increasingly in the competition of international combines for world markets, illustrated the changed attitudes of British economic forces towards the Empire after the war. No longer could they afford to risk American displeasure by holding on to colonial barriers against international trade, especially if such attempts were to involve a spate of colonial wars. Only where there seemed to be a danger of communism succeeding colonial rule would defence of Empire be recognized as part of the battle to protect the 'free world'. On the contrary, it was progressively recognized that racial conflict might well provide new opportunities for communist gains. (The Americans recognized this feature of mid-twentieth century life in the empires of European states long before they were compelled to concede that the same principle might apply to their own homeland.) Of at least equal importance was the fact that overseas investors and commercial interests were now looking to a long-term future of profitable business in the colonies. The large concerns, in particular, realized that this might not, and probably would not depend on continued British rule, at least in West Africa. It would be more likely to depend on British business building confidence with emerging élites or, where still entrenched, with the old feudal rulers. It might be tricky to decide which individuals or groups would be most likely to survive in power under self-government, but it was increasingly recognized as fatal to allow British business interests to be associated with the preservation of colonial rule.

Whilst this attitude held generally true in West Africa, the situation was somewhat different in the white-settled lands in the east and centre of the continent. Here the expectation was that Europeans would become the successor rulers to Whitehall. There were a few qualified exceptions – in Central Africa the Booker interests and the Rhodesian Selection Trust saw the light earlier than others – but most British businesses fully expected East and Central Africa to follow the example of South, rather than of West Africa. This did not mean that the great corporations were any more inclined to throw their weight into the preservation of imperial rule than their colleagues in the west; but it did involve them in the tortuous path first, of participating in the efforts of Europeans in Kenya, Uganda, both Rhodesias and Nyasaland to remove Colonial Office rule so as to establish independent, white-controlled governments, and then suddenly changing direction in order to keep their place on the road now clearly leading to African independence. It was, however, the trade and investment prospects of the successor regimes which attracted them rather than the preservation of British political authority. By this time they realized anyway that Britain could only retain colonial power by engaging in wars as disruptive as that in Algeria.

The economic environment, then, was ripe for decolonization. Without the changed character of Britain's economy and the new direction taken by her major economic interests British political control over Africans would have not been concluded at this time. As we have seen, the gap in military power between Britain and her colonial subjects had never been so wide.

Yet, equally, whatever the environment, if there had not also been a virile movement amongst Africans to rid themselves of colonial rule, decolonization would not have followed the course that it did. Although the British forces supporting colonial rule were in retreat, they had not reached the point of flight seen, for instance, in Belgium after 1957.

There is no simple description for the outlook of Africans after the second world war. Their feelings are commonly termed 'nationalist', but, with very few exceptions, they had never lived in nation states. They had certainly never been governed as nations under colonial rulers. They had been subject peoples, governed by institutions and officers whose final authority lay in Westminster. It is true that a form of diarchy had increasingly arisen as colonial councils, under governors, had been accorded greater powers. Such local governments stimulated some ambition for statehood, but as the units of administration hardly ever coincided with social or cultural entities, the achievement of nationhood was a different matter. The fact was that Africans, to a much greater extent than their colonial cousins in Asia or the Caribbean, had little, if any national heritage to which they could nostalgically refer. They had strong localized traditions and cultures, but, with few exceptions, these had never been politically organized into nation states even before colonization. One of the usual and most potent forces capable of mobilization in the cause of decolonization was therefore almost entirely absent from Africa.[1]

Yet there is no doubt that anti-colonial emotions gripped many Africans. We have seen earlier that some Africans had never accepted the colonial status. Opposition to the imposition of alien rule was widespread from its inception and continued in an active and often violent form well into the first world war. Of even deeper import, however, were the efforts made by Africans to plan their own social and political future. The Fante Confederation of the 1870s provided an early example. The Aborigines' Rights Protection Society of 1897 organized defence of land rights in the Gold Coast. Professor Du Bois, an American Negro, took the lead in stimulating pan-African ideals and initiated a number of conferences to develop them from 1900 onward. In 1918 a Gold Coast lawyer, J. E. Caseley Hayford, founded the National Congress of British West Africa which sought African participation in colonial governments and some form of unity between the four West African territories ruled by Britain; for a few years it became active in both the Gold Coast and Nigeria. In the following decade the West African Youth League strove even more forthrightly to achieve unity in British West Africa. As increasing numbers of

[1] For greater political details of the decolonization period see John Hatch, *A History of Post-War Africa*, (André Deutsch, 1965).

African young men went to study in London and other British cities, political theories and their application to the African scene became a constant subject of discussion. The emphasis during the inter-war period was usually on gaining greater representation in the colonial institutions set up in their homelands and on the need to create a wider African consciousness. The West African Students' Union, founded in the mid-twenties, provided the liveliest forum for these discussions. During the same period, too, Herbert Macaulay, grandson of Nigeria's first African bishop, founded the Nigerian National Democratic Party. Its object was to press for self-government within the British Commonwealth, but although it was able to gain some publicity in Lagos during the periodic elections to the Legislative Council, it never succeeded in attracting serious support outside Lagos.

During this inter-war period most West African political activity arose from ideas and ambitions which were essentially middle-class in origin. As progress was made, albeit slowly, in medical facilities, education, social amenities and economic life – the inevitable consequence of accelerated economic activity – Africans began to join the professions as teachers, doctors, lawyers and clergymen. As we have seen, there had always been merchants and businessmen in West Africa, together with a handful of professional men. Their ranks now swelled, though they still only constituted a minute proportion of the African inhabitants and were concentrated mainly near the coastal regions. Together with the expanding legion of students seeking their education in Britain, they began to constitute a class which was absorbing European thought and breaking away from the tribal milieu.

This growing circle accepted its appointed place in the new liberal setting of the post-Versailles world. The concept of 'self-determination' propounded by Woodrow Wilson, Lenin and the League of Nations may have been vague, but it created a new international atmosphere in which liberal-minded people could revel without too much questioning. It was marked by the 1923 Devonshire Declaration, reaffirmed by Passfield in the 1929 Labour government, promising that African interests in Kenya would be considered paramount; the independence of Eire in 1921; the 1926 Balfour Declaration accepting Dominion equality with Britain, put into constitutional form by the Statute of Westminster in 1931; the passage of the 1929 Colonial Development Act, recognizing for the first time a small imperial responsibility for economic development in the colonies. The Indians were able to make use of the new trend to secure some advance towards self-government, debates on colonial policies began to be heard at the League of Nations and, for a time, it even became fashionable to suggest that all colonies should be taken under an international wing.

On this new international stage, although the Indians supplied the leading characters in colonial scenes, Africans clearly had a role, if a minor one. But those who had contact with European society, almost all drawn from wealthy families, usually followed the political fashions of Europe. They sought reform, equal salaries and opportunities in the professions, greater representation in colonial institutions, more schools and universities. They discussed international issues like the mandates system and vague notions of pan-Africanism, but they hardly considered any direct challenge to the actual institution of imperialism. Nor was this surprising, for not only did most of them depend for their living on their place in the imperial system, but there was as yet little basic challenge to imperial foundations in European thought. Africans came into contact with communists, socialists and radicals in Britain, accepting some of their ideas on both policy and organization, but one has only to examine the actions of the 1929–31 Labour government to realize how remote the idea of destroying imperialism was from British politics.

The 1930s saw a change. The world economic crisis sharpened the issues and aggravated tensions. Investment and trade fell abruptly. Prices of primary products slumped and, if imperial preferences provided some cushioning effect, they also narrowed the market for colonial producers. The invasion of Ethiopia in 1935 shocked even middle-class *évolué* Africans by revealing that Europeans were still capable of imperial expansion; appeasement towards the Italians by Britain and France began to disillusion the African élite with the good faith of their own European friends. Yet these Africans were caught up in the same dilemma as the progressives of Europe; they recognized that Britain and France were still pursuing imperial interests, yet realized at the same time that the Nazis and Fascists were propounding policies not only imperialist but openly racialist. They therefore continued, with reservations, to regard the British and French as their friends. Very few Africans stood outside the conflict and treated it as an intra-imperialist struggle, as Nehru and Gandhi did.

Nevertheless, out of the maelstrom of the 1930s emerged a more radical attitude in West Africa. With the return of Nnamdi Azikiwe from his studies in American universities and of Oladipo Davies from the London School of Economics, the complacent outlook of the middle class in Nigeria and the Gold Coast was increasingly challenged. Azikiwe began to use the press, first in Accra and then through his own *West African Pilot* in Nigeria, to attack not only discrimination but the continuation of colonial rule. Davies and Azikiwe used their influence within the Nigerian Youth Movement, originally formed to protest against poor education, to turn it into the first national movement of Nigeria. The organization still tended to be led largely by the middle class, but Davies and Azikiwe helped to broaden its appeal by attracting some urban workers. They also persuaded it to adopt a platform calling for independence and autonomy within the British Empire, a sharp challenge to the reformists. But the radical orientation of the Movement did not last long. The more bourgeois Yoruba from Lagos and the commercial west began to dominate its organisation, adding communal to political differences amongst its members.

Communal consciousness was also retarding political organization in East Africa. It had been the Kikuyu who had taken the lead in protest against British policy in Kenya. They came into more direct contact with European interests than any other community because they lived beside the white farms and their homes skirted the suburbs of Nairobi. They therefore found their avenues of expansion blocked, whilst in the city they suffered both from unemployment and discrimination. Moreover, in Nairobi they heard the strident voices of white settlers proclaiming their intention of taking over the government of the country themselves.

The only serious political organization established during the interwar period, the Kikuyu Central Association founded by Harry Thuku, was essentially confined to the single tribe. It adopted a sophisticated attitude towards land rights, unemployment and discrimination; but it still revealed its traditionalist outlook by a heated reaction to attempts made by missionaries to abolish the practice of female circumcision. And when the Kikuyu set up their own schools in competition with the missionaries, it was as much in order to combat attacks on their tribal traditions as to provide more educational opportunities for their children. In the meantime, Jomo Kenyatta, who had been secretary of the Association, was in London studying anthropology and, more importantly, discussing political organization with communists, members of the Independent Labour Party and left-wingers from the Labour Party.

Other varieties of communalism also influenced anti-imperialist resistance in north-east and southern Africa. In Egypt the pseudo-independence granted by Britain in 1922 was followed by periods in which power alternated between the court and the Wafd moderate nationalists. But beneath the surface cynicism was growing, particularly amongst the younger generation, as little was achieved in land redistribution or industrial employment. The pan-Islamic concept attracted considerable support in Cairo from those who rejected European influences. This marriage between revolt against harsh economic realities and dogmatic religion conceived the Moslem Brotherhood, an organization which appealed both to the utopianism of the poor and to those whose disillusion with politicians led them to take an anti-parliamentary pose.

In the south the main communal influence was neither tribal nor religious; in both South Africa and Rhodesia it was racial. Rhodesia hardly produced an industrial working class during the inter-war years. Her small white population lived as masters within a feudal society in which the conquered Africans were ruled as vanquished subjects, supplying servants and unskilled farm or service labourers. But in South Africa an environment existed which theoretically was more conducive to class organization than any other in the continent. Mining of minerals required a large labour force of skilled and unskilled workers; the manufactures and services which arose out of mining activity needed a similar workforce. Farming was conducted on a much lower plane of organization and efficiency, but it needed workers. From such a diverse economic society it was inevitable that professional and intellectual classes should also appear. Moreover, the need to maintain high profitability from the mines and to modernize agriculture inevitably led to increased exploitation of the workers, especially at times when the gold mines appeared to be approaching exhaustion.

In these circumstances it could have been expected that in South Africa the conditions were ripe for strong working-class organization concentrated against white rulers given power by Britain to act as imperialist agents, and against mining and manufacturing owners who garnered much of their capital from Britain and America.

The fact that this did not occur was almost entirely due to the racial character of the South African labour force. At crucial moments in the 1920s the white workers put colour consciousness and the preservation of their privileged position as labour aristocrats before working-class solidarity. They attacked their employers in 1922, but more because of fear that African workers might be given a chance to compete with them than to defend themselves against exploitation. And when, a few years later, African workers reached the climax of their struggle for trade union rights, they were offered little support from white workers. On the contrary, it was the white workers in the South African Labour Party who formed an alliance with Hertzog and his Afrikaner nationalists to enforce further helotry on the Africans. Any chance of social revolution in South Africa was thus postponed whilst the Afrikaners consolidated their political power and established an alliance with capital to preserve the migratory labour system and to depress African wages. The Afrikaners, with tacit consent from the English-speaking community, chose to create a state-controlled capitalist structure in which the internal market would be deliberately restricted in order to preserve their racial fanaticism. It might be an unpopular decision amongst manufacturers, but it could be maintained so long as the economy was underpinned by the gold mines, where cheap labour was welcomed, and by continued capital investment from abroad. British political influence virtually disappeared after the first world war; but the continuing profitability of South Africa as an investment market persuaded British capital to provide the means by which state control of economic organization and social structure could be consolidated. In South Africa the imperial torch was handed over by Britain to the white community, who used it to impose colonial rule over their own non-white subjects.

Over most of Africa during the inter-war years the movement against colonial rule appeared incipient rather than openly challenging. The masses were still almost entirely engaged in traditional agriculture. Their frustrations were expressed through schismatic or messianic religious sects rather than in political organization. Amongst a small proportion of Africans outside the subsistence economy, however, three groups or classes had begun to emerge, first and most clearly in

West Africa. There were the traditionalists, chiefs and their henchmen, who usually worked with the colonial authorities; there was a professional, business element, sometimes related to chiefly families, usually with close connections with Britain, intent on reforming the existing structure and securing a better place in it for themselves; thirdly, there were the beginnings of an urbanized leadership, whose contacts in Britain were usually with left-wing politicians, who were just starting to recognize that the logic of their adoption of political democracy must lead to an attack on colonial rule itself.

The effects of the second world war were to strengthen the position of the third group, greatly expand their numbers and extend their outlook to territories previously slumbering under unchallenged British rule. It was from this group, sometimes temporarily allied to the middle class, that was to come the leadership against the roots of colonial rule.

In the second world war, as in the first, thousands of Africans were to witness white men killing each other by the most horrific means scientific minds could devise. They listened to the propaganda and counter-propaganda, realizing that the 'Christian civilization' brought to them from Europe soon discarded its teaching on the supreme value of Truth when its various communities quarrelled with each other. Now they also saw that the Europeans were vulnerable when an Asian, non-white nation, Japan, captured the British, French, Dutch and American empires in Asia. They also found that their French-speaking brothers were involved in the bitter quarrels between two rival French governments, Vichy and de Gaulle, both seeking support from French Africans. They heard or read of the passionate debates in South Africa and Rhodesia as to whether it was safe to arm black men; on the other hand, many of them saw a country ruled by black men for the first time when they participated in the liberation of Ethiopia from Italian rule and the restoration of the Emperor. They learnt in Burma and India that other coloured subjects of the British Empire were organizing for total independence, for the complete removal of British rule. In short, the second world war destroyed the European mystique on which so much of imperial rule depended.

Africans may have felt that in Nazism they were fighting a philosophy aimed at their own dignity and human identity as well as helping to defend their imperial masters; but the concept of innate racial superiority could never survive the war experience amongst Africans, even if Europeans were less ready to accept the logic. The fact that by the end of the war the East African forces numbered 228,000 and West African 146,000 shows that the experience was considerable.

The war also bequeathed an Africa different in significant respects from the pre-war continent. This time important campaigns had been fought right across the northern part of the continent itself. Mobilization of war supplies had been organized in many African countries. Roads, railways, harbours and airfields had been either newly built or greatly improved. Production in both agriculture and industry had been considerably increased to supply the insatiable maws of war. Towns and cities had grown enormously as a result and having gained this momentum, urbanization was maintained after the war. Lagos, for instance, which had been a small town of some 75,000 inhabitants in 1914, had grown to 230,000 by 1950 and to 675,000 by 1962, and during the same period Accra's population increased from 20,000 to 135,000 to 325,000. Enugu, a village of only 15,000 residents in 1939, had grown to a sizeable town of 35,000 by 1945 and to 60,000 in 1953. Similar patterns were to be seen in Nairobi, the Northern Rhodesian copper towns, in Salisbury and Bulawayo. Urbanization brought release from the disciplines of tribal life, and an exchange of ideas between people from different communities. Social life became more diverse and stimulating, many cafés and bars were opened, public transport had to be provided, new types of houses supplied, and new household goods produced. Expanded town life naturally stimulated the local market; it also led urbanized Africans to organize modern social associations on a serious scale for the first time. Trade unions were established, some with the help of the British trade union movement, an activity encouraged by Britain's new Foreign Secretary, Ernest Bevin, and his protégé, Arthur Creech Jones, who became Colonial Secretary. (Though it was to become significant that the unions established under the aegis of the T.U.C. were always strongly advised by that body to remain aloof from politics.) Ex-servicemen's associations, market women's groups, sports clubs, religious and educational bodies, all provided increasing experience in organization for the growing number of Africans in the towns. Newspapers proliferated, giving increased opportunities for debate and argument in their columns, and by the end of the war, with prices high, shortages of

9

258 The History of Britain in Africa

goods, returning servicemen unable to find work, there was plenty to debate and many issues inviting organized pressures.

By the end of the war, too, not only was a little of the wealth produced by increased economic activity beginning to rub off on to a few African shoulders, but the consequences of pre-war educational opportunities were becoming apparent. In the immediate post-war years, for instance, nearly 120,000 children were at school in the Gold Coast, over 600,000 in Nigeria, over 250,000 in Kenya and about 170,000 in Northern Rhodesia.[1] These might be very small percentages of the total child population; but as literate individuals in African society they had a particular significance for the growth of political consciousness. Immediately after the war university colleges were established in the Gold Coast, Nigeria, Uganda and the Sudan. These institutions, though often conducted on British classical lines, offered extended opportunities, previously only supplied by Fourah Bay in Sierra Leone, for higher education and the experience of student debate and organization.

It was in these turbulent circumstances that the first serious African political organizations were founded. In the Sudan the Graduates' General Congress, formed in 1937, raised the cry for self-determination soon after the war ended. The Congress divided in 1945 between the Ashiqqua party supporting Egypt and the more conciliatory Umma. Azikiwe and Macaulay, influenced by the radical attitudes of Nigerian students, formed the National Council of Nigeria and the Cameroons in 1944. In the same year the Nyasaland African Congress was set up, mainly by civil servants and chiefs. Two years later the Northern Rhodesians federated their welfare societies throughout the country in defence against the political ambitions of the European community; the federation was later to graduate into a Congress. In Kenya a new organization, the Kenya African Union, was established in 1944 and secured backing from Luo and Kamba as well as from the Kikuyu although the latter remained its largest supporters. 1947 saw the formation of Dr Danquah's United Gold Coast Convention.

Almost all these organizations aimed to represent as broad a cross section of the population as possible and usually demanded some form of 'self-government'. They owed much of their inspiration to the

[1] Lord Hailey, *An African Survey*, Oxford 1956, p. 1,258.

Indian Congress, often adopting the same name, and seeking support in a similar way from as many different sectors of society as possible. Usually they were federal-type organisations, linking together a variety of separate bodies without provision for an individual membership of their own. Their response was to a general sense of resentment against alien rule and a desire to secure increased representation for indigenous inhabitants in established colonial institutions. Usually they were led by a mixture of professionals and intellectuals who had contact with left-wing circles in Britain. They had, with the notable exception of Azikiwe, as little conception of the roots of imperialism or of the future structure of their countries as had their friends in Britain.

These organizations were an African reflection of the prevalent attitudes towards imperialism amongst Fabians and Labour Party colonial experts in London. When Arthur Creech Jones was appointed Colonial Secretary in 1946 he became the official representative of this outlook. Passionately devoted to the cause of colonial reform, he nevertheless accepted the general bi-partisan approach to colonial policy assumed in Britain to be essential for continuity of policy. Under the influence of Lord Hailey, Britain's trusteeship approach was now extended into the field of social development. Hailey, Oliver Stanley from the Conservative Party, and Creech Jones, all accepted that in the post-war world Britain had a responsibility to ensure better living standards and social services for her colonial subjects. This would entail the imperial government exercising greater influence over the policies of the colonial governments in the colonies, taking the initiative in London and providing some of the funds for development. It also implied that 'good government' and social progress should take precedence over 'self-government' or any serious attack on the economic controllers of colonial economies.

This outlook was particularly fitted to Labour's post-war perspective of welfare reformism. It found a ready response from leaders like Ernest Bevin and the trade union cohorts whom he represented, always suspicious of intellectuals obsessed by politics who had no concern with the bread and butter needs of either colonial subjects or British workers! In any case, Bevin was speaking for many in the Labour Party when he told the House of Commons, 'I am not prepared to sacrifice the British Empire, because I know that if the British Empire fell. . . . it would mean the standard of life of our constituents would fall considerably.'[1] Creech Jones, despite his sincere desire to reform the Empire, rejected the idea that a Labour Colonial Secretary had the responsibility of introducing socialism into the colonies. He declared that it was 'contrary to the spirit of British policy to force people into particular moulds because a Secretary of State or his particular party thinks it good for them.'[2] He thus revealed his belief in bi-partisan continuity; but it might have been more accurate to suggest that it was the colonial governors rather than the colonial people who might object to socialist directives from Whitehall.

So reform was to be confined to social welfare and slowly increased representation in colonial institutions. British companies in the colonies might be expected to contribute more to such welfare schemes and, as in Northern Rhodesia, it might be held that the natural resources of a colony really belonged to it. But when it came to control of the economy, both Creech Jones and John Strachey, the Minister of Food, were agreed that nationalizing an organization like the United Africa Company was out of the question. Labour's conception of economic development was represented by the Overseas Food Corporation, the Colonial Development Corporation and marketing boards such as those for cocoa in Nigeria and the Gold Coast. (The Fabians failed to persuade the Secretary of State to set up a Colonial Mining Corporation because it might be resented in the colonies. They equally failed to convince their former chairman that he should not increase the political influence of Northern Rhodesian Europeans.) Such public corporations were to cooperate with colonial governments in finding the means to attract private development capital, whilst providing the infrastructure to facilitate the operations of private business and industry.

On the political front the prescription was for gradual advance in indigenous representation as social and economic conditions improved and a class of politicians and administrators emerged replete with British habits, attitudes and values. Creech Jones revealed his outlook by an address in Cambridge in 1948 when he declared, 'our conception of African development is based on Western political philosophy, and as far as we can see at present, that of the African leaders is based

[1] House of Commons 21.2.46.
[2] J. M. Lee, *Colonial Development and Good Government*, Oxford, 1967, p.75.

on the same ideas.' It was assumed that 'natives' in the colonies would acquire British administrative routines if they were provided with an example for long enough. The exercise of political democracy, first through local government and then at the national level, would be taught by the same colonial officials. The fact that democracy might involve conflict between organized social classes – as had occurred in Britain – was too dangerous a thought to be contemplated. After all, this was not how the official classes regarded British politics; the 'Establishment' ruled the country, whilst the politicians played their game of musical chairs according to the accepted rules. It was not surprising, therefore, that when the Colonial Office defended the Gold Coast Burns' constitution against an official commission's verdict that it was 'outmoded', it aggrievedly pointed out that the constitution had been approved by press, public and Legislative Council. What the colonial officials failed to perceive was that it was no longer sufficient to claim legitimacy because some black faces had replaced white. In situations like that of the Gold Coast, traditional chiefs and British-trained lawyers were no longer acceptable as representatives of the people, even though they were black; nor would institutions be acknowledged as democratic because of the skin colour of those occupying their benches.

British colonial officials and politicians might have been warned of the change taking place in African attitudes from a pan-African conference held in Manchester in 1945. It is true that communists and left-wing socialists had held many anti-colonial conferences and this might have been just another insignificant gathering held in a dingy hall by the tiny band of faithfuls. It is also true that pan-African conferences had been held internationally since 1900, without provoking any revolution. But anyone with a knowledge of Africa could have noticed something different in Manchester. Du Bois was still chairman, as he had been in previous gatherings. But this time an alliance had been formed between the most militant anti-colonialists in Britain, who were West Indians, and new African leaders with their feet firmly planted in their own societies. Padmore, James, Milliard, Makonnen, were well-known West Indians seen at most left-wing anti-colonial meetings; they were accompanied by Jomo Kenyatta, already a seasoned organizer of Kikuyu protest from the 1920s; Wallace Johnson, with experience in his own Sierra Leone and other

West African colonies; Peter Abrahams, a South African Cape Coloured writer who knew something of non-European protests on the Wit-watersrand; Kwame Nkrumah, whose experience in his own Gold Coast was limited, but who had already caught Azikiwe's eye and had learnt his political organization amongst African and Negro students in the United States.

These men met together to hammer out a programme for the removal of colonial rule from Africa. No longer content to haggle over the niceties of constitutional reform, they proclaimed, 'We are deter-mined to be free. . . . Therefore, we shall complain, appeal and arraign. We will make the world listen to the facts of our conditions. We will fight in every way we can for freedom, democracy and social better-ment.' This might be demagogic language, the words might be taken from European political experience, but it was not the tone of com-promise or reform. It had the spirit of agitation, of revolution.

If the Colonial Office chose to disregard Manchester's warning, its political analysts could have predicted that British policies themselves were bound to effect drastic changes. The period 1944–51 was a time of new constitutions. But if the loose, declamatory, congress type of organization sufficed to air post-war grievances, convincing British governments that constitutional or social reform was necessary, it was not equipped to fight elections on popular suffrage. This required a degree of local mass organization of which the middle-class-led protest movements were incapable. Thus the grant of constitutions in which elections were to be held on a franchise which included a number of genuine workers and peasants inevitably forced the forma-tion of modern political parties. They might break away from the old congress-type body, as did Nkrumah's Convention Peoples' Party, or transform their congress into a party, as Kenyatta attempted with the Kenya African Union and Azikiwe with his N.C.N.C.; but, whatever the method, this period of new constitutions was bound to see the appearance of African political parties.

Even before the new constitutions paved the way for popular elections, circumstances began to develop which invited mass organiza-tion. Post-war discontents erupted into revolt of various types in several colonies during the 1940s. In the Gold Coast there were strikes in the mines, a boycott of foreign stores, protest marches from ex-servicemen, and twenty-one were killed in subsequent riots. In Nigeria one of Azikiwe's newspapers was fined for sedition, whilst strikes and threats of strikes revealed the new militancy of trade unions. In Buganda discontent broke out against the feudal outlook of the aristocrats who ruled the country. In Kenya Kikuyu land grievances against their neighbouring white farmers mingled with resentment against lack of employment in the towns. These spontaneous discontents provided ready ammunition for the nascent political parties, for it was not of a character which appealed to the conservative, middle-class leadership. In any case, it could only be capitalized by the organization of urban masses in West Africa and a combination amongst the same kind of people along with the peasant farmers in the East. This was a task beyond the capacities of the wealthier, upper middle-class professionals and merchants who led the older type of organization like the United Gold Coast Convention; it could only be accomplished by the lower middle class cadres recruited by an Nkrumah to mobilize mass support behind a programme of action. 'Self-government now', easily translated into 'freedom now', provided the kind of rallying cry which could appeal to mass audiences. Strikes, boycotts, non-violent demonstrations, could readily be organized under the attractively simple slogan of 'positive action'. When Nkrumah and his lieutenants went to gaol charismatic martyrdom completed the pattern.

Yet the influence of Britain was still strong. The Gold Coast revolution was quickly transformed into a gentlemanly agreement. Whether the Colonial Office officials could see the realities of the colonial scene or not, Sir Charles Arden-Clarke, governor of the Gold Coast, certainly could. Although Nkrumah was in prison at the time of the 1951 elections, the governor released him as soon as it was clear that his C.P.P. had secured the support of the electorate. Arden-Clarke recalled his situation in a reminiscent article: 'My choice was fairly simple: if I did not release him we would not even make a start with working the Constitution; and if I did release him, he would find it very difficult to refuse to work the Constitution or give it a trial, even though it might be called "bogus and fraudulent". So he was released. He came up to see me, and I asked him to form a Government.' Nkrumah's response to the governor's action was equally appropriate to the best British manners. 'I would like to make it absolutely clear', he declared on his release, 'that I am a friend of Britain. I desire for the Gold Coast Dominion status within the Commonwealth.'

Ghana's attainment of responsibility for her own domestic affairs set the whole of West Africa inexorably on the road to independence. As soon as it was proven that Africans could control a modern state machine – and why should it have been thought that Africans were any less capable of doing so than anyone else? – West Africans were accepted into the same stream of British policy which had previously swept Canada, Australia, New Zealand and South Africa into statehood. British interests were no more threatened by black faces in Christiansborg Castle than they had been by pink in Canberra, Ottawa or Pretoria.

A few minor delays occurred in the 1950s, usually occasioned by communal fears. The approach of independence in Ghana provoked a revival of traditionalist pride in Ashanti. Three-way suspicions between Hausa-Fulani, Ibo and Yoruba, forced the Nigerians to experiment with various types of federal constitution, postponing their independence until 1960. In Sierra Leone tensions between the tribal communities of the hinterland and the more sophisticated Creoles on the coast, together with suspicions between the Mende and Temne tribes delayed independence there until 1961. Gambia tried to sort out her relations with surrounding Senegal and had to convince herself and the British that she was large enough to become an independent state. But by 1951 the die was cast; franchises were to become universal (except for Northern Nigeria's sex discrimination); parties would fight elections – the C.P.P. in Ghana, the S.L.P.P. in Sierra Leone, the N.C.N.C., Action Group and N.P.C. in Nigeria; victorious parties would form governments; their governments, supported by majority parties in the legislatures, would ask for sovereignty and the British parliament would pass independence acts. As the Sudan had gained independent status by the same means in 1956 and the Somali Protectorate was due to join her brother Somalis in 1960, political decolonization in non-settler Africa was now inevitable.

Political independence, of course, did not bring imperialism to an end. Unilever's United Africa Company, which at the end of the war was responsible for a third of all Gold Coast and Nigerian imports and exports,[1] did not leave with the proconsuls. The company might

---

[1] See Reginald H. Green and Ann Seidman, *Unity or Poverty*, Penguin 1968, pp. 109 sqq.

find it more expedient under African government to bequeath the retail trade to the locals, but only to transfer its investment into the production of consumer goods, cold storage, assembly of vehicles, drinks, cement etc. In fact it often found that African governments were more sympathetic than their colonial predecessors. As they hoped to protect local production, which the colonial rulers had refused to do, and as U.A.C., as part of the huge Unilever combine, had such a strong bargaining power, marketing opportunities could actually increase after independence. It was sufficiently strong to maintain its low wage policy and even to insist on importing many of the materials it processed for the African market rather than use local products.

The United Africa Company illustrates most distinctly the power of European economic forces in Africa both before and after independence.[1] As part of the huge Unilever combine its operations constituted only one sector of that institution's international activities. Indeed, although the growth of the company's capital expenditure after the second world war was phenomenal, its increase in Africa was modest. For instance, between 1951–55 and 1961–65 its capital expenditure in Britain rose from £32 million to £136.4 million; in the rest of Europe from £43.1 million to £144.6 million; in Africa, however, it only increased from £30 million to £39.9 million. Nevertheless, for Africans the operations of U.A.C. were deeply significant.

Before the first world war William Lever had been mainly interested in the raw materials he believed he could find in Africa. He expected much from his plantations in the Congo and from commercial activities such as those conducted by the Niger Company. From the Africans his company brought palm oil and kernels, cocoa and coffee, groundnuts, timber, hides and skins, which it sold on the world market. To the Africans it sold salt, flour, cotton, textiles, beer, hardware and sundry miscellaneous small goods. It is worth noting that the U.A.C. seems to have prospered when Africans were given good prices and declined when they were offered less money for their goods.

The growth of the African company and its standing within the Unilever empire can be judged from the fact that immediately after

---

[1] Charles Wilson, *Unilever 1945–1965*, Cassell 1968. Most of the factual information provided in this section on the U.A.C. is drawn from this official source – but not, of course, the conclusions.

9*

the second world war U.A.C. and the plantation companies provided between one-third and one-half of Unilever's total profits and one-quarter of its total turnover. It operated in several African regions as well as its traditional habitat in the west. In East Africa it had acquired Gailey and Roberts, a heavy equipment firm, in 1937. After the war this branch of the company assembled tractors, machinery, vehicles, bicycles, electrical goods. In South Africa it expanded from Lever's original three manufacturing centres, Johannesburg, Durban and Cape Town, buying up small businesses, producing margarine, soaps, ice-cream. Its operations had a similar character in Rhodesia where it saw the opportunity to replace imports coming from South Africa.

Nor was the U.A.C. confined to British Africa. Its French section, Niger France, operated in fourteen states, a quarter to a third of its turnover being in the Ivory Coast. This section was sufficiently successful to provide one-third the total turnover, one-fifth the total capital and one-quarter the total profits of the U.A.C. in Africa.

But it was the company's activities and policy directions in West Africa which most clearly demonstrate the significance of European capitalist enterprise in post-war Africa. The first important change arose from the creation of marketing boards and the parallel system of licensing buying agents. This had the effect of transferring control of produce buying from expatriate firms to African agents. Seeing the trend U.A.C., began to divert its activity into acquiring or building up retail business. The Kingsway stores, of which there were four in Ghana, eleven in Nigeria and one in Sierra Leone, provided the most noteworthy examples. And these businesses were largely capitalized by ploughing back into them about half the profits in order to create new investment. They became some of the main controllers of imports in the countries where they operated.

But around the time of independence retail trade and import control began to come under African control. The U.A.C. was again quick to recognize the signs, but it may well have made some miscalculations. Its object was to redeploy the capital it had invested in trade into light manufacturing industries which might develop import substitutes. During the 1950s the prospects looked fair and there seemed no reason to persuade the British government to delay independence. It was assumed that the new African regimes would be grateful to have the advice and support of experienced European entrepreneurs. The success of its efforts to sell itself as an ally of the nationalist leaders seems to have led the U.A.C. into believing that its future was assured. To some degree it had misread the course of nationalist actions in the economic field and the probability of political instability.

At first it seemed to the U.A.C. that prospects in Ghana were most promising. With a dense population and the comparatively high annual per capita income of £94, together with rapid development in education, social services and economic infrastructure, this country appeared a sound investment. In fact the investment programme was agreed with the Ghana government in 1958. A new town called Samreboi was built to service a ply-wood mill. In association with Heinekens a brewery was started at Kumasi. In the new town of Tema a detergent plant was built, whilst in association with the government a printing company was founded, a vehicle assembly plant was established and the company acted as agent for caterpillar tractors. What had not been foreseen was the government's increasing determination to control the country's economy. So the extent of government spending, the restrictions on imports and the campaign against repatriation of profits all began to undermine the U.A.C.'s influence in the economy.

Nigeria and the Ivory Coast also seemed promising fields for investment. Both were prepared to allow some luxury production as import substitutes and in each there was a growing demand for new clothes, garages, petrol stations, cars, refrigerators in shops, radio and television sets, which could all be either manufactured or assembled. The lack of radical ideology amongst the rulers of Nigeria and the close friendship of the Ivory Coast leaders with France seemed sufficient insurance against the kind of policies which were being adopted in Ghana.

By the time of independence in 1960, U.A.C. was on the point of almost total withdrawal from produce purchase and merchant business in Nigeria. Her redeployment cost 2,500 Africans in the lower grades their jobs, but this was unlikely to cause the kind of unrest which might have been expected in Ghana. Again timber attracted interest, particularly in Sapele, and the company went into business in affairs like cold storage, a meat factory, ice-cream – in conjunction with Walls – beer and stout brewing, in partnership with Guinness, cement production, with Portland Cement Company, car hire, as Niger Motors, a vehicle assembly plant at Apapa.

It can be seen, therefore, that the U.A.C. operated at the heart of European investment in West Africa, often bringing in other European firms with special technical knowledge as partners. The new perspective of the post-independence period was that the prospects were most inviting in new light industries which could produce substitutes for imports and therefore escape from the closing net of diminishing overseas balances. Profits would be partly used as new capital, or repatriated where possible. But Africans were also encouraged to buy shares so as to involve them in the whole operation, and local banks were taken into partnership. Where possible governments were also brought in. Many Africans were also employed by the company – forty per cent of its managerial posts in the continent were held by Africans in 1965 – which had been accustomed to train its higher-grade employees in technical schools or in Europe.

The U.A.C., therefore, can be seen as the chief agent in West Africa for the spread of the capitalist ethic and the involvement of governments, institutions, public leaders and the general population in it. It had to meet the handicaps of former colonial economic policy, the lack of transport and communications, the orientation of most economic life towards the coast for the purpose of export. During the re-deployment period from its old merchant function to the new productive policy it suffered a relative decline. Between 1955 and 1965 its share of Unilever's total African capital sank from 27 to 15.3 per cent. Yet it had invested in seventy-two factories in tropical Africa, provided commercial management in fifty-five and technical management for thirty-four. With the beginnings of oil exploitation in Nigeria it found a new stimulant to the provision of goods and services; in 1963 production was 3 million tons of crude oil; in 1966 20 million tons.

Yet by now the U.A.C. and its fellow companies were under heavy pressure, not so much from deliberate government policies but from events. The Congo plantations had lost about £1.5 million. African governments, even when sympathetic to foreign capitalists, were forced to try and retain a greater proportion of their national wealth at home. The official historian of Unilever remarks somewhat sourly, 'the governments of developing countries are not the only ones to allow themselves to overspend and run into balance of payments crises: but they are specially prone to do so, partly through lack of experience, partly because their situation often justifies heavy spending abroad.

The fundamental truth here should not be lost sight of. Foreign investment in a country expands that country's economic equipment. If it
yields profits, it must increase the country's national income. These
profits cannot therefore be a net burden on the local community. It
must be for the government of the community to see that facilities
are normally provided for the transfer of dividends as an accepted
charge against the national balance in recognition of the services
provided by the capital investment.' Professor Wilson also fulminates
against the critics of overseas capital investment: 'But joined to the
political risks already mentioned – the risk of expropriation without
compensation, savage taxation deriving from xenophobia, or the denial
of the right to repatriate profits – they still help to bedevil the future
of private investment in the *developing* economies.'

To those who consider that the wealth of the world and the labour
of its inhabitants should be available to whoever can exploit them, this
argument is autoptical. From the viewpoint of the labourers, of governments in the lands where the wealth is found, of ministers trying to plan
a modern standard of life for peoples to whom one dividend would
represent a year's income, it is open to rather deeper scrutiny.

Investment in West African minerals also continued unbroken by
political independence. The Sierra Leone Development Company,
mining iron ore, accounted for nearly one-third of the country's
exports in 1960 and was preparing to expand production. The assumption that Sierra Leone is a poor country can only be maintained by
restricting observation to the life of her people; wealth is there, but
most of it has always been sent out of the country. There has never
been any intention of using the ore to build a local iron and steel
industry to serve the needs of West Africa.

With the discovery of oil another product of world importance
joined West African exports. Shell alone is estimated to have invested
a greater sum in Nigeria than the total manufacturing investment in
that country. By 1964 the company claimed to have sunk £130
million in its Nigerian industry.[1] It looked as though West Africa was
to join North Africa and the Middle East as part of the industrial
world's oil empire. And, although oil might provide increased national

[1] Green and Seidman, *op. cit.*, p. 118.

revenues for independent Nigeria, it was, of course, owned and controlled from abroad, with the product almost entirely exported.

Independent governments tried various methods of securing greater
control over the companies exploiting their country's resources or, at
least, of ensuring that their treasuries gained greater benefits from their
operations. Nkrumah and his colleagues took the strongest initiative.
They used the Cocoa Marketing Board to accumulate surpluses which
they could use for state participation in the national economy. They
built their own shipping line, national commercial enterprises and
cocoa-processing plants. They tried to organize the cocoa-producing
nations in order to secure greater bargaining power in price determination. A National Trading Company, formed on the foundations of a
private business taken over by the state, competed in the import trade.
Exchange control, import licensing and legislation regulating private
business curtailed the operations of foreign concerns. Yet even the
Ghanaians could not prevent VALCO, supported by the governments
of both the United States and Ghana, from actually planning to bring
bauxite from America or the West Indies to feed the smelter built in
Ghana, rather than using Ghana's own supplies or those of Guinea.
Nothing could more clearly demonstrate the precautions taken by
international firms to ensure that control of the total productive
process should never be entrusted to one of the new states – nor better
illustrate the need for regional planning in Africa itself.

Despite these attempts to discipline overseas economic operations
in his country, Nkrumah finally failed. But his failure is less to be
accounted to his policies than to his failure in carrying them out. The
policies would have brought more of Ghana's economy under Ghanaian
control and provided the basis for building a progressive, self-sustaining economic life. It was the inefficiency, nepotism, corruption and
extravagance of those who were responsible for their execution which
led to failure, not mistaken policies.

The victory of decolonizing forces in West Africa did not necessarily
presage parallel developments in the rest of British Africa. It was
certainly clear by now that the political rule of the British would be
ultimately withdrawn from the whole continent, but the timetable
was uncertain and the character of the successor regimes obscure.
East and Central Africa consisted of colonies of white settlement and
until the beginning of the 1960s passionate arguments continued as to

whether the principles applied in West Africa were appropriate to Kenya, Uganda, Tanganyika, Nyasaland and the Rhodesias. At least until 1959 the British Conservative Party pursued a policy towards these countries more closely approximating to that in the pre-Union Cape Colony than to the attitude which was bringing independence to West Africa.

Two central issues governed the outcome of this debate. First, it had to be seen whether the white settlers with political pretensions, those in Kenya and the Rhodesias in particular, could mobilize sufficient force to assert political power over their African populations. They were given the chance, though, with the exception of Southern Rhodesia, they never secured unreserved support from the imperial government. Until the mid-1950s the 60,000 Europeans in Kenya were allowed to advance towards the same position as had been assumed by their cousins in the Cape Colony and Southern Rhodesia. It was not expected that Europeans in either Uganda or Tanganyika would be strong enough to imitate them, but it was thought that a federation of the three territories might sustain 'good' and white government for the whole region if the Kenyans proved themselves.

The Mau Mau rebellion ended this dream. Frustrated by land discrimination, unemployment, interference in tribal traditions and the cold-shouldering of Kenyatta's K.A.U., the Kikuyu, together with some Meru, Embu and Kamba, broke into violent revolt. Their warfare was conducted by medieval, quasi-mystical tactics to secure modern ends. The oath-taking ritualistic methods employed had little in common with the tactics of political parties in the rest of the continent; their objectives – removing discrimination, land reform, urban employment – were very similar.

The significance of the Mau Mau, however, was that it proved that the Europeans of Kenya were too few to meet the challenge of modern African political protest. Tom Mboya and his colleagues demonstrated their capacity to organize political activities even under the restrictions of the emergency. And Mau Mau itself could only be contained by the use of British military strength. The situation was therefore clarified by the rebellion. Europeans in Kenya were not strong enough to rule the country without continued British support. If they were left alone they would face the growing pressures of African political protest.

Their history showed little evidence of ability to abdicate voluntarily; so another war could be foreseen. In these circumstances Britain saw it as her interest to mediate whilst there was still time. For a few years British Conservative politicians tried to compromise by introducing various types of 'multi-racial' political balances. When they found that these would not appease the Africans, who used them only in order to increase their pressure, capitulation to the principle of popular democracy as practised in West Africa was inevitable.

The second factor was the degree to which Britain was able and willing to use her resources in order to impose her policies on recalcitrant colonies, but the Suez invasion settled the issue and showed that the days of gunboat colonial policy had passed. In future Britain would support the successful forces in her colonies, even if she had to wait some time before being able to identify them.

In the meantime Julius Nyerere was proving in Tanganyika that Nkrumah's strategy could succeed in the vastly different environment of East Africa. He based his approach on the power of a mass party, organized throughout the country. Leading it with firmness, tact and good humour, together with the use of his special advantage at the United Nations as representing a Trust Territory, he steadily pressed a retreating Colonial Office towards granting independence. He had little trouble with his Europeans, less than a third of Kenya's community and perhaps somewhat abashed by their neighbours' experience with Mau Mau. In fact, he showed those Europeans and Asians with foresight that their security depended on popular democratic government. In teaching this lesson and securing the cooperation of leading Europeans and Asians, Nyerere certainly eased the transition towards African government in Kenya.

Nyerere's quiet revolution also helped to kill the idea of a white-governed East African Federation. Uganda had been so agitated at the prospect that the Kabaka of Buganda, the most powerful traditionalist monarch, rebelled against British authority and was exiled in consequence. Though delayed by internal disputes, the revulsion against white rule thus expressed ensured that Uganda, once she could find the means of developing a national consciousness superseding communal and traditionalist loyalties, would follow the Tanganyikan example. So white settler rule, whether territorial or federal, was decisively rejected throughout East Africa. As British policy was now firmly marching along the decolonization road, the only alternative was African government based on popular election.

This verdict was facilitated by the fact that no major economic interests were involved in preserving European hegemony in East Africa. White farmers and businessmen, Asian traders and small industrialists, absorbed most foreign investment. Mining of soda in Kenya, copper in Uganda and diamonds in Tanganyika, never involved the large combines. This factor prevented the white settler lobby at Westminster ever gaining serious support in the City, which, in any case, was surely convinced after the mid-fifties that European rule in East Africa could only be imposed at the cost of further expensive wars. It also enabled post-independence African governments to show what could be achieved in controlling foreign capital, at least where the large corporations were not operating. The Uganda Development Corporation dominated industrial output in that country, whilst Nyerere ensured that about seventy per cent of Williamson's diamond profit accrued to his treasury.[1] His 1967 Arusha declaration, proclaiming a policy of nationalization in banking, insurance, commerce and some industry, accompanied by austerity and anti-corruption measures, demonstrated a determination, unparalleled in Africa, to exercise African control over the country's economy and to develop social justice amongst his own people. His example was partially followed the next year by Kaunda in Zambia.

If the massive corporations were little interested in East Africa, the picture in Central Africa was in complete contrast. Here were to be found Anglo-American and the Selection Trust in copper, Imperial Tobacco, Dunlops, Booker Brothers, Stewart and Lloyd, Metal Box, Turner and Newall, British Oxygen, De Havilland, and many others. In the five years following the war £150 million was added to the pre-war £50 million British investment in the Rhodesias, whilst the public debt holding rose from £10 million to £100 million.[2] The Rhodesias certainly became a profitable field for British investment in the post-war period. Northern Rhodesia provided the classic example of a colonial mining enclave. Between 1937 and 1956 output rose from £12 million to £115 million, dividends and royalties from

[1] Green and Seidman, *op. cit.*, p. 121
[2] Brown, *op. cit.*, p. 282

£5.5 million to £34 million.[1] The country's exports, almost entirely composed of copper, provided over eighty per cent of her money income, whilst payments leaving the country varied between a quarter and a half of her export revenues.[2]

Southern Rhodesia, on the other hand, was a white-settled colony, having been ruled first by the British South Africa Company and then, after 1923, directly by the white settlers. Her exports, a third of them tobacco, provided between forty and sixty per cent of her national income.[3] Transfer of profits and dividends again played a prominent part in export earnings, though not as large as in the northern territory, whilst much of the domestic savings from the white settlers were channelled to London rather than being invested in economic development in the territory.

Yet, despite this large-scale economic interest in the Rhodesias, the political issue remained the same as in East Africa. Could the white settlers, numbering between 200,000 and 300,000 compared to under 100,000 in East Africa, control the governmental machine against the political pressures of the Africans? If they could, capitalist interests and politicians would be prepared to support them as they had in South Africa. If there were risks of serious disturbance, especially of a form requiring British military assistance, allegiances would have to be reconsidered.

It seemed at first that the Europeans were sufficiently powerful to establish a modified form of South African regime. The white Southern Rhodesians, ruling a conquered African population, had demonstrated the possibility. They had maintained political stability and developed a growing European market as immigrants poured in from Britain after the war, attracting considerable investment. But the settlers were greedy. As immigration increased, pressure rose on the social amenities suitable for the comfortable colonial-style life which attracted Europeans. Materials, skilled labour and services were scarce. The whites looked enviously, as they had before the war, at Northern Rhodesia's copper wealth.

The scheme for federation of the two Rhodesias and Nyasaland which

[1] Brown, *op. cit.*, p. 183
[2] Green and Seidman, *op. cit.*, pp. 102–3
[3] Green and Seidman, *op. cit.*, pp. 102–3

was put into operation in 1953 made good capitalist sense for the settler community. Southern Rhodesia had greatly benefited from the war through expenditure by the forces and enforced import substitution in manufactures. If copper profits could be restrained from expatriation through taxation, the two Rhodesians could accumulate capital, as the South Africans had done, to build up their own manufacturing industries, thus becoming economically self-sustaining. Even many members of the British Labour Party believed that federation would be good for the economy of Central Africa. What they did not realize was that it depended on the maintenance of cheap African labour in the mines, where white trade unionists were fighting for the retention of the racial differential, and that it represented the white capitalist alternative to African government which alone could harness wealth production to the people's needs.

Conservative politicians, aided by divided views within the Labour Party, fought hard up to 1959 to preserve the federation. They were even prepared to prejudice peaceful political advance in East Africa lest it might undermine European hegemony in the Rhodesias. As late as March 1959, Lord Perth, from the Colonial Office, was telling Rhodesians that 'so far as our general colonial policy is concerned, a halt is being called to the rapid advance of colonial territories to independence. For Tanganyika, for example, we are proposing a long-term programme.'[1] This speech was made less than three years before Tanganyika's independence and in the midst of the few months which finally killed the multi-racial concept in East and Central Africa.

Federation became the Achilles' heel of European Central Africa. What the Europeans had not realized was that Britain was bound to allow some political rights and provide for certain electoral systems in her protectorates, Nyasaland and Northern Rhodesia, in concert with her general colonial policy. These were bound to stimulate African political activity and the growth of parties; even the restricted, highly qualified federal franchise would have the same consequence. And, although the Europeans might be able to hold the line in the Federation and in Southern Rhodesia, they could hardly expect to do so in the northern territories. There were simply not enough Europeans, whilst the presence of the Colonial Office in Lusaka and

[1] Sir Roy Welensky, *Welensky's 4000 Days*, p. 139

Zomba, with its responsibility to Westminster, would open up channels of debate constantly eroding white supremacy.

So, from a state of quietude before the argument on federation opened in 1951, the morrow of federation found Nkumbula and Kaunda in Northern Rhodesia, Nkomo in Southern Rhodesia and Banda, Chiume and Chipembere in Nyasaland, organizing modern political parties. At first they were of the congress type, but as electoral opportunities in the federation and the territories widened, each party began to organize its branches, determine a constitution, debate policies and strengthen its machinery. The Europeans had ignored the lesson taught by South Africans: that any political rights accorded to the masses must foster political organization, eventually fatal to an oligarchy.

So when the trial of strength opened in 1959 the outcome in Nyasaland and Northern Rhodesia was inevitable. Emergencies might be declared in Southern Rhodesia and Nyasaland; Africans might be killed; leaders like Kaunda, Banda and Nkomo might be imprisoned. As had been found in the rest of British Africa, this only led to martyrdom and in its turn to that charismatic leadership which represented the last nail in the federal coffin. The white community had shown, as in East Africa, that it could not govern without provoking conflict and relying on British help. Henceforth it was doomed to be abandoned by British interests. They quickly turned to making their peace with African leaders destined to become successors to the British governors and to Huggins, Welensky and their white colleagues who had failed to hold the succession. As in East Africa, feeble attempts might be made to stave off the inevitable or to modify the shock, but 1959 saw the defeat of the federal concept and of the white oligarchy which had gambled on its success; the conclusion of federation in 1963 was no more than a funeral four years after the death. The independence celebrations in Malawi and Zambia in 1964 marked the conception of new national lives. The strength of African organization within the British colonial context had successfully challenged European hegemony, forcing it to display its weakness to those most concerned to measure its capacity for preserving that form of stability likely to provide safe conditions for investment.

The collapse of federation and the founding of Malawi and Zambia still left open the issue of Southern Rhodesia. Here the situation was quite different, for the Europeans had been in political control for

over forty years and had preserved the basic elements of stability. They
had learnt only part of the South African lesson, allowing their Africans
minimal rights and ruling them as conquered subjects. What remained
to be seen was whether the rupture from Zambia would seriously
weaken the Rhodesian economy and if contact with the north had
stimulated the African population to political organization capable of
challenging white hegemony. In the meantime, other factors entered
the scene. Rhodesia was left as the residual problem of the British
African Empire. With the remainder of her African dependencies
now independent states (Bechuanaland became the independent state of
Botswana, Basutoland became Lesotho, in 1966; Swaziland followed
in 1968), Britain had to calculate whether her interest lay in appeasing
the Rhodesian Europeans or in preserving her relations with black
Africa. In the event she did neither, ineffectually refusing to recognize
the 1965 Rhodesian unilateral declaration of independence, but failing
to convince the Africans that she was genuinely trying to replace white
oligarchic rule by black democracy. Both the political and the economic future of Rhodesia lay poised in the balance; on the one hand,
European Rhodesia had become entirely dependent on the support of
the South Africans and Portuguese; on the other, she was refused
recognition by the rest of the world, despite the pressure of British
Conservatives, some closely linked with Rhodesian business. Meanwhile, guerilla fighters began to infiltrate across her borders, the
standard bearers for the inevitable eventual attack of black Africa on
the white southern redoubt.

Chapter 11

The Post-Independence Decade

The decade following the initiation of decolonization with the independence of Ghana in 1957 was a period of turbulence in Afro-British relations. During these years some thirty new African states were created. European imperial political control almost disappeared from the continent. The flood tide of African independence was followed by mutinies, civil wars, revolutions and *coups d'état*. Such violence took place, we should remember, in a world which also saw political assassinations in North America, civil wars in South America, international wars in Asia, and civic rioting almost everywhere. It was an age of violence in which the degree of brutality seen in Africa was probably somewhat less than the average – particularly if one remembers that Africans were plunged into the midst of sudden revolution as European government was replaced by African.

On the other side Britain was living through a period in which, almost overnight, she found herself for the first time in four centuries without an empire. Brought up on the assumption of inherent world power, many British people reacted emotionally to the sudden removal of imperial status and many more continued to assume that former colonial subjects would remain subservient in outlook to British leadership. As to the new insecurity caused by the loss of her empires were added the uncertainties of frequent economic crises during this period, it is not surprising that attitudes towards events in Africa tended to be emotive.

Relations between the two peoples during this cataclysmic period were the product of the previous four hundred years' experience. As a result of this historical experience both faced the new circumstances with certain assumptions already formed, if only in the subconscious. On the African side, although a few people who remembered the pre-colonial days were still alive, most attitudes had been strongly influenced

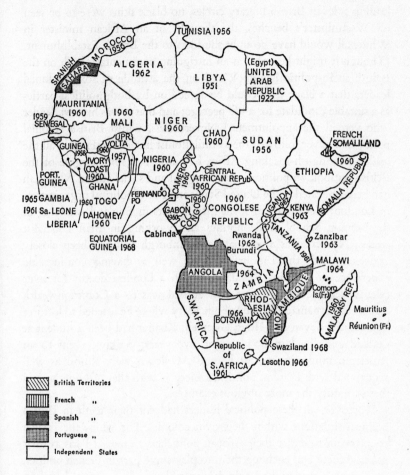

TUNISIA 1956

MOROCCO 1956

SPANISH SAHARA

ALGERIA 1962

LIBYA 1951

(Egypt) UNITED ARAB REPUBLIC 1922

MAURITANIA 1960

1959 SENEGAL

1960 MALI

NIGER 1960

CHAD 1960

SUDAN 1956

FRENCH SOMALILAND

GUINEA 1958

UPR VOLTA 1960

1957

IVORY COAST 1960

GHANA

NIGERIA 1960

CAMEROON 1960

CENTRAL AFRICAN REPub 1960

ETHIOPIA

SOMALIA REPUBLIC 1960

PORT. GUINEA

1965 GAMBIA

1961 Sa.LEONE

LIBERIA

1960 TOGO

FERNANDO PO

DAHOMEY 1960

GABON 1960

1960

CONGO

Cabinda

CONGOLESE REPUBLIC

1960

UGANDA 1962

KENYA 1963

EQUATORIAL GUINEA 1968

Rwanda 1962

Burundi

TANZANIA 1961

Zanzibar 1963

ANGOLA

1964

ZAMBIA

MALAWI 1964

MOZAMBIQUE

Comoro Is.(Fr)

1960

MALAGASY REP.

Mauritius

Réunion (Fr)

S.W.AFRICA

1966 BOTSWANA

RHOD ESIA

Republic of S. AFRICA 1961

Swaziland 1968

Lesotho 1966

British Territories

French   ,,

Spanish   ,,

Portuguese   ,,

Independent States

5 Africa today

by the British impact. Africans in British colonies had never drunk as deeply from the cup of British culture as their francophone cousins had from the wine of French civilization. No African poets took leading roles in British literary circles, no black skins were to be seen on Westminster's benches, the thought of an African minister in Whitehall would have brought shudders to the British Establishment. (Though it might be noted as an intriguing commentary both on the British socio-political outlook and on the attitude of some colonial leaders that a black man could be agreed on by both political parties as a suitable candidate for a life peerage; and that it was his own leader who vetoed the appointment.) Nevertheless, whilst British colonial policy had never followed the assimilationist line of the French, all the leaders of English-speaking Africa had absorbed some degree of the British outlook on political, constitutional and social affairs. Nkrumah had been educated in the United States and learnt political organization in London; Kenyatta had spent fifteen years in England, studying at the London School of Economics and working in British socialist circles; Nyerere was a graduate of Edinburgh and had been closely associated with the Labour Party as well as having considerable experience in America; Banda had been a London doctor for over twenty years; Kaunda's first visit abroad was to a Commonwealth conference organized by the Labour Party where he listened to lectures by Aneurin Bevan and Hugh Gaitskell; Khama had been a student at Oxford and lived in London for five years; Azikiwe went to an American university, whilst he and Awolowo were almost as well acquainted with London political society as with that of Nigeria; and these are only the more obvious examples.

Moreover, all these political leaders had cut their teeth in British political situations within their own colonies. For whilst the French were trying to entice their African politicians to regard Paris as their political focus and enabling them to play some part in French politics, the British were building colonial assemblies and executives based on the British model. So, inevitably, English-speaking African politicians emerged into an environment in which they had to use British political techniques. They formed parties – when they were allowed to do so – they organized branches to woo electorates, claimed inherent rights based on British democratic principles, engaged in debating, built trade unions and declared strikes; eventually, they became ministers with departments of civil servants and, perhaps most importantly, they learnt the value of going in deputations to Westminster to lobby Members of Parliament and try to influence British governments. Most of their political reading, writing and speaking was not only in the English language, but drawn from British political concepts. And much of their social life, of course, was conditioned by what they saw in Britain, or from British settlers and officials in their own lands.

Yet every African leader became increasingly aware that the institutions bequeathed by Britain's Colonial Office and the British-based political tactics employed to attain independence would not satisfy the needs of their new states. Tiny élite groups might have absorbed British ideas; the mass of Africans remained in their domestic environment, following African cultural forms, religions, family relations and habits of mind. This was never more clear than in the example of Mau Mau, which was as much a revolt against European mores as a nationalist uprising. But the factor was present in every state to a greater or lesser degree, and it was impressed on the consciousness of African leaders very shortly after they had taken over political control from their imperial masters.

This did not imply, however, that all European attitudes were immediately discarded on the morrow of self-government. Indeed, many of these persisted, further exacerbating the tensions which had already appeared. For instance, in several states nationalist movements had so impressed their followers with the handicaps represented by colonial rule that immediately improved conditions were expected to succeed the withdrawal of the imperial power. They were expressed most stridently by those associations which had come into being in response to the demands of anti-colonial agitation. Thus within nationalist parties and trade unions claims for higher wages quickly followed independence. But the new indigenous governments could only admit such claims from the minority of organized urban workers at the expense of still further widening the gap between the few industrial, commercial and service workers in the towns and the mass of peasants in the countryside.

Every African leader was therefore caught in the dichotomy of needing to maintain some of the techniques he had learnt from Britain, whilst at the same time introducing elements of African attitudes and traditions into his governmental amalgam. It is hardly surprising that in seeking a viable balance disturbances arose.

On their side, with confidence undermined by their rapidly changing national and social status, the British people tended to judge African events by exclusively British values. The euphoria which grew during the 1950s as Britain was thought to be adopting a magnanimous policy of voluntarily ending her imperial powers and setting up miniature Westminsters all over Africa quickly evaporated. The pictures of little British parliaments, all replete with Speaker's wigs, maces, lounging ministers and members on leather benches, offered the British public an escape from the guilt of a century's authoritarian imperial rule. It was assumed that these British institutions would continue to reflect the glory of the British political system. When they were seen to be modified or totally destroyed the British took comfort in the narcissistic concept that Africans really could not be expected to maintain the high standards of Britain – entirely neglecting the self-evident fact that this form of parliamentary institution had only satisfied the needs of Britain and a few European communities at a particular stage of their national development.

This post-imperial attitude was seen most clearly in reactions to the Commonwealth. Most British people and a considerable section of the British press assumed that the new African states would be content to accept a junior role in a British-centred and white dominion-dominated organization. They expected the Commonwealth to continue to hold its annual family meetings in London, embellished with pictures of the monarch surrounded by her loyal colonial premiers, talking in bromides but reassuring the British populace that it was still cushioned from the foreigners' world by the Empire. Even the shock of Indian republicanism had been softened by the Anglophile streak in Pandit Nehru, and if it might seem not quite in line with tradition to see dark-skinned heads of state being received in friendly fashion by British Royalty, this had its exotic excitement too.

Even before the independence era really got under way the first blow fell. Six months before his country attained independence, Julius Nyerere warned the Commonwealth prime ministers that Tanganyika would not join the club if South Africa remained a member. To many British this was appalling lèse majesté; after all, South Africa might now be ruled by rather rough men, but she was the country of Smuts, was governed by Europeans and had been an original member of the Commonwealth.

This, however, was only the start of the irreverance introduced by Africans. They began to question whether Britain was more than one equal member of the club, whether the conference should automatically be held in London, then to put the British prime minister in the dock over his policy towards Rhodesia. To many in Britain this new brash attitude shown by African leaders was felt as an affront to the one great British institution which might have assuaged the sense of imperial loss and there was thus a tendency to lose interest in the organization, to regard it as a miniature United Nations, to retreat still further into a 'little England' posture, and to blame Africans for the decline of the once proud 'British Commonwealth'.

There was therefore widespread criticism, sometimes amounting to abuse, when disturbances began to occur in post-independence Africa. The single-party state, restrictions on trade unions and the press, arrests and deportations, all brought their share of condemnation. Curiously, the same degree of criticism did not appear from the same quarters when military regimes began to replace civilian governments in certain countries. Of course, there was much to criticize. In such revolutionary situations some regimes did undermine the rule of law; and when judges are brought under the control of the executive the liberty of the individual is certainly jeopardized. The public executions which took place in one or two states cannot be defended on any grounds of humanity or decency. Then again, some Africans who had inherited the power and offices of colonial rulers outbid the colonialists in ostentatious living, whilst many of them succumbed to the temptations offered, indulging in corruption and nepotism. It is patronizingly insulting to Africans to excuse such practices by placing sole responsibility for them on those who offered bribes.

It is also true that most of the British public was shown such a confused and chaotic picture of events in the Congo that it appeared as though total savagery had broken out. Few knew of the international machinations behind the scenes, whilst some large-circulation publications completely distorted the role of the United Nations there, clearly in order to discredit its actions. It is also true that what little news could be gleaned out of Zanzibar tended to suggest that brutal excesses had taken place there, whilst the horrors of civil war in Nigeria needed no exaggeration to impress their inhumanity. Nevertheless, there was always a section of news media in Britain which reported such events in a different light from, for example, the violence of the United States, the brutalities in Vietnam or the oppression in South Africa, Angola and Mozambique. A racist element certainly coloured the presentation of such news.

This attitude was not universal in Britain. Certain newspapers, periodicals, radio and television stations tried to present a balanced picture and even to analyse the causes of these events. Some attempts were made to place them in the world-wide context of general violence. Various private organizations were also established both to publicize the African case and to act as host to visiting African leaders. But two weaknesses prevented the British public ever really being able to assess the situations with objectivity. One small section of the British press and of the organizations developed such an attitude of automatic apologia for anything that happened in Africa that its patronizing outlook became counter-productive; it simply came to be regarded as the black man's apologist. The second failure was caused by widespread ignorance of African history. Because so few British people – even journalists and commentators – knew anything of the background, thought or social traditions of Africa, little serious understanding of the causes of African crises could be offered, even by sympathizers. So again, somewhat egocentric judgements were made even when no malice was present. This was perhaps most obvious in the treatment of Nigeria. After being falsely portrayed as the most hopeful example of an African democracy based on British principles, sympathetic commentators were left without explanation when the federation began to disintegrate in violence. They had failed to look behind the superficial covering of parliamentary forms to the historical communal tensions which British imperial rule had papered over. And by conveniently ignoring the open corruption which flourished under this system they remained in ignorance of the deep resentment which was growing as corrupt wealth marched alongside dire poverty. In short, these commentators, sympathetic towards Africa though they were, by failing to gauge African sensitivities, had left their readers or listeners entirely unprepared for the passions which were let loose in Nigeria and consequently unable to understand their causes.

It was this absence of comprehension about the realities of African life and the outlook of Africans, rather than the hostile intent of the few, which presented the gravest threat to relations between Britain and Africa during the 1960s. British people were thinking of Africa in terms of massacres, civil wars, the deportation of Europeans, interference with judges, starvation, the erosion of parliaments, single-party 'dictatorships', and anti-British declarations; whilst Africans were thinking of the Suez bombardment, the imposition of white federation on Central Africa, support for the South Africans, Portuguese membership of NATO, the introduction of the Cold War into the Congo, the refusal of military force to suppress Ian Smith's rebellion in contrast to the air-lift to extricate Europeans from Stanleyville, the supply of arms to Lagos alongside the offer of food to the victims in Biafra, support for Americans in Vietnam, British obsession with acceptance into the European Economic Community of rich nations, contrasted with their decreasing concern for the poverty of their former colonies. It is true that all these factors which created the nuance of feelings between the two peoples would have been hedged with reservations in more rational, secure times; but it is equally true that it was these considerations which affected the outlook of Africans and British in the immediate post-independence period; and it was these attitudes which often influenced speeches, writings and policies.

Two main themes dominated Africa's approach to the post-independence era and neither was seriously appreciated in Britain. The first was the search for economic in addition to political sovereignty; and the second was a determination to play a role in international society equal to that of longer-established states. As we have already seen, after independence the influence of foreign capital rarely diminished and often increased. Every African government was left with an economy which was essentially dependent. Exports, usually limited to one or two raw materials and produced by mainly unskilled African workers, played a dominant role in the economy; so did imports of manufactures and capital goods. Most of this foreign trade was dependent on the former colonial power, which also provided almost all foreign investment and economic aid, most of which was concentrated on developing the export commodities. The internal markets were very small, government revenues insufficient, local savings inadequate and many of them expatriated overseas, whilst there was a general dearth of trained personnel.

The objective of all African governments was to change this status of economic dependence into one of independence. Various methods were tried according to differing local circumstances and the outlooks of the local leadership. A choice between two main policies emerged: either continued reliance on western capital in the hope that self-sustaining economic development might eventually appear, as in some other former dependencies; or taking the risk of antagonizing the traditional capital suppliers in the metropolitan countries by diversification of economic relations and greater state control. The Ivory Coast, other French-speaking states, Nigeria, Sierra Leone and Malawi provide examples of the former tactic; Ghana and Guinea were at one time leading exponents of the latter. After the deposition of Nkrumah Tanzania initiated an even bolder experiment in the control of foreign capital, to be followed in 1968 by Zambia, though here conditioned by her heavy dependence on copper production. Kenya came somewhere between the two approaches, though foreign investment in commerce, light industry and agriculture showed little sign of diminishing influence after independence.

Reactions in Britain to these differing policies were sharply divergent. Nkrumah's Ghana became the *bête noire* of much of the British press. Nyerere's Tanzania suffered the same fate, albeit in somewhat less virulent terms. Nigeria was usually held up as the example of how democracy could work in Africa until the 1966 coup shattered that illusion. Meanwhile most foreign capitalist interests exerted what pressure they could to persuade African governments to offer attractive terms for external investors and to desist from controls which would limit freedom of action for private capital. In other words, they resisted the growth of economic independence by the new states. This attitude was usual but not universal amongst foreign capitalist interests; some, especially amongst bankers, saw the benefits to their profits of high-level economic activities which could only be secured through long-term state agreements on commodity prices and markets.

In British economic and public opinion, however, little sympathy was shown towards those African governments which tried to experiment with socialist policies. There were a few economists, like Balogh, Seers and Kaldor, together with the Frenchman, René Dumont, who gave practical help to these efforts. The liberal press tried to show some sympathy but in general very little was known about either the policies or their objectives and still less about the vision of the people who promoted them. Most of the press and many public figures never allowed their ignorance to inhibit their condemnations. Thus those African countries which, in varying ways, tried to apply socialist methods to their economies by gaining greater indigenous control, the U.A.R., Ghana, Tanzania, and Zambia, were the most abused by the British press and conservative sections of British public life. It was the compliant, the regimes which collaborated most readily with Western capitalists, in Nigeria, Sierra Leone, Malawi and, to a lesser extent, in Kenya, who were given the most uncritical treatment. And, of course, South Africa and Rhodesia could always count on support from those who recognized their 'kith and kin' as governing oligarchies as well as business and commercial partners.

The foreign policies of independent African states followed closely their economic outlook. Those who adopted radical economic policies also embraced the attitude of 'non-alignment' on the international scene. Because all African countries had been governed under colonial rule as part of the Western bloc, it was imperative for those who wished to remove their new states from the Cold War syndrome to make overtures to communist and neutralist countries in order to achieve a position of equilibrium. Moreover, they were more likely to gain assistance from such quarters in their efforts to escape from the tentacles of foreign capital than from Western Europe or the United States. For a time the prospect of joining the 'Bandung' group of non-aligned nations seemed to offer the best hope of attaining this position in the world of diplomacy, but by the time that African states were gaining independence that group was rapidly declining. It was therefore soon realized by African leaders concerned with an international role that Africa must create its own international group. The ideals of pan-Africanism had been preached throughout the century by men like the American Negro, Du Bois, the West Indian, George Padmore, and later by all the leading African nationalists, Kenyatta, Nkrumah, Wallace Johnson, Azikiwe, Nyerere and Kaunda. It was natural, therefore, for the leaders of the new states to turn to intra-African organization.

Yet the division between radical and conservative persisted in the organization of international bodies. The Casablanca and Monrovia groups threatened to split the continent into hostile camps, though the

Pan-African Freedom Movement of East, Central and Southern Africa, formed under the guidance of Nyerere and Kaunda, encountered no such difficulties. By 1963, however, African leaders had recognized the dangers of schism and were able to sink their differences to the extent of establishing a single continental institution, the Organization of African Unity. The creation of this body could not, of course, remove every cause of friction between African states. Its early years saw it frequently under strain from conflicts between the Somalis and Kenya and Ethiopia, the constant confusions of the Congo, attitudes to the former colonial powers, the spate of military coups in West and francophone Africa, the Nigerian civil war, the fear of subversion between groups with contrary ideologies. But Africans, on the morrow of gaining control over their own states, had achieved what no other continent had ever established, a continent-wide supra-national form where differences could be discussed, quarrels assuaged and future policies prepared.

Africans never visualized the O.A.U. as an alternative to the United Nations. Indeed, membership of the U.N. was one of the objectives of the campaigns for independence. African delegates were quick to take advantage of their membership rights, using the U.N. and many of its constituent bodies as forums in which to attack the remnants of colonialism, white oligarchies and the foreign adventures of the great powers. They placed great value on the U.N. as an international body which could undermine racialism throughout the world and tended to judge other states by the part they played in the U.N. on this issue – even though it often consisted of no more than casting votes on resolutions.

These international activities tended to irritate certain sections of British opinion. It was suggested that the Casablanca radicals were intent on overturning the moderate regimes, that the O.A.U. was a farce, that African delegates at the U.N. were only concerned with making trouble for the West. Above all, few sections of British opinion seemed capable of recognizing that the communist-capitalist conflict which they took for granted as the vital feature of the twentieth century world seemed irrelevant to many African leaders. British publications were particularly vicious in attacks on Nkrumah for his association with the Russians and reflected the same egocentric attitude when Nyerere made friends with the Chinese. They neglected to remember that African nations had been compelled to serve the West under colonial rule, that they wished to become unattached states on the international stage, and that, although most of their technicians and professionals invariably still came from the West, when Britain hesitated to recognize the revolutionary regime in Zanzibar or help to build the vital Tanzania-Zambia railway, African leaders had to look elsewhere for support and assistance. So instead of welcoming the sight of African leaders taking a genuinely international initiative by trading and discussing with nations of all political persuasions, any step they took outside the Western enclosure was regarded with suspicion.

The climax of international tension between Africa and Britain arose over the Rhodesian affair. To Africans the test was seen in simple terms. In 1964 they had seen Britain and America cooperating with Belgium in an air-lift to rescue Europeans trapped in Stanleyville. They had experienced the use of British troops against African opposition to colonial rule. When Ian Smith illegally declared Rhodesia independent in 1965, therefore, they waited to see whether Britain would use the same military methods to suppress a white man's revolt. That she did not do so, that her prime minister actually announced before the declaration that she would not do so, proved conclusively to Africans that Britain applied separate standards to white and black men.

In Britain the situation was viewed from a different angle. In London it was realized that although Southern Rhodesia had nominally been a colony, no British government had ever administered it. The British South Africa Company was responsible until 1923 and after that it was governed on the lines of the Cape Colony in pre-Union days. Although a governor represented the monarch and Britain had final authority, administration and policy were actually in the hands of the local legislature and executive which controlled its own civil service, police and armed forces. Thus Britain was left with responsibility but devoid of power. As the conflict between the Rhodesian government and Britain approached it was clear that the British government could only assert its authority by armed invasion. As most of the white settlers who were defying Britain had recently emigrated from Britain, this would have involved sending British forces to attack British people – a similar situation to the American Civil War, but with greater logistical problems. At this moment, in the second half of 1965, Harold Wilson's government had a majority of only three in the House of Commons. The deployment of British forces in this manner was therefore seen as a political risk which might lead to the government's defeat and almost certainly to its loss of the next general election. By the time that Wilson had won the 1966 election and had assured himself of a large majority in the Commons the psychological moment for the use of military means had passed. The Rhodesians had settled down to circumvent economic sanctions, had mobilized South African and Portuguese support and had succeeded in building a vociferous lobby in Britain. In the meantime, Britain's economic difficulties had increased and would certainly have been exacerbated by threats to invade Rhodesia.

Thus African suspicions of British double standards were confirmed. Nyerere, after quarrelling with Wilson over Rhodesian policy at the 1965 Commonwealth Conference, broke off diplomatic relations – in accordance with an O.A.U. resolution ignored by most of its members – when he saw that the most Britain would do to discipline the rebel Smith regime was to impose a limited set of economic sanctions. Relations with Zambians, who stood to suffer most from Rhodesian intransigence and from the sanctions policy, rapidly deteriorated. The rest of Africa looked on cynically, convinced that here was sure proof of the white man's hypocrisy when faced with the anti-democratic ambitions of his own kind.

During the thirteen months which followed the Rhodesian Front's declaration of independence repeated efforts by the British Government to negotiate a settlement with Ian Smith on conditions which would have granted independence without democratic rule increased the general cynicism and the anger of Kaunda and Nyerere. It was only when the Rhodesian Front rejected the terms drawn up on the *Tiger* in December 1966 that the tide in Afro-British relations slowly began to turn. When Wilson honoured his pledge to declare that in future independence would not be granted before majority rule had been established and secured U.N. support for sanctions, the slide in his reputation in Africa was halted. In the second half of 1967 George Thomson, the Commonwealth Secretary, began to rebuild bridges by visiting Nyerere, despite the absence of diplomatic relations, had discussions with Kaunda and, after meeting Smith, made it clear that no basis for a settlement with the Rhodesian Front now remained. When Britain sponsored a resolution, passed unanimously by the Security Council, giving mandatory force to comprehensive sanctions against the Rhodesian regime, Africans began to gain some little confidence in Britain's determination not to allow the Rhodesian Front to perpetuate its white oligarchic rule. They remained sceptical over the effectiveness of sanctions, if only because South Africa and the Portuguese colonies continued to offer loopholes for Rhodesian trade and Britain made it apparent that confrontation with the South Africans could not be contemplated, even when South African forces were sent on to British soil to aid the Smith regime; but at least the British government had begun to convince Africans of its good faith within the prescribed limits of a refusal to use force or to use any form of coercion against South Africa. This confidence, however, extended only to a Labour government; by this time the Conservative Party had almost abandoned its original support for sanctions or democratic condition for a settlement and appeared ready to negotiate with the Rhodesian Front on almost any terms.

In the last quarter of 1968 the modicum of trust in Labour's integrity over the Rhodesian issue which had slowly returned to African leaders was again shattered, this time perhaps finally. Despite Mr Wilson's original declaration that he would never talk to the rebels, in spite of the pledge not to grant independence before the establishment of majority rule, and even after the Prime Minister had declared that he would never trust certain key figures in the Rhodesian Front, the British government initiated further negotiations with Ian Smith and his colleagues on H.M.S. *Fearless*, moored in Gibraltar harbour. In certain respects the *Fearless* proposals made even greater concessions to the Rhodesian white supremacists than those of the *Tiger*, and therefore gave Rhodesian Africans less protection. On his return to Salisbury Ian Smith and his ministers rejected certain of the proposals even after George Thomson had negotiated further with them in Rhodesia itself. But none of this was important to the African leaders concerned with British policy. The simple, and very stark, fact was that Wilson and his government were obviously and openly trying every manœuvre they could devise to break their own word. Either independence was to come before or after majority rule had been established; no six or six hundred principles could alter that straightforward alternative. No 'nice calculations of two seats less or two seats more' (Wilson) could be substituted for this crucial choice. Acceptance or rejection by Smith and his colleagues was irrelevant. Nor could the single-minded test of African leaders be diverted by sophistry. To them the Labour government had shown by its re-opening of negotiations that all its pretensions of democratic principle at the United Nations and within the Commonwealth were insincere. Its post-*Tiger* policy had been forced on it against its will by Smith's refusal to cooperate. The pledge of 'no independence before majority African rule' was an equivocation if not a perjury. The government had exposed its lack of will to defeat the racial supremacists and establish democratic institutions in Britain's last African colony.

Whether the Rhodesian whites and the British government ultimately found a *modus vivendi* for agreement, as was now generally expected, or the bargaining continued inconclusively, Labour in Britain had now burned its boats. There was no longer any reason for African leaders to trust its word and they would not be so foolish as to do so. They had learned by bitter experience that in British politics pledges, promises or guarantees must be taken to apply only to the day, or perhaps the hour, on which they are given. The experience of Wilson's Rhodesian policies thus finally destroyed the confidence of those Africans originally most friendly to British Labour in its government.

This unfortunate fact did not, however, remove Rhodesia from a role in British-African relations. Now convinced that no British government could be trusted to prevent Rhodesia following the tragic path of South Africa, the Africans realized that their last defence lay in guerilla warfare. It seemed likely that this strategy would have to be used eventually against South Africa if white supremacy were ever to be undermined there and it had been in progress in the Portuguese territories for some years. The British failure in Rhodesia ensured that the front line would be the Zambezi rather than the Limpopo. Guerillas had been active in Rhodesia since August 1967, but early experience had shown that it would take many years to mount the volume of attacks needed to challenge the strength of the Rhodesian security forces, reinforced by those of South Africa. In particular, it would obviously be some time before the guerillas were strong enough to convince the Africans living inside Rhodesian borders that they were going to win – and thus secure their all-important support. But the length and difficulties of the task did not deter African governments, nor the alliance of Rhodesian, South African and South-West African freedom fighters. They simply realized that more organization, money, equipment and training were essential.

But where would Britain stand in this war? This was now to be the crucial issue determining all future relations between Britain and black Africa. Some Africans, including important leaders, had become completely cynical over the British position after the *Fearless* talks, predicting that she would support the Rhodesian and South African whites, perhaps even sending troops to help them. Rhodesia had now become not only a no-man's land between minority white and majority black rule; it was an African Delphi, where the truth about Britain's real racial principles was to be sought.

Reduced to its simplest terms, what Africans were asking the Europeans and Americans who controlled most of the vital sectors of international life was whether the twentieth century was to evolve one world or two. To many Euro-American minds, not least those in Britain, this question could only refer to the Cold War context. But this outlook appeared irrelevant and myopic to Africans. They were posing the question in an entirely different context. They wished to know whether the Euro-Americans sought a continuation of the imperial world which they had dominated, in which the white skin was a passport to power, in which the industrialized world drew on the wealth of the non-industrialized without making any serious effort towards equalizing relations between the two, in which the social, economic and political standards of Euro-America were assumed to be universal. If this was to be the answer, then the world would certainly be divided into two; for Africans, like Asians and Latin Americans, rejected the concept of the universality of European culture and the permanent inferiority which this implied. They were determined to develop their own cultures, preferably as part of an integrated but diverse single world community; but if this were rejected, within the non-European community which held the concept in common. Similarly, they were determined to participate in those international decisions, both economic and political, which affected their own peoples. They hoped that this opportunity would arise out of the development of the United Nations, but if the white great powers insisted on maintaining their domination, Africans would seek strength through cooperation with other ex-colonial states. It was in this mood that African leaders addressed themselves to the daunting tasks of developing their new nation states out of the conglomeration of communities thrown together haphazardly by the imperial powers, seeking to marry what was useful in their colonial tutelage with the constructive aspects of their own traditions, using those modernizing techniques which did not destroy the African genius for human relations. The same objectives governed their search for foreign policies which would guarantee human rights to their fellow beings in other ex-colonial territories and in those countries still under minority rule.

The onus for answering this crucially significant question lay with European and American states. They alone possessed the power to determine whether there should be one or two worlds, for the answer depended on whether they were prepared to share the economic and political strength they had acquired during the age of industrialism within a single world community or were determined to try and preserve their privilege. The determining factor in this decision would be which type of social structure emerged within each of the developed states. Many Africans were disappointed to find that the communists of Russia and Eastern Europe appeared to be following the short-term materialist goals of the capitalist West. The aid they received from the East seemed to be just as closely geared to the objectives of seeking spheres of influence and powers of interference as that from the West. Often, too, African states found that their economic relations with communist countries were dominated by the national economic interests of the Eastern Europeans, as, for example, when they discovered that their products were being taxed out of competitive prices in communist markets.

African leaders were also bitterly disappointed with the performance of Harold Wilson's Labour government in Britain during its first few years of office. Many African public men – Nyerere, Kaunda, Kenyatta and Nkrumah were notable examples – had had close personal relations with the Labour Party during the years in which they were building their parties and mounting their anti-colonial campaigns. They desperately hoped for a Labour victory in the expectation of greater assistance and cooperation in their developmental experiments and more positive action in combating racial discrimination than could be expected from the traditional defenders of the capitalist system, the Conservatives. The Labour government's policies over Rhodesia, South Africa, immigration of coloured Commonwealth citizens and the Nigerian civil war brought disillusion. It was felt that Labour supported the United Nations with greater sincerity than the Conservatives and devoted a greater part of its foreign policy to U.N. affairs, certainly in banning arms to South Africa. But the deepest concern centred on Britain's external economic policies under Labour. The creation of the Ministry of Overseas Development and the easier terms it offered for economic help were appreciated, as were the special difficulties experienced by the British economy. Yet what brought most doubts to African minds was the extent to which a Labour government conceived itself as leading Britain into a socialist posture on world affairs. The apparent obsession with gaining entrance to the European Community seemed to be staking Britain's future as essentially a part of the rich industrialized world, a rejection of the participation in the wider community of peoples striving to achieve a universally balanced international society. It was hardly consistent with a socialist approach to a world divided between rich and poor. And when Nyerere and Kaunda began to put traditional socialist principles into practice, by taking commercial undertakings, banks and some industries under state control, little interest or encouragement was forthcoming from the British Labour Party. Nor did it seem as though Labour in office was concerned about the activities of those large capitalists concerns which both strongly influenced British life and dominated ex-colonial economies. Indeed, they were encouraged to expand their trade with South Africa, just as investment in that country was also welcomed. Yet, as must have beome clear from everything above, a continuation of capitalist activities would inevitably provoke still further strife in African countries, with increasing damage to Afro-British relations.

A decade after the independence era opened, therefore, future relations between Africa and Britain seemed likely to depend much more on British decisions than on African policies. There were certainly some minor irritations in Britain over the actions of some African states – over their attitude to the Gibraltar issue at the U.N., for instance, or the pusillanimous criticism levelled by French-speaking

Africans against the French evasion of Rhodesian sanctions and supply of arms to South Africa. Such irritations would no doubt continue; but they were miniscule compared with the profound issues of British policy on which Afro-British relations would fundamentally depend.

Two main factors in British policy would crucially determine the character of these relations. First, they would depend on the extent to which Britain accepted or rejected the proposition that her national interests would be best served by committing herself primarily to the developing world, to investing in the growth of new industrialization projects in non-industrial states, to building new markets for her goods and services. If this policy were once adopted, it would necessarily follow that politically Britain would throw her weight behind the forces combating white racialism in southern Africa and within Britain herself. If the policy were rejected Britain would inevitably become a minor part of the rich, white, developed world, increasingly faced by the hostility of the poor, coloured nations. Her relations with Africa would be determined by this group of rich states, but would lose all individual significance as the wider conflict grew. Evidence increasingly pointed to the probability that this conflict would open in southern Africa, where rich, powerful white societies confronted poor, but determined black communities. The time was rapidly approaching when the rest of the world would have to commit themselves to one or the other.

The second factor would be the path taken by the British Labour Party. If that party continued to aim at running a capitalist system more efficiently than its rivals, it would be forced to confine itself to governing Britain as part of the rich white world, with policies essentially determined by superpowers. In this case the contribution to socialist experiment taking place in Africa would be of little concern to it. If, on the other hand, the party were to commit itself to the international class struggle between rich and poor, the efforts of African socialists would be seen as highly significant. For not only would they form a new factor in the international socialist community, but they would also be recognized as intimately linked with the horizons of British socialists. The trading interests of Britain would then be seen to coincide with the needs of developing Africa, whilst empathy between African and British socialists would open the door to cooperative planning for mutual benefit.

On the African side one important factor was likely to influence
future relations with Britain. As we have just seen, British decisions
would determine whether or not significant relations could flower in
the new situation, with African states independent and Britain seeking
a post-imperial role. But African attitudes would also have at least
some effect. In Britain the more progressive, rational observers could
look with sympathetic understanding on the violent upheavals which
shook independent Africa, particularly when the history of imperial
rule was recalled. What left no cause for sympathy was the cynical
use all too frequently made of public office for private profits, together
with ostentatious displays of luxury living and prestige spending of
both private and public funds. Such attitudes were strongly criticized
when exhibited in affluent societies; in a continent where almost everyone lived on bare subsistence, they were an affront to social justice
which could only provoke unreserved condemnation. They had
certainly often led to an alienation of sympathy amongst British
people genuinely friendly to Africa and Africans. If Africa had a claim
on the understanding and goodwill of British socialists, they had an
equal right to expect social morality from African socialists. Fortunately, the most important of them, especially Nyerere and Kaunda,
set a fine example, taught austerity during scarcity as part of their
socialist message and strongly criticized those who practised the capitalist standards of ostentatious living. In many ways they resembled the
earlier non-conformist socialists who not only professed but acted
from deeply-held principles. It was on a forthright, uninhibited dialogue
between men like these and those British socialists prepared to use the
same candid language that the future of Afro-British relations now
rested.

During the four centuries in which the British and African peoples
had been in contact with each other the technical superiority of Britain
had always been a dominant factor. From slave trading days, through
the period of normal commercial trading into the era of imperialism
and on to the independence decade, Britain had been the senior
partner, often the master. Her ships sailed to African coasts, took
African captives across the Atlantic, her factories used the palm oil
and groundnuts, her rich bought the ivory, she sent missionaries, traders,
hunters, eventually soldiers and administrators to the continent. Even

when imperial power was waning, it was British parliaments which determined the pace of African self-government and finally passed independence acts. Above all, it was British firms which sought the minerals of Africa, which developed modern markets, invested, bought and sold, exported what could be used in Britain, imported British manufactures, formed the economic cores of African economies, even after political independence had been achieved.

Technical power forms one of the elements in a society's culture, but it is by no means the only one. In technological skills Britain was more advanced than Africa – and, indeed, for almost two centuries, than the rest of the world. But African society did not disintegrate under her impact as, for example, the inhabitants of the West Indies, America and Australia did from contact with European cultures. Much of African society had an inner strength, a resilience, which not only preserved its basic elements, its communal cohesion and pattern of personal relations, but planted them in the Caribbean and the Americas. Despite the destructive effects of the slave trade and imperialism and the cultural assaults of Christianity, science, technology and commercialism, the essential features of African society have remained widely unscathed.

Nevertheless, British culture, aggressive and expansionist from the sixteenth century onward, has made a much deeper impact on African society than African influences on British life. During their four hundred years' acquaintance Britain has offered Africans her commercial practices, religion, education, medicine, technology, social values, economic organizations and administrative structures. To Britain have come some aspects of African music, poetry, art, perhaps some influences from African human relationships, from the enthusiasm and optimism of Africans. But although the British cultural impact has been deeper, evidence of Africa's social strength has been revealed in the manner in which she had discriminated in her acceptance and rejection of those cultural gifts. Now that political imperialism has disappeared, that discrimination is being even more consciously applied. For, after the three-quarters of a century in which African society was largely controlled by Europeans, independent Africa has had to return to pre-imperial times in order to restructure her societies. She is restoring those African elements which are still relevant and which were submerged under the Europeans, and retaining only those European contributions which fit the new cultural patterns. And because the British took their cultural exports to Africa from their own egocentric experience, assuming them to be part of a universalist concept, the rejection of some of their values by Africans before and after independence often induces a patronizing attitude in Britain which undermines relations. The British are not noted for their tolerance of cultural diversity. In their view of African society the contempt which they commonly display to differences from the familiar may be complicated by a national feeling of guilt still prevailing from memories of past sins. On the African side, affection from personal acquaintance and for those British contributions which seem valuable is often laced with scorn for British materialism, insensitivity and cynicism.

Of course, these are generalizations. It should always be remembered that there are many different kinds of Britishers and even more varying types of African. There is little in common between, say, Hastings Banda and Gamal Nasser, William Tubman and Julius Nyerere, or Chief Sobhuza and the late Tom Mboya. Similarly, in Britain, it would be hard to find much in common in the attitudes towards Africans shown by Fenner Brockway, Enoch Powell, Michael Foot, Harold Wilson, John Collins, Tony Crosland, Humphrey Berkeley, Patrick Wall and Alec Douglas Home. Yet all these men, and many others in both continents, have and will have an influence on the relations between Africa and Britain.

It is now apparent that both Britain and Africa find themselves during the second half of the twentieth century in extraordinarily fluid eras of their development. Britain has to learn how to live without the empire which provided the strongest bulwark of her world power, to determine the objectives and values of her post-imperial society. Africa, for the first time able to plan her national societies by using scientific techniques, and simultaneously entering the international community, has equally to determine her ideals and rebuild her structures to achieve them. Both Britain and Africa will be affected by external influences; both will have some impact on each other in their future development; their relations will certainly be conditioned by the ideas which prevail in each society, by the men who control power.

In Africa the independence decade which followed Ghana's achievement of sovereignty in 1957 witnessed three major attempts at radical reorganization, designed to build the kind of state capable of meeting new challenges. Nasser sought a centralized economic power which could provide the foundations of a peasant socialism, but the extreme pressures of population expansion and his marriage to Arab chauvinism constantly thwarted him. Nkrumah also tried to create a centralized control over his economy, seeking to mobilize Ghana's wealth and, with the aid of modern technology, create a state-directed industrial society capable of providing European standards of life for his people. His inability to prevent his lieutenants from forming themselves into a luxury-seeking, élitist class progressively out of touch with the masses, his administrative inefficiency and his lack of control over his party bureaucracy destroyed the experiment.

The third attempt to build a new form of African state is probably the most important for Afro-British relations. Most sections of British opinion were hostile to Nkrumah and Nasser, partly because they both rejected much of the British heritage and spurned British guidance, partly because of excesses in each regime. It remained to be seen how the British would react to Nyerere's policies in Tanzania, for, in many ways, these rejected the British legacy more completely than either of the others. Nyerere has succinctly enunciated his basic principles: 'The basis and the ultimate aim of African socialism is the enlargement of the family. The true African socialist. ... regards all people as his brothers – as the members of a family which is growing continually. Ujamaa therefore – or Family-Community – is our interpretation of socialism. It stands in opposition to capitalism, which attempts to establish a happy society on the basis of exploitation of the people by the people. And it likewise opposes doctrinaire socialism which endeavours to found its happy society on the philosophy of the inevitable conflict between man and man'. This creed and its practical application were laid down in the Arusha Declaration of 1967. It is based on self-reliance and social equality. Foreign aid is not rejected, but is to be controlled and used only to strengthen the self-help plan. Certain crucial sectors of the economy are to be directed by the state. Every citizen in Tanzania is expected to contribute to cooperative efforts, most by increasing agricultural production through cooperative schemes and by building self-reliant villages. Wages and salaries are strictly controlled to ensure that the country moves towards equality, whilst everyone in public life is forbidden to acquire high incomes. Above all, the British model of administration is being reorganized to fit the needs of this new Tanzanian society. This involves discarding the multi-party system, with its divisive implications, creating a single-party state, with the party representing a national cohesion, though encouraging debate and discussion within it on national policies. The concept of building a unified nation through common purpose renders the British administrative structure obsolete if not obstructive. The pattern of a non-political civil service, the separation of executive, legislature and party, cannot serve the cohesive purposes of such a policy. Therefore the legacy of the colonial structure is being dismantled and replaced by a system in which the party itself represents the determining forum of national life and becomes the supreme authority over both parliament and government. Of course there are many dangers in this concept as in any political system. But it is certainly an important if experimental contribution to socialist philosophy.

The lessons of Tanzanian successes and failures in applying their socialist theories to the problems of the new African state will be observed and used by other Africans. President Kaunda of Zambia showed signs of adapting them to his own very different circumstances in 1968, though his copper wealth and the comparatively highly paid community of copper miners gave his country such a sharply differentiated society as to raise higher obstacles to egalitarianism than those faced by Nyerere.

But the essential factor determining future Afro-British relations will be the degree of imaginative open-mindedness shown by British people when such experiments are made by Africans. Will Britain remain egocentric, judging all constitutional structures against the model of her own institutions, or will she make the imaginative effort to understand the different problems faced by Africa's leaders, evaluating the experiments critically but sympathetically and constructively? Can she even conceive the possibility of learning something herself from them?

It seems certain that the answer to these queries will be largely determined by the direction taken in British politics. Not only are these African experiments socialist in character, aimed at controlling wealth production for the benefit of the whole community; but they are radical, even revolutionary departures from the manner in which Britain governed her African colonies. They cannot therefore be expected to be either understood or appreciated by British conservatives of either party. It is no coincidence that in their early stages the policies of Nyerere and Kaunda found greater sympathy in Scandinavia than in Britain. Understanding, sympathetic criticism, cooperation, on which healthy Afro-British relations depend can only develop from the growth of an open-minded section of British socialists aiming at the same objectives as these African socialists, seeking to change the British economic system which encourages capitalist enterprises to dominate both British and African economic life. On the other hand, if the African socialists fail to win support for their ideas and the more conservative methods of men like Banda, the military leaders of West Africa or some of the Paris-oriented French-speaking regimes prevail, the relations between Africa and Britain will continue on the capitalist semi-colonial basis approved by the conservative politicians and economic magnates of Britain.

These alternatives extend into the international field. Britain is still equivocal over the vital issue of race, whether it has to be faced within her own national community or in her attitude to southern Africa. Her relations with Africans are bound to be deeply affected by the way she treats other non-Europeans in her own country and by her attitude towards the racial war developing in Rhodesia, South Africa, and the Portuguese territories. At the same time, African policies in their non-aligned posture will affect Britain and her outlook on Africans. The British people – or some of them – may be able to appreciate Africa's refusal to judge every international issue according to its significance to the communist-anti-communist conflict. But this requires the creation of a new set of criteria for international attitudes and such criteria, to be sincere, will have to be equally applied to every issue – to the invasion of Czechoslovakia as well as to Vietnam, to Chinese violence as much as to South African, Greek or Portuguese. The Africans, with little to lose, have a unique opportunity to create new standards of international morality; but these will have to be impartially applied if they are to be accepted as anything higher than cant. If they are, they may well appeal to the younger, more idealistic section of the British people, weary of hypocrisy and cynicism in international relations.

Two focal factors will therefore determine the future course of Afro-British relations, both of paramount significance to each of the peoples concerned. Will Britain resign herself to an increasingly minor role in the segment of the world she has been largely instrumental in creating – the world of industry, of commerce, of finance, the world of comfort and luxury, of materialism, of atomized human relations, of individualism, anonymity and loneliness – the rich, white, Euro-American world? Or will she seek the means of creating a single human community, or finding the way to close the widening chasm between that world and the other world of mankind's coloured masses, of poverty, hunger, sickness, early death, of communal cohesion, spirituality, social responsibility? – the kind of task for which the new Commonwealth is admirally fitted. Both worlds have much to offer the other, but they find themselves helplessly in conflict, for members of each can see little beyond their own immediate interest, frightened to look into the future, to escape from the familiar and meet the revolutionary changes in attitude for which human survival cries out. It could be that British and African participation in the Commonwealth might provide this significant change.

For the African the choice is as stark. Are Africans to be content to cling to the skirts of European society, offering their pittance to the affluent community which still seeks their products to feed the industrial maws, hoping to receive charitable doles for their servility, leaving the control of their lives in the practised hands of the 'civilized world'? Or are they to build on the strength of their own cultures, asserting their own virtues, banishing their own vices and using only those techniques of the Euro-Americans which preserve and deepen the harmony of their own society?

It would be foolish to speculate as to which of these choices Africans and the British people will make. From all the evidence presented here, however, it is reasonable to conclude that the only hope of future relations between Britain and Africa being based on mutual respect, dignity and equality is for Africans to assert control over their own economic, social and political life, building nations on genuinely African foundations; and for the British people to seek a new international role, free from domination by the 'western camp,' leading the way with other free-minded, humanistic nations in merging the 'two worlds' into one humanity.

Select
Bibliography

It is clearly impossible to compile an adequate selection of source books covering a period of four hundred years. The following suggestions are simply offered as a guide to further reading; many of the books mentioned contain comprehensive bibliographies on their special fields. For the sake of clarity I have concentrated on three divisions of my subject: the history of African societies; the British social scene; the analysis of Afro-British economic relations.

African Societies

J. F. Ade Ajayi and R. Smith, *Yoruba Warfare in the Nineteenth Century*. Cambridge and Madison, Wisc., 1964

Roger Anstey, *Britain and the Congo in the Nineteenth Century*. Oxford, 1962.

John Atkins, *A voyage to Guinea, Brazil and the West Indies*. 1737.

E. Axelson, Ed., *South African Explorers*. Oxford, 1964.

James Barber, *Rhodesia, the Road to Rebellion*. London and New York, 1967.

The Book of Duarte Barbosa. Hakluyt Society, London, 1918.

Heinrich Barth, *Travels and Discoveries in North and Central Africa, etc.*, London, 1857–8; new ed., London and New York, 1965.

Ibn Battuta, *Travels in Asia and Africa*. London, 1929.

George Bennett, *Kenya: A Political History, The Colonial Phase*. Oxford, 1963.

Norman R. Bennett, *Studies in East African History*. Boston, 1962.

Geoffrey Bing, *Reap the Whirlwind*. London, 1968.

J. W. Blake, *Europeans in West Africa*. Hakluyt Society, 1924.

E. W. Blyden, *The Prospects of the African*. London, 1874.

William Bosman, *A New and Accurate Description of Guinea, etc.* London, 1705.

T. E. Bowdich, *Mission from Cape Coast to Ashantee*. London, 1819.

R. Brown, Ed., *Leo Africanus*, Hakluyt Society, 1896.

James Bruce, *Travels to Discover the Sources of the Blue Nile in the Years 1768–1773* Edinburgh, 1790, 5 vols.

A. T. Bryant, *Olden Times in Zululand and Natal*. London, 1929.

Raymond Leslie Buell, *The Native Problem in Africa*. London and New York, 1928 and 1965.

Sir Richard Burton, *First Footsteps in East Africa*. London and New York, 1966.

Cadamosto, *Voyages I.O. 1507.* In the Collection, Paesi navamente retrovati, Vicenza.

H. A. C. Cairns, *Prelude to Imperialism.* London, 1965; published as *The Clash of Cultures.* New York, 1965.

Robert Campbell, *A Pilgrimage to my Motherland, etc.* New York, 1861

Gwendolen M. Carter, *The Politics of Inequality.* New York, 1958.

Dunduz Chisiza, *Africa—What lies Ahead?* New York, 1962.

A. & J. Churchill, *Collections of Voyages and Travels.* (1723, Vol. 5).

H. Clapperton, *Journal of a Second Expedition into the Interior of Africa.* London, 1826.

Thomas Clarkson, *History of the Rise, Progress and Accomplishment of the Abolition of the African Slave Trade by the British Public.* 1839.

Sir Reginald Coupland, *The British Anti-Slavery Movement.* 1933; 2nd ed., London, 1964.

Sir Reginald Coupland, *The Exploitation of East Africa 1856–1850.* London, 1939.

Brodie Cruickshank, *Eighteen Years on the Gold Coast.* Vol. 1. London, 1853.

Philip D. Curtin, *The Image of Africa.* Wisconsin, 1964.

Basil Davidson, *The African Past.* London and Boston, 1964.

Basil Davidson, *Black Mother.* London and Boston, 1961.

Basil Davidson, *A History of West Africa.* London and New York, 1965.

Basil Davidson, *Old Africa Rediscovered.* London, 1959; published as *The Lost Cities of Africa.* Boston and Toronto, 1959.

Basil Davidson, *Which Way Africa?* London, 1964.

Martin R. Delany, *Official Report of the Niger Valley Exploring Party.* New York, 1861.

K. Onwuka Dike, *Trade and Politics in the Niger Delta, 1830–1885.* Oxford, 1956.

E. Donnan, *Documents Illustrative of the History of the Slave Trade to America.* (Carnegie Institution, Washington, D.C. 1931).

W. E. B. DuBois, *The World and Africa.* New York, 1965.

Paul Edwards, Ed., *Equiano's Travels.* London and New York, 1967.

J. V. Engharevba, *A Short History of Benin.* Ibadan, 1960.

The Interesting Narrative of the Live of Olaudah Equiano, or Gustavus Vasa, the African, written by Himself. London, 1789.

Ifor L. Evans, *The British in Tropical Africa.* Cambridge. 1929.

J. D. Fage, *An Introduction to the History of West Africa.* Cambridge, 1962.

S. Herbert Frankel, *Capital Investment in Africa.* London, 1938.

G. S. P. Freeman-Grenville, *East African Coast, Select Documents.* London, 1962.

G. S. P. Freeman-Grenville, *A Medieval History of the Coast of Tanganyika.* London, 1961.

Christopher Fyfe, *A History of Sierra Leone.* Oxford, 1962.

Lord William Hailey, *African Survey.* Oxford, 1938, 1957 and 1968.

Richard Hakluyt, *The Principal Navigations, Voyages, Traffiques and Discoveries of the English Nation.* 1598–1600.

Robin Hallett, *The Penetration of Africa to 1815.* London and New York, 1965.

Sir W. Keith Hancock, *Smuts, The Fields of Force, 1919–1950.* Cambridge, London, New York, 1968.

Sir W. Keith Hancock, *Smuts, The Sanguine Years, 1870–1919.* Cambridge, 1962.

J. D. Hargreaves, *Prelude to the Partition of West Africa.* London, 1963.

Vincent Harlow and E. M. Chilver, ed., *History of East Africa.* Vol. 2. London, 1965.

John Hatch, *A History of Postwar Africa.* London and New York, 1965.

Melville J. Herskovits, *The Human Factor in Changing Africa.* London and New York, 1963.

Thomas Hodgkin, *Nationalism in Colonial Africa.* London, 1956.

Thomas Hodgkin, *Nigerian Perspectives.* London, 1960.

Cecil Howard, Ed., *West African Explorers.* London and New York, 1951.

Guy Hunter, *The New Societies of Tropical Africa.* Oxford, 1962; New York, 1964.

Richard Jobson, *The Golden Trade.* London, 1623; Teignmouth, 1904.

Samuel Johnson, *History of the Yorubas.* London, 1921; new edition London, 1966.

Robert W. July, *The Origins of Modern African Thought.* London and New York, 1968.

Kenneth Kaunda, *Zambia Shall be Free.* London and New York, 1962.

Cornelius W. de Kiewiet, *A History of South Africa.* Oxford, 1941–1966.

David Kimble, *Political History of Ghana.* Oxford, 1963.

Mary Kingsley, *Travels in West Africa.* London, 1897.

Kenneth Kirkwood, *Britain and Africa.* London, 1965.

W. L. Langer, *The Diplomacy of Imperialism.* New York, 1935.

Lord Frederick D. Lugard, *The Dual Mandate in British Tropical Africa.* London, 1929 and 1965.

Ian D. Macrone, *Race attitudes in South Africa.* Johannesburg, 1957.

William M. Macmillan, *Bantu, Boer and Briton.* 2nd revised ed., Oxford, 1963.

John Marlowe, *Anglo-Egyptian Relations, 1800–1956.* London, 1965.

Colonel R. Meinertzhagen, *Kenya Diary, 1902–1906.* London, 1957.

Robert Moffat, *Missionary Labours and Scenes in South Africa.* London, 1842.

Francis Moore, *Travels into the Inland Parts of Africa.* London, 1738.

E. D. Morel, *Affairs of West Africa.* London, 1902 and 1968.

E. D. Morel, *Red Rubber.* London, 1906.

George Peter Murdock, *Africa: Its Peoples and Their Culture History.* New York and London, 1959.

Robert Norris, *Memoirs of the Reign of Bossa Ahadee, King of Dahomey.* London, 1789.

Roland Oliver and Anthony Atmore, *Africa since 1800*. Cambridge, 1967.

Roland Oliver and Gervase Mathew, Ed., *History of East Africa*. Vol 1. London, 1963.

Roland Oliver, *The Missionary Factor in East Africa*. London, 1965.

Roland Oliver and J. D. Fage, *A Short History of Africa*. London, 1962.

Roland Oliver, *Sir Harry Johnston and the Scramble for Africa*. London, 1957.

J. D. Omer-Cooper, *The Zulu Aftermath*. London, 1966.

Capt. W. F. W. Owen, R.N., *Narrative from Voyages to explore the Shores of Africa, Arabia and Madagascar*. London, 1833.

Mungo Park, *Travels in the Interior Districts of Africa, etc.* London, 1799.

J. H. Parry, *Europe and a Wider World, 1415–1715*. London, 1949 and 1966; New York, 1966.

William Paterson, *A narrative of Four Journeys in the Country of the Hottentots and Caffraria*. London, 1790.

Alan Paton, *Hofmeyr*. New York and London, 1964.

Margery Perham, *Lugard*. 2 vols London, 1956 and 1960.

Margery Perham and R. E. Robinson, Ed., *History of East Africa*. Oxford, 1965.

J. Pinkerton, *A general Collection of the Best and Most Interesting Voyages and Travels*. London, 1814.

G. Ravenstein, Ed., *A Journal of the First Voyage of Vasco da Gama*. Hakluyt Society, 1898.

Charles G. Richards and James Place, Ed., *East African Explorers*. London, 1960.

E. A. Ritter, *Shaka Zulu*. London, 1955.

Ronald Robinson and John Gallagher, *Africa and the Victorians*. London and New York, 1961.

Robert I. Rotberg, *A Political History of Tropical Africa*. New York, 1965.

Robert I. Rotberg, *The Rise of Nationalism in Central Africa, 1873–1964*. Cambridge, Mass. and Oxford, 1966.

Edward Roux, *Time longer than Rope*. London, 1949; Madison, Wisc., 1968.

João dos Santos, *Purchas His Pilgrimes*. Glasgow, 1905.

I. Schapera, Ed., *Livingstone's Private Journals, 1851–1853*. Berkeley, Calif. and London, 1960.

C. G. Seligman, *Races of Africa*. London and New York, 1957.

F. C. Selous, *Travel and Adventure in South-East Africa*. London, 1893.

George Shepperson and Thomas Price, *Independent African*. Edinburgh, 1958.

William Smith, *A New Voyage to Guinea*. London, 1744.

Andrew Sparman, *A Voyage to the Cape of Good Hope, etc. 1772–1776*. London, 1785.

R. Stanley and R. Neame, Ed. *The Exploration Diaries of H.M. Stanley*. London and New York, 1961.

A. J. P. Taylor, *The Struggle for Mastery in Europe*. Oxford, 1954.

G. M. Theal, *Records of Southern-Eastern Africa*. (1900 Vol. 6).

Leonard M. Thompson, *The Unification of South Africa. 1902–10*. Oxford, 1960.

C. B. Wadström, *Observations on the Slave Trade*. London, 1789.

Eric A. Walker, *A History of Southern Africa*. London, 1960.

James A. Williamson, *A Short History of British Expansion, The Modern Empire and Commonwealth*. London and New York, 1964.

Thomas Winterbottom, *An Account of the Native Africans, etc*. London, 1803

H. A. Wyndham, *The Atlantic and Slavery*. London, 1935.

British Social History

W. Ashworth, *An Economic History of England 1870–1939*. new ed., London, 1960.

Asa Briggs, *The Age of Improvement, 1780–1867*. London and New York, 1959.

Asa Briggs, *Victorian Cities*. London, 1964.

Sir J. Clapham, *An Economic History of Modern Britain, 1830–1914*. Cambridge, 1930–38.

G. D. H. Cole and R. W. Postgate, *The Common People*. London, 1938.

W. H. B. Court, *British Economic History 1870–1914*. Cambridge, 1965.

W. H. B. Court, *A Concise Economic History of England since 1750*. Cambridge, 1954.

Frederick Engels, *The Condition of the Working Class in 1844*. new ed., London, 1967.

R. C. K. Ensor, *England 1870–1914*. Oxford, 1936.

C. R. Fay, *Life and Labour in the Nineteenth Century*. Cambridge, 1956.

J. R. Green, *A Short History of the English People*. London,

Elie Halevy, *History of the English People in the Nineteenth Century*. 2nd rev. ed, London, 1949–65.

J. L. and B. Hammond, *The Town Labourer*. new ed., London, 1966.

J. L. and B. Hammond, *The Village Labourer*. new ed., London, 1966.

Eric J. Hobsbawm, *Industry and Empire*. London, 1968.

Harold J. Laski, *The Rise of European Liberalism*. London. 1936.

Henry Mayhew, *London Labour and the London Poor*. London, 1967.

A. L. Morton, *A People's History of England*, London, 1938.

Charles Loch Mowat, *Britain between the Wars, 1918–40*, new ed. London and Chicago, 1955.

J. H. Plumb, *England in the Eighteenth Century*. London and Baltimore, 1950.

A. F. Pollard, *Factors in Modern History*. London and Cambridge, Mass., 1952.

S. Pollard, *The Development of the British Economy, 1914–1950*. London, 1962.

Eileen Power, *Medieval People*. 10th ed. London and New York, 1963.

J. B. Priestley, *English Journey*. Heinemann, 1934.

Richard H. Tawney. *The Agrarian Problem in the Sixteenth Century*. new ed. London and New York, 1967.

Richard H. Tawney, *Religion and the Rise of Capitalism*. London, 1926; New York.

A. J. P. Taylor, *English History, 1914–1945*. Oxford, 1965.

Edward P. Thompson, *The Making of the English Working Class*. London, 1963 New York, 1964.

David Thomson, *England in the Nineteenth Century*, London, 1964.

David Thomson, *England in the Twentieth Century*, London, 1964.

R. Tressell, *The Ragged-Trousered Philanthropists*. London, 1955.

G. M. Trevelyan, *Social History of England*. London, 1944.

A. William-Ellis and F. J. Fisher, *A History of English Life*. London, 1960-63.

Economic Relations

Thomas Balogh, *The Economics of Poverty*. London, 1966; New York, 1967.

F. Benham, *Economic Aid to Underdeveloped Countries*. Oxford, 1961.

J. D. Bernal, *Science and Industry in the Nineteenth Century*, London, 1953.

C. A. Bodelsen, *Studies in Mid-Victorian Imperialism*. London, 1960.

Michael Barratt Brown, *After Imperialism*. London, 1963.

A. K. Cairncross, *Home and Foreign Investment. 1870–1930*. Cambridge, 1953.

G. D. H. Cole. *Intelligent Man's Guide through World Choas*. London, 1932.

René Dumont, *False Start in Africa*. Rev. ed. London and New York, 1969.

Reginald H. Green and Ann Seidman, *Unity or Poverty*. London, 1968.

H. J. Habbakuk, *American and British Technology in the Nineteenth Century*. Cambridge, 1962.

Nigel Heseltine, *Remaking Africa*. London, 1961.

J. A. Hobson, *Imperialism* (1902). 3rd ed. London, 1938; rev. ed. Ann Arbor, Mich.

W. G. Hoffman, *British History, 1750–1950*. London, 1965.

A. H. Imlah, *Economic Elements in the Pax Britannica*. Harvard, 1958.

J. M. Keynes, *Essays in Persuasion*. London, 1931.

L. C. A. Knowles, *Economic Development of the British Overseas Empire*. London, 1928.

J. M. Lee, *Colonial Development and Good Government*. Oxford, 1967.

V. I. Lenin, *Imperialism: the Highest Stage of Capitalism*. London, 1948; San Francisco, 1956.

W. A. Lewis, *Economic Survey 1919–39*. London, 1949.

E. Lipson, *Economic History of England*. London, 1934.

P. C. Lloyd, *Africa in Social Change*. London, 1967; rev. ed. New York, 1969.

Gunnar Myrdal, *Economic Theory and Underdeveloped Regions*. London, 1957.

W. B. Reddaway *et. al.*, *The Effects of U.K. Direct Investment Overseas: an Interim Report*. Cambridge University Press, 1967.

W. Schloete, *British Overseas Trade from 1700 to the 1930's*. London, 1932.

Andrew Schonfield, *Attack on World Poverty*. London, 1960.

Andrew Schonfield, *British Economic Policy since the War*. London, 1958.

J. R. Seeley, *Expansion of England*. London, 1883.

K. M. Stahl, *The Metropolitan Organisation of Britain's Colonial Trade*. London, 1937.

Sir Dudley Stamp, *Our Developing World*. London, 1960.

John Strachey, *The End of Empire*. London. 1959; New York, 1964.

E. Varga and L. Mendelsohn, *New Data on Lenin's Imperialism*. New York, 1940.

P. Larmartine Yates, *Forty Years of Foreign Trade*. London, 1960.

Index

Abeokuta, 126, 150, 151; Egba of, 152, 153
Abdurahman (leader of Cape Coloureds), 219
Aborigines' Rights Protection Society, 250
Accra, 80, 257
Achimota, Gold Coast, 233
Aden, 133, 187
African Company, 59, 61
African Lakes Corporation, 163
African National Congress, 219
African People's Organization, 218
Agriculture, 22, 23, 28; during slave period, 103, 107; in E. Africa, and the reserve system, 211–15
Akim kingdom, 81, 82
Akwamu empire: rise and decline of, 80–1
Algeria, Algerians, 133, 166, 177
Algiers, 22
Allada (slave centre), 80
Almoravida, 38, 40
Amiens, Treaty of (1802), 136
Anglican Society for the Propagation of the Gospel, 113
Angola, 166, 284
Anti-Slavery patrol. *See* Royal Navy
Antwerp, 19, 20
Apapa, Nigeria, 267
Apartheid, 139
  See also Segregationist policies
Arabia, and the Arabs, 13, 14, 15, 18, 22, 25, 33, 36, 37, 129, 130, 163; conflicts with the Portuguese, 92; and the slave trade, 129, 145, 157–8, 199; financial relations with Indians, 131; revolt against Khedive's rule, 134; some absorbed into Swahili population, 156; conflict with the British in Zanzibar, 199–200
Arden-Clarke, Sir Charles, 263
Arusha declaration (1967), 273, 300
Ashanti empire: slave trade, 72; partnership with the Dutch, 82; conquers Denkyira and Akim, 82; conflicts with the Fante, and treaty with the British, 117–20, 149; renews attacks, 121–3;

Wolseley's expedition, and break-up of the empire, 123; British conquest of, 198–9, 207
Ashanti peoples, 81, 264
Ashiqqua party (Sudan), 258
Asiatic Journal, 101
Asquith, H. H., 218
Association for the Discovery of the Interior Parts of Africa, 93
Atlantic Charter, 243
Australia, Australasia, 107, 113, 171, 174, 205, 245, 264,
Austro-Hungary, 172
Awolowo, Chief, 280
Azikiwe, Nnamdi, 233, 253, 258, 259, 262, 263, 280, 287

Badagri, 149, 150
Baganda, kingdom of, 235; ally of the British, 214; people, 164, 200
Baikie, Dr, 126, 127
Baker, S. W., 159
Balfour Declaration (1926), 251
Banda, Dr Hastings, 276, 280, 299
Banks, Sir Joseph, 93
Bantu, 135, 137, 140
Barbados, 54, 55, 56, 57
Barbary, 11, 34, 51
Barber, Francis, 144
Barbosa, Duarte, on the trade of East Africa, 30–1; on the port cities of the east, 31–2; on the kingdom of Benemetapa, 32–3
Bargash, Sultan, 130–1
Barotseland, 163
Barth, Heinrich, 94, 112
Basutoland, 137, 140, 235; transferred to Union of S.A., 218; becomes Lesotho, 277
Bathurst, 52, 115
Bechuanaland, 137, 168, 187, 235; British protectorate declared, 186, 200; transferred to Union of S.A., 218; independence, 277